A
LIST
OF
THINGS
THAT
DIDN'T
KILL
ME

A LIST OF THINGS THAT DIDN'T KILL ME

A MEMOIR BY JASON SCHMIDT

Farrar Straus Giroux / New York

Farrar Straus Giroux Books for Young Readers
175 Fifth Avenue, New York 10010

Copyright © 2015 by Jason Schmidt
Printed in the United States of America
Designed by Anne Diebel
First edition, 2015
1 3 5 7 9 10 8 6 4 2

macteenbooks.com

Library of Congress Cataloging-in-Publication Data

Schmidt, Jason, 1972–
    A list of things that didn't kill me / Jason Schmidt.
        pages cm
    Summary: "In his searing, honest, and ultimately inspiring memoir,
Jason Schmidt tells the story of growing up with an abusive father, who
contracted HIV and ultimately died of AIDS when Jason was a teenager"—
Provided by publisher.
    ISBN 978-0-374-38013-7 (hardback)
    ISBN 978-0-374-38014-4 (ebook)
    1. Dysfunctional families.   2. Drug addiction.   3. Sexual abuse.
4. Family violence.   I. Title.

HV697.S347 2014
362.19697'920092—dc23   1\2015
[B]

                                                          2014013170

Farrar Straus Giroux Books for Young Readers may be purchased for business or
promotional use. For information on bulk purchases please contact Macmillan
Corporate and Premium Sales Department at (800) 221-7945 x5442 or by email at
specialmarkets@macmillan.com.

For Tricia, who makes everything possible

Author's Note

"I'm not making up any of these stories I'm telling you tonight. Um . . . except for one. Except for the fact that the banana sticks to the wall when it hits. That's the only one. Everything else is true."

—Spalding Gray, *Swimming to Cambodia*

The names and identifying characteristics of many of the people described in this memoir have been changed, and some characters are composites. This has been done to protect the innocent, and give everyone else plausible deniability. I have also engaged in what I understand to be a memoirist's usual prerogative to fiddle with time, dialogue, and small details. Quotes are meant to convey my memory of the gist of conversations as I recall them.

Finally, because a lot of people have asked me about my recall, and the level of detail in my writing, I feel like I need to explain something about how these stories have been preserved over the years. One of my earliest memories is of riding a tricycle across town when I was three years old. I described that memory to my father when I was about seven years old, and he confirmed that it had, in fact, happened. Then he told me his memory of it, fleshing out the story for me. For years afterward, I retold the story to friends and family, and occasionally thought of it myself. When I was in a familiar place that I hadn't visited in a long time, I would flash back to that long-ago tricycle ride, and the sensation of navigating through dreamlike associations with obscure landmarks. Twenty or thirty years passed, and now I've written the story down. Is it a memory, or a story about a memory? I have no idea and, for purposes of this memoir, I have chosen not to be particular. But quite a few of the stories in this book are like that. Whether a story becomes more or less true after frequent retellings is, of course, a matter of opinion, but they're accurate to the best of my recollection.

And that's about it.

Everything else is true.

A
LIST
OF
THINGS
THAT
DIDN'T
KILL
ME

Prologue

"There is no way to tell his story without telling my own. And if his story really is a confession, then so is mine."

—Captain Benjamin Willard, *Apocalypse Now*

When I was sixteen years old I came home from school one day and found my dad crawling around on the kitchen floor in a big pool of blood. He was down on all fours with a dishrag, trying to mop it up, but there was a lot of blood and it was a small dishrag so things weren't going very well. When I walked in from the back hallway and saw what he was doing, it wasn't immediately obvious where the blood had come from. I stopped in the doorway and stood there for a minute, hoping he'd notice me and offer some kind of explanation. But he just kept scrubbing away.

"Dad," I said, after a pause. "Hey, Dad."

He finally looked up at me and smiled placidly.

"I fell," he said. Now that he was looking right at me, I could see that some of his hair was caked into a sticky mess on one side of his head. A little knot of tension let go in the back of my skull. Once I knew the blood was his, I knew what to do: I went to the phone in my bedroom and called a cab. I thought about calling an ambulance, but I wasn't sure Medicaid would cover it and the last thing we needed was another bill we couldn't pay. When I came back out a minute later, Dad had gone back to scrubbing at the blood. Same patch of floor, same dishrag. He hadn't even rinsed it.

"Dad," I said.

He didn't respond.

"Hey!" I said. "Dad!"

He looked up at me slowly, like he was seeing me for the first time. This was how it was with him now. Everything happened at one-quarter speed, and half of it ended badly. Watching him use a step stool or a kitchen knife was enough to give me nervous fits.

"Come on," I said. "We need to go downstairs and wait for the cab."

I tried to make it sound fun, like we were going on a trip to the park.

"Cab?" he said. "No . . . I have to . . . we . . . have to clean this up."

"No, it's okay," I said, still talking to him like he was a reluctant child. "I'll clean it up when I get home. Come on. We have to go."

"Go?" he muttered.

"We have to go. Downstairs. For the cab."

"Oh," he said, looking like he was trying to remember something. "Okay. Um."

He tried to stand up, but I could see right away that it wasn't going to happen. The linoleum floor was slippery from all the blood, and Dad was profoundly stoned on painkillers. He went up, he came down. Went up, came down. I watched him flop around for a minute longer than I probably should have, then

4

I stepped in and hoisted him onto his feet. Once he was standing he started looking around and patting his pockets.

"I need . . ." he said.

"You're fine," I said. "Come on."

I managed to get him out onto the landing and down the stairs. I was worried about the stairs, but he didn't weigh anything. I carried him down in my arms, like a baby. When we got outside, we sat down on the front steps and waited for the cab. The building we lived in was an old house that had been subdivided into apartments, so it had a proper porch and a small front yard.

We waited longer than I expected to. Longer than I wanted to. Holding still this long had been hard for me lately. If something bad or scary didn't happen every few minutes, I started to worry that someone somewhere was saving it up for me.

"My son'll be home from school soon," my dad said.

I looked over at him. He was staring out at the street. I wasn't sure I'd heard him right until he followed it up with "He's doing really well in school."

When I understood what was happening I closed my eyes and took a deep breath.

"He's got the whole world in front of him," Dad continued. "Anything he wants to do. He's . . . he's doing really well. He'll be . . . really well."

I thought, not for the first time, how satisfying it would be to kill my father. How easy. To just fucking kill him.

I went back and forth with myself about whether it was a good idea. There was the whole getting caught thing, but, really, that wasn't a significant problem. He overdosed on his pain meds all the time. Once or twice a month, I had to sit next to his bed, timing the intervals between his breaths on my cheap digital watch. If he didn't take one at least every two minutes, I was supposed to call 911. But that would be the time to do it. If

I just held a pillow or a damp cloth over his face one of those nights, I doubted anyone would ask questions.

My real hesitation was that I might regret it. Probably not right away, but eventually. If I lived a really long time. And I never wanted to regret anything to do with my dad. When he died—which would happen soon, with or without my help—it was important to me that I'd have the moral authority to despise his memory for the rest of my natural life. So, fine. If taking care of him until he died of natural causes was what it took to establish for good and all that I was different than he was, then the insurance was cheap at the price.

Dad kept muttering about how great Jason's grades were and how bright Jason's future was, but I tuned him out. I dug at the peeling paint on the front porch stairs with the toe of my sneaker. When the cab arrived, I got Dad up and helped him into the back seat.

"Swedish Hospital emergency room, please," I said to the driver.

When we got there, I eased Dad onto the curb and leaned in to pay the cabdriver.

"There's some blood on your seats," I said, tipping him with my last five dollars. "You have to clean it with bleach water. Wear gloves."

He looked at me like he had no idea what I was talking about.

"Gloves?" I said, making totally incomprehensible gestures, like jazz hands. "You have to wear gloves. His blood's poison. You understand poison? You have to wear gloves."

The cabdriver gave me a look and nodded. I handed him the money and he drove away. Then I got my dad up again and helped him along through the automatic doors, into the emergency room.

It was a slow day at the hospital or something. When they saw me come through the doors they all came running: a couple of nurses and an orderly with a gurney.

"What happened?" one of the nurses asked.

"He fell and hit his head," I said. "But be careful with him. He's got AIDS."

They all skidded to a stop. One of them put on a pair of elbow-length gloves and helped me get Dad onto the gurney. The others left and came back in blue plastic moon suits with huge Plexiglas face shields.

"I feel sick," Dad said, as the hospital people surrounded him on the gurney.

"We've got him," one of the space-suited nurses said to me. I stood back while they wheeled him into an exam room. One of the orderlies barely managed to get a bedpan in front of him before he sat up and vomited into it. It was a wet, focused explosion, like he was breathing fire. The nurses started giving each other instructions in those loud, barking tones they use, while one of them talked to my dad, trying to keep him calm. Trying to keep him awake. Every so often one of them would ask me a question: What was he on? Did he have any allergies? How long ago did this happen? I answered their questions and wished Dad had one of those conditions where vomiting and passing out actually meant the end was nigh. That this would be over soon.

I don't know how long I stood there before I looked down and noticed I was covered with his blood.

1

My first memory is of riding my tricycle under a pale blue sky, down streets lined with compact houses and generous yards. I rode toward things that pleased me—the shape of a tree, the spacing of telephone poles, an arrangement of power lines above the street. I rode down the middle of the street, so cars would be able to see me.

I didn't feel worried or afraid. It was a beautiful day. I took my time. When the door of one of the houses opened and I heard my mother call, "Jason?" I smiled and waved at her.

She brought me inside. Her living room had a big picture window that faced onto the street. The curtains were drawn back, and the room was full of light. Most of the floor space was taken up by a large wooden loom, but there was a couch and a big overstuffed chair farther back in the living room, near the kitchen. There was a small square trunk next to the chair. The shape of the loom, the pedals and the rows of steel wires, reminded me of a piano. I sat on the couch while Mom called Dad on the telephone. Dad showed up a little while later, and I sensed that I was in trouble so I crawled under the loom, but nobody yelled at me. He sat down on the couch, and she sat down on the chair.

"Honestly," he said. "I didn't even know he was gone."

"That's not very comforting," she said.

Then they were quiet for a while.

"It's more than a mile, Mark," she said.

"I know," he said. He looked at me then, and I could tell he didn't know what he should say. What he should think.

They talked for a while longer, then he took me home.

It was the summer I turned three years old; the summer of 1975.

* * *

My dad and I lived in a dark brown house with a gently sloping roof, a wood-slat exterior, and windows that opened out like little doors instead of sliding up and down the way windows were supposed to. It was built in a flatter, more sprawling style than most of the other houses in town. I didn't like it. It was the only house on a dead-end street in the middle of a giant field. There were no other kids nearby. There were never any people walking on the sidewalk or playing ball out in the field. When I went outside, all I heard was wind.

The street ended a block past our house, where a heavy galvanized steel chain was stretched across the road between two metal posts. The posts were made of thick metal pipes that had been driven into the ground and filled with concrete. They were painted bright yellow, and the chain was locked in place with a bulky rubber-coated padlock. The blacktop road ended at the chain. Beyond that, it was a dirt road, covered with gravel, that went toward a large, low building in the distance.

I spent a lot of time contemplating the mystery of the posts and the chain. Someone had gone to a great deal of trouble to put them there, but they seemed like a poor solution to a problem that didn't really exist. If someone really wanted to go on the dirt road, all they had to do was drive into the field and go around the posts. And yet I never saw it happen.

Of course, people did dump garbage near the posts, and I

never saw that happen either. So maybe the chain did serve some function, even if it was just to keep the garbage on our side of the posts. One day I went outside and found a burned-out mattress lying in our driveway. I had no idea how it had gotten there. All the cloth and stuffing had burned away, leaving nothing but the metal springs and frame, like the bones of some poorly evolved dinosaur. I climbed onto it and started bouncing as hard as I could. Cartoons had given me the idea that a really enthusiastic bounce would launch me ten or fifteen feet into the air, but I didn't seem to be able to get more than a few inches of clearance. At some point, Marianne came out and told me to be careful on that thing.

I looked back at her, as she held open the screen door that led out of the house and onto the driveway—a plump hippie with a wild mop of curly brown hair. She had a wide face with sunburned cheeks; strong nose, weak chin. She looked sleepy. She sounded sleepy; she had a scratchy voice, like someone who'd just woken up. She wore loose blue jeans and a baggy T-shirt. She didn't live with us but she was around a lot, and she seemed to want to look after me. Most of my dad's friends ignored me.

"I'll be careful," I said.

She nodded and went back inside.

Everything else I remember about that house amounts to a small collection of moments. I make guesses about when they happened, or in what order. The last memory is the only one I'm sure of.

* * *

I was hiding in my dad's closet, watching him through a crack in the door while he did something he didn't want me to see. I felt clever for catching him, but I didn't understand most of what I saw.

I tried to make up a story that would explain what he was doing, but whenever I thought I understood what was happening, he did something else that surprised me: burning silverware with a lighter; holding a hot spoon between his knees; tying a piece of rubber around his arm. No story I could come up with explained what he'd done so far, let alone anticipated what he'd do next. At some point the whole ritual reached a kind of climax and he sat there on the bed for a while, like he was doing some really deep thinking. Then he stood up and started hiding his collection of strange implements in various small wooden and metal boxes around the room; the rubber tubing went in one box, the spoon in another box, and so on.

I waited until he left the room, then snuck out of the closet and opened the last box I'd seen him touch.

I recognized the thing in the box as something that doctors used. I even had some idea what it was for, though I didn't know the word for it. It was a little plastic tube with a wire-thin needle poking out of one end. The other end had a blue plastic plunger with a rubber tip, which was used to push liquid through the needle. I didn't know what Dad had been doing with it, but I knew the pointy metal needle meant I shouldn't touch it. I closed the box and left the room.

* * *

I was in the living room. I wasn't doing anything, just sitting quietly and watching. Marianne was standing across from me. She was wearing jeans and a T-shirt and a black vest. The curtains on the front window were open, and there was afternoon light coming in behind her, framing her in two giant golden rectangles. The living room was cluttered, and she was making her way carefully toward the back of the house. She had one hand on the wall, like she needed help staying upright. In her other hand, she had a glass jug full of red wine. She lifted the jug to her lips and took a swig, then shivered and shook her head like the flavor had hit her wrong.

* * *

It was nighttime. I was in the living room. My dad and some of his friends were sitting around the coffee table in front of the couch. A lamp hanging down from the ceiling cast a circle of glaring white light on the glass surface of the table and made the rest of the room disappear. The adults were laughing and playing a game where they tore pages out of a magazine. The page I could see had a glossy picture of a bright blue ocean and a wide blue sky. The sky was full of hot air balloons, and the balloons were all the colors of the rainbow. The adults tore the page into strips, rolled the strips up into tubes, and used them to inhale lines of white powder off the tabletop, into their noses. Sometimes after they snorted some of the powder, one of them would rub his nose with the heel of his hand and squint his eyes. I thought it must hurt to snort that stuff.

* * *

I woke up when someone knocked on our door. Maybe it was that same night, maybe some other night. Everything was dark until someone opened the door and the porch light shone into the living room. I could see that whoever had opened the door was silhouetted against the light, peeking cautiously out to talk to someone on our porch. They spoke in quiet tones, like they didn't want to wake up the neighbors. Not that we had neighbors. After a few minutes, someone else went to the door to see what was going on. At some point another person turned on the overhead light in the living room and stepped back to open the front door wider.

There were men on the porch, and then they were coming into our house. They weren't like us. They weren't our people. The one I could see best, the one in front, wore big square glasses with brown plastic frames. He had shaggy medium-length brown hair. He was wearing denim pants and an ugly white button-down shirt with black stripes that were broken up by symbols from playing cards: diamonds, spades, hearts, and clubs. He was holding a big silver gun in his right hand, like the kind in cowboy movies, but shinier. There were a few other men behind him, similarly dressed.

One of them had a chrome-plated shotgun that he was holding in both hands—one hand on the stock, one hand on the pump—but he didn't look like he expected to do anything with it. I noticed that the wood on the grip of the pump slide was a light blond color and seemed dirty in the place where his hand rested on it. The shotguns our friends owned were all made out of dark blue metal and had dark wood grips on the pumps, or just had two short barrels side by side and big pistol grips instead of rifle stocks. I thought this man's shotgun was supposed to look cool because it was so shiny, but it really just looked like a toy. It was tacky.

There were four or five of these men. Two came into the house. The one with the tacky shotgun stood by the door. One or two more stood on the porch.

There were five or six of our people in the house; me, my dad, Marianne, and two or three men whose names I didn't know. The men with the guns were talking to our people, and our people seemed ashamed and scared and angry at the same time. They didn't want to make eye contact with the armed men. They moved like they wanted to run or fight, but they were forcing themselves to move slowly and stand still. I kept looking around, trying to understand what was happening.

When I glanced back toward the door I saw police officers standing in the doorway, in blue uniforms. On TV, cops were the good guys, so I thought we were probably going to be all right. Marianne came over and picked me up, then sat in a chair next to the front door with me in her lap. The armed men didn't seem interested in her. She sat me on her lap while the men with the guns talked to my dad and his friends, and told the police where to go. I started to get the idea that not only were the strangers cops, in spite of their plain clothes, but that they were actually the cops in charge.

The uniformed police started to make their way into the house. They walked around freely, turning on lights and looking in rooms without asking permission. I didn't know you were supposed to ask permission to walk around in someone else's house until I saw the police officers not doing it. I realized I might have been mistaken about things being okay because the police were here. Finally, I understood that something was going very wrong; it was just taking a long time to actually happen. I heard a noise, like someone dropping an armful of wood, and looked through the doorway that led into the kitchen. There was a cop in there with a long pole, tearing panels off the ceiling.

I looked at my dad. He was talking to the man with the silver pistol.

That's my only clear memory of my dad from that time: thin, medium height, with a beard and a receding hairline. Dark skin. Long, dark, wispy hair. He had a high forehead, strong cheekbones, and a large, straight nose. Some people thought he looked Arabic. He was wearing a sleeveless undershirt and a pair of bellbottoms. His wide, sensitive mouth was tight with fear and anxiety. Marianne reached up and grabbed my arms, like she thought I might try to get off her lap, but she didn't say anything. I could feel the fear in her—the tension in her leg muscles and the way she held her body perfectly rigid behind me. I kept expecting her to say something about how

15

everything was going to be okay, but she was completely focused on the men with the guns.

Later that night, some people came to collect me. I never went back to that house again.

* * *

10-08-75
0900

RECEIPT FOR REMOVAL OF
BELOW LISTED ITEMS FROM
ON OR NEAR THE PERSON OF

MARK CRAIG SCHMIDT (02-05-50)
AKA: MARK CHRISTIANSEN

AT = 1395 W. 15ᵀᴴ St, Eugene

ON = 10-06-75 AT APPROX 2350 HRS

ITEM #1: ONE LARGE POWDER
FOLD CONTAINING WHITE
POWDER MATERIAL REPRESENTED
TO BE COCAINE.

#2: ONE BAGGIE OF WHITE
POWDER MATERIAL REPRESENTED
TO BE COCAINE.

#3: 1320⁰⁰ CURRENCY
REMOVED FROM LEFT FRONT
PANT POCKET OF SCHMIDT.

2

My dad was born in Los Angeles, California, in 1950. He had a mother and a father and two older brothers. My grandfather, John, was the son of Hungarian immigrants with a German surname. John served in the Navy during World War II, came home, and got a job operating construction cranes during the postwar West Coast building boom. My dad's mother died when Dad was in high school. My grandfather remarried to a woman named Margaret. Margaret and my father did not get along, so my father left home when he was still comparatively young. At some point, he met my mother. The two of them got married and, when my dad was twenty-two, I was born.

These are the things I can prove.

My dad, when he told me the story of his life, always framed it in terms of *Leave It to Beaver*. Until he was about twelve, he said, his life was just like that TV show: nuclear family, stern authoritarian father he called "sir," a politely maternal mother; clean house, big yard, meat and potatoes for dinner. All the boys had crew cuts. They wore slacks and shirts for school, suits for church, jeans and T-shirts during summer vacation. A guy in white coveralls and a flat cap delivered their milk twice a week, and candy bars cost a nickel.

Dad's mother, who had grown up during the Great Depression, used to tell her kids that they needed to appreciate everything they had—that nobody in the history of the world had ever had it this good, and probably nobody ever would again. If history had seasons, my dad and his brothers were born during the warmest, gentlest, most bountiful summer anyone had ever seen. But it wouldn't last, because it never did. When Dad talked about his childhood, he talked about it like a perfect day at the beach.

Then, in a different kind of mood, he'd talk about having been born premature. He said his parents had resigned themselves to the fact that he was going to die while he was in the hospital, and they never seemed to know what to do with him when he didn't. He said he never felt like part of that family. That he was always a runt compared to his older brothers. That he made up for it by being smarter, and that his father and his brothers resented him for it, particularly the middle brother, Paul.

"Paul used to do this thing," Dad would say. "Where he'd sit on me while he loaded his BB gun. Then he'd get off me, let me run, count to five, and start shooting. One time he got me in the knee and we had to pry the BB out with a screwdriver. I blackmailed him for everything he had, then told on him anyway. That was Paul to a T. He was the kind of guy who, if there was a piece of cake in the refrigerator and our parents told us not to eat it, not only would Paul eat it—but then he'd leave the empty plate in the refrigerator. That was the kind of stupid your uncle Paul was."

I once asked my dad's oldest brother, my uncle John, what my dad was like when he was a kid. Uncle John confirmed Dad's version of events in more ways than he probably meant to. He said Dad was extremely precocious, but that he'd always been sickly on account of being born premature.

"Like his hair," Uncle John said. "If you grabbed him by his hair, it'd just come out in your hand. In big clumps."

3

A lot of what happened when Dad got busted was a mystery to me, during and afterward. Years later he told me there was some kind of bureaucratic screwup and the social worker who was handling my case sent me to Texas, where my mom's parents had recently settled. Only once I got down there, nobody knew what to do with me, so I spent one night in a foster home before being shipped to California, where I stayed with my other grandparents—John and Margaret—in Torrance, the blue-collar suburb of Los Angeles where my dad and his brothers had grown up. I didn't follow any of it. Afterward I had a vague memory of airplanes, and stewardesses being nice to me. At some point someone gave me a stuffed raccoon.

Dad's explanation of what befell him back in Eugene was, if anything, less clear than his description of what had happened to me: he was arrested, charged, and spent some time in jail. Then his friends bailed him out while he was awaiting trial and, somehow, he ended up on probation. The whole process took several months. Then he had to find us a new place to live and deal with other hassles that arose from the arrest. That took a few more months.

* * *

Not long after I arrived in Torrance, my grandparents took me to Disneyland. It was my first experience with a completely manufactured environment of faux finishes and fake people. I was disappointed to learn that Mickey Mouse was really just a guy in a stupid costume, but I appreciated the experience afterward because it gave me some context for my grandparents' house, where they had a real brick fireplace that they'd gone to the trouble to paint red—except for the mortar, which they'd painted white. The food all looked like food. In fact, it often looked exactly like the pictures of food on the boxes that Grandma took it out of before she cooked it—but it still tasted like cardboard. The furniture all looked like it should be comfortable: the couches were new and clean, the tables and shelves were store-bought (instead of improvised out of stolen packing containers), and the blankets and pillows looked fluffy and inviting. But the textures were all wrong. Everything was dry and soulless and unpleasant to the touch. I later realized that it was because every object in the house was made out of polyester and plastic.

Even my grandparents themselves seemed like escapees from the theme park. Grandpa was gruff and stoic. He spent most of his time sitting in his recliner—a piece of furniture I'd seen on TV but had never encountered in person—watching sports broadcasts that I didn't understand, and ignoring me. Grandma, who'd never had any children of her own, seemed to go the other way: no matter where I was or what I was doing, her attention followed me like a spotlight. She dressed me up in tight polyester clothing, cut my hair short, dragged me to church every Sunday, and started telling me—constantly, it seemed like—about Jesus and how wonderful he was. Her reactions to everything surprised me. I felt like I was constantly breaking rules nobody had told me about but that everyone seemed to expect me to just know.

The only thing in the house that made sense to me was Grandma's Yorkshire terrier, Tigger. He was dirty, and he stank, and he hated my living guts, either because he was jealous of my arrival in the house or because he was a furry little demon from hell. But his dislike of me was the only thing in that house that seemed authentic. I appreciated it in a way, even if I also sort of wanted to kick him into traffic when Grandma was looking the other way.

I was there for eight months before my grandparents handed me over to another team of stewardesses, who put me on another plane and took me to another airport. Only this time, when I made my way up the weird metal hallway into the airport, Dad was waiting for me at the other end. He didn't seem to recognize me at first. He looked over my head for a second before his eyes settled on me, and he got a curious, questioning look on his face.

"Holy shit," he finally said. "What the fuck have they got you wearing?"

4

Eugene was a college town, which is to say that it had been a small town once upon a time—a lumber town, a farming town, a textile town—that had been taken over by its college. The college that ate Eugene was the University of Oregon. City people had come to that small town from all over the country, to work or study at the U of O, and they'd brought their city money and city ideas with them. In the sixties and seventies, those city people were flower children, baby boomers with a taste for sex, drugs, and loud music. Most of them were just passing through. The ones who decided to stay were back-to-the-earth hippies who used their parents' money to buy farms outside of town and turn them into communes. Or they were people like my dad, who serviced the drug pipeline that kept all those college students in grass, smack, acid, and blow. There were still people in and around Eugene who thought of themselves as being from Eugene; who worked in lumber or farming or textiles. But to my dad and his friends, those people were like the Indians who used to spend summers in the rich Willamette River Valley before the whites came along and took it all away from them. Eugene's townies were a historical curiosity whose time had come and gone. They were the police. They drove the buses and taught in the schools. And it may at some point have occurred to someone in my dad's circles that the townies also repaired the streets and the sewers, kept the water running and the lights on—it may have occurred to someone at some point that the people they considered the least relevant were actually the most important. Or maybe that kind of big-picture thinking was still another ten or fifteen years away for the revolutionary vanguard of hard partying and free love that my dad imagined himself to be a part of. Mostly, we just avoided the straights, as we called them, and mistrusted them. And for me it all boiled down to one simple rule that even a child could remember: Never tell them anything.

Our world was not a great place for kids. Not to say there weren't a bunch of us kids running around. As Dad often said, you get a lot of people taking drugs that make them forgetful and horny, you're going to get a lot of kids. But most of us existed by default. Abortion was effectively illegal in all but four states until the year after I was born, so a certain number of us were just accidents. And some of us were the product of short-lived attempts at normalcy. My dad often told me that he and my mom had gotten married and had me because they thought that, by acting normal, they could become normal. It only took them a year or two to realize that wasn't going to work out. Then they went back to being a couple of strung-out fuckups—only now I was along for the ride, too. A lot of the kids

in our crew had a story like that. So we inhaled a shitload of secondhand pot smoke. We got taken to cow pastures to help pick
magic mushrooms. We went to noisy, confusing concerts, and we
often had really exciting birthday parties. But the rest of the time
we got left home alone a lot. And we watched a lot of television.

* * *

As eager as I'd been to leave my grandparents' house in California and get back to my dad and Eugene, I found the transi-
tion from Torrance a little jarring. When Dad came to get me
in the airport, he was wearing a bright red headscarf to cover
his receding hairline, a green silk shirt, and tight denim bell-
bottoms. He had a large gold nose ring, piercings in both ears,
a sort of dramatically sculpted beard and mustache, and a big
brass bracelet on his left wrist. And, of course, the peace sign he
had tattooed on the back of his left hand, in the crotch between
his thumb and forefinger.

He gave me a hug and a kiss, and called me "Boo," which
was his nickname for me when I was a baby. At almost four
years old, I still got some comfort from it. I was glad to see him.
Glad to be home. But I felt people staring at us, and part of me
wished he could have toned it down a little, just for the airport.
The airport was straight territory, and I was tired of getting
disapproving looks from these people: in eight months with
my grandparents, I'd never blended in, never felt like one of
them. In my memory, it was just eight months of these looks.

Dad felt my hesitation and quieted down until we got my
luggage and caught the bus back to town. Then he asked me
about Grandma and Grandpa, and what they'd told me about
him while I was down there. I told him he hadn't come up much
in conversation, which was true. Then he asked me about the
rest of it, and I told him about how they'd forced me to get a

haircut, and how Tigger used to snap and growl at me when nobody was looking, and how I had to go to church every Sunday. The only good part, I said, was that Grandma had set me up with this cool deal where I was going to live forever.

"Hold on," Dad said. "What was that last part?"

"Well," I said, "Grandma told me that if I invited Jesus into my heart, I'd live forever. So I did it in the kitchen one time. I said, 'I invite Jesus into my heart.' So now I'll live forever. That's what she said, anyway."

Dad was quiet for a minute while he thought that over. The bus was mostly empty, and I wanted to sit on his lap because the bus seats were uncomfortable. But he didn't like me climbing on him, so I just waited for him to say whatever he was going to say. He was obviously building up a pretty good head of steam about it.

"Did Grandma tell you who Jesus really was?" he asked after a while. "How he was born, in the manger, and the three wise men?"

Since I'd been with my grandparents over Christmas, I'd heard the story a bunch of times. I told him the parts I could remember, but he started shaking his head before I was even halfway through.

"Yeah," he said. "That's a government lie. The truth is, Jesus was part alien."

I blinked. "Part alien?"

"Yeah."

"Like, from Mars?" I asked, thinking of Marvin the Martian in Bugs Bunny cartoons.

"Yeah," Dad said. "Only a lot farther away than that. Aliens have been coming to Earth from millions of light-years away, and they've been doing it for thousands of years, in secret. Then, about two thousand years ago, they decided to try to communicate with us. So they used a technique called artificial

24

insemination to get Mary pregnant with an alien baby that would look like us and talk like us but have some of the traits of an alien. That's why she could give birth even though she was a virgin—she'd never had sex, but the alien technology made her pregnant. And the star of Bethlehem was a spaceship. Like a flying saucer. The wise men followed it because they knew that it was hovering above the place where Jesus was being born, making sure everything was okay. And the reason Jesus had all those powers, like healing the sick and walking on water, was because he was part alien—so he was telekinetic and telepathic. The aliens sent Jesus here to teach people to love each other, but the people in charge realized he was a threat to the system, so they had him killed. After he was dead, this narc named Paul corrupted his message and turned it into a mind control tool for the government. And that's what your grandma was teaching you in church."

I thought this over for a while. Dad had always said a lot of things to me that didn't make sense in the moment, but usually if I just let my brain chew on them long enough I could start to get the flavor of what he meant.

"So . . ." I said. "Jesus was an alien. From . . . another planet."

"Half alien," Dad said. "His dad was an alien. But he was born here, and his mom was human."

"And he was here to make us be nice to each other."

"Yeah," Dad said.

"So the government killed him."

"Right."

"Why?"

"Because the government maintains control by tricking poor people into killing each other. If people did what Jesus was telling them to do, they'd get together and share everything and stop killing each other and the government would stop working. So they killed him."

25

"Why did the aliens want us to be nice to each other?"

"Because they're smarter than we are. They can read minds and travel faster than the speed of light, and they know that the only possible future is peace."

"So the bad guys killed Jesus. And now . . ."

"The government that killed Jesus was the empire of Rome. But that government eventually became the church. So now the church lies about what Jesus actually said, in order to control people's minds."

I thought about my grandparents, and everything I'd heard at their church, and how Grandma was constantly telling me what not to say and what not to do and making me wear different clothes and get my hair cut. And I had to admit Dad's explanation made a lot more sense than anything my grandparents had said.

"Wow," I said after a while. "Poor Grandma. She's got it all wrong."

"Yeah," Dad said. "She does. But don't you feel sorry for that woman. She's got it all wrong because she wants to."

* * *

Our people usually lived in sort of leftover houses. Dad was always talking about history, and the movement of money and jobs—it was an obsession he'd learned from his mother—so I knew how we came to have these places. They were houses that had been built by straights during some period of prosperity—a lumber boom, farm boom, or textile boom—and then abandoned for various reasons when things got bad again. In the big cities, middle-class white people were heading out to the suburbs to get away from black people, Mexicans, gays, and other undesirables; white flight, people called it. In Eugene, the straights had been migrating out of town since World War II. New telephone lines, power lines, and highways built since the war had made it possible for a blue-collar worker to buy a giant ranch house on a cheap five-acre lot in the middle of nowhere, drive to the mall to shop, drive to church to worship, and drive to the hospital to see the doctor. That idea seemed to appeal to a lot of Eugene's straights, so they left town in droves to move to suburbs and exurbs like Dexter, Junction City, and Cottage Grove. And, after they were gone, our people moved into their nice old houses in town, dug their nice old furniture out of the landfills, and turned the factories and hardware stores where they used to work into artists' lofts and coffee shops. The only problem was that our people weren't great at taking care of things, or fixing things after they were broken, and we were generally too poor to hire anyone else to do it. So after a couple of years a lot of those nice old houses started to get pretty run-down.

The house my dad had found for us while I was in California was one of those leftover houses. It was an old Dutch farmhouse on Hayes Street. Dad said it was older than the rest of the neighborhood—older than the streets, even—which was why it was backwards, with a small glass-paned door facing toward the street and an elaborate porch and sunroom facing toward the alley behind the house. It had a big front yard and a backyard that was shaded by an enormous willow tree. The tree had a tire swing hanging from it. It probably would have been the perfect house for an almost-four-year-old except that nobody had taken much care of it for a couple of decades. The walls and ceiling were water-stained from old leaks in the roof. The yard was overgrown and full of scrap lumber and junk, and the kitchen was infested with giant black wood ants and mice. There was no central heating or even baseboards—just a huge wood-burning stove in the living room—so the house was always cold. Everything smelled a little bit like soil and rotting wood. The floor in the bathroom was soft—and not in a good way.

I explored the whole place at a dead run that first day. The best part was that I had my own room on the first floor—about ten feet square, with fourteen-foot ceilings. There was a giant water stain that covered most of the ceiling and part of one of the walls, and the plaster had fallen off in the middle of the stain, exposing the gray wood laths underneath. There was a morning glory growing through a crack in the window frame, and the carpet was worn down to the jute, but my old brass bed was in there, with my antique dresser and a box of my old toys from the house we'd lived in when Dad got busted.

"Pretty," I said, fingering the big white flowers on the vine that came through the window frame.

"Yeah," Dad said. "We can pull it out in the fall, when it dies back."

*　*　*

We shared the Hayes Street house with two housemates from Dad's network: a young Jewish lesbian named Beth, who dreamed of starting a commune, and a truck driver named John who worked for an anarchist trucking cooperative called Starflower, that delivered natural foods all up and down the West Coast. Dad wasn't especially tight with either of them, but they were our people in all the ways that mattered—they were friends of friends, and they knew how to keep their mouths shut. Not that Dad had anything too heavy planned while we were on Hayes Street. He was on probation after getting arrested, so he'd enrolled in drafting classes at the local community college and signed us up for welfare, food stamps, and whatever else he could get to cover at least part of the shortfall from his lost drug dealing income.

Beth wasn't around much, but John's work schedule meant that he was home for big blocks of time, including some weekdays. Dad, who never missed an opportunity to impose on someone else's generosity, had talked John into keeping an eye on me while Dad was at school. It was understood that keeping an eye on me just meant that John had to be home—he didn't actually have to be in the same room as me or anything. Dad had me on what he hoped was an accelerated schedule for self-reliance.

The first time Dad left me home alone with John I managed to hold out for a couple of hours before I got bored enough to go upstairs and see what he was doing. I had some idea I wasn't supposed to be up there, so I snuck up the stairs, and found him sitting on the floor in front of a coffee table, painting tiny lead figures of knights and monsters. When he saw me watching him, instead of getting mad he invited me over to see what he was doing.

"What are those?" I asked.

"Part of a game," he said. "Like checkers, or chess. But much more complicated. Do you want to learn?"

John had a way of talking about things that made me nervous and excited. He wasn't much to look at—just a pudgy blond hippie with feathered hair and a wispy mustache. He had small buckteeth and round cheeks that made him look a little like a rabbit when he smiled, and most of his clothes were too tight because he'd bought them about fifteen pounds ago. But there was something else about him—like he knew a secret, and he was always just about to tell me what it was.

His room ran the length of the house and had low sloping ceilings, with his bed at the far end under the window. I went over and looked at the collection of little figures he had on the coffee table in front of him. They were interesting, but the comparison to checkers or chess cooled my interest. Rules made me anxious.

John watched my face for a minute, then said, "Or if you want, I could read you a story."

"Read me a story?" I asked. My dad read to me at bedtime sometimes, and it was one of my favorite things.

"Can I play with these while you read it?" I asked, gesturing to his collection.

"Sure," he said. "In fact, this story is about people like that."

"Okay," I said.

While I started drawing up battle lines with orcs and knights on the coffee table, John went over to the milk crate next to his bed, took a book out of it, and sat on the floor. He fussed with the book until he found the page he wanted, then leaned back against the mattress and box spring and started to read.

"In a hole in the ground," he said, "there lived a hobbit. Not a nasty, dirty, wet hole, filled with the ends of worms and an oozy smell, nor yet a dry, bare, sandy hole with nothing in it to sit down on or to eat: it was a hobbit-hole, and that means comfort."

5

My dad's childhood ended when he was twelve. That was when one of his junior high school teachers molested him. He never talked much about the thing itself. When he told the story, he usually talked about the aftermath; about telling his mom, his mom telling his dad, his dad telling the police, and the arrest and trial that followed. At some point in the process— the arrest, or the trial—the story got out. The teacher was prosecuted, but when it was over Dad had to go back to a school where his teachers and his classmates all knew that he'd been sexually intimate with a man. The law at the time said that if a rape victim—a woman—didn't fight back "to the utmost," she was assumed to have consented. That legal standard didn't apply to my father because he was a child—and a boy. The teacher could be convicted for other things. Most forms of homosexual sex were felonies under California State law in 1962, to say nothing of the charges arising from sexual contact with a child. But people wondered.

Dad didn't talk about being beaten up, or harassed or called names. What he talked about was that nobody ever looked at him the same way again. His classmates. His teachers. His dad and his brothers. Even the cops who made the arrest looked at him sideways. The only person in the world who stood by him through the whole thing was his mother. When she died of lung cancer a few years later, it felt like a malicious cosmic joke. When Grandpa married Margaret the fundamentalist Christian, that was the punch line.

Somewhere along the way, the boy who would become my dad started to take a turn for the genuinely antisocial. He talked a lot about having various conflicts with Margaret, then doing things specifically calculated to aggravate her: having big parties at the house, and going out of his way to make it obvious to her that he was doing a lot of drugs and having a lot of sex. It didn't take very long for things to escalate to the point where he had to move out on his own.

What Dad did during the time between leaving home and when he moved to Eugene was always a little fuzzy. He had a lot of sex, took and sold a lot of drugs, and traveled around south and central California. At some point he met my mom, but I never got the details. I don't even know what city they met in. Their families knew each other somehow, but Dad was from L.A. and Mom was from San Francisco. Dad went back and forth between the two cities a lot. Maybe Mom did, too. I know that when they met, they were both strung out. Mom had just gotten out of a mental hospital. That was when straight life had betrayed her—when her parents had her locked up. I always figured that shared sense of betrayal had to be the basis for their mutual attraction.

Whatever it was that drew them together, their joint mission seemed to be the simulation of some mythical lifestyle called "normal." They had a huge church wedding, with a tux and a big white dress and lots of professionally staged photos. Dad kept his hair short most of the time they were together. Wore straight-leg jeans and plaid shirts. And he quit dealing and worked a couple of regular jobs, which was not his usual thing. When they moved to Eugene, Dad said it was mainly because Eugene seemed like such a quaint little town—like Mayberry RFD, but full of hippies. It seemed like the kind of place they could have a house with a yard, and a dog, and a kid.

Dad invited his father and stepmother up, to see the normal house he rented with money from his normal job; his normal wife and his normal life. I've got snapshots of them all having lunch: Mom and Dad holding me while Grandpa and Margaret sit or stand awkwardly nearby. Dad and Mom with big fixed grins, Grandma and Grandpa looking like they wish they were somewhere else.

All the photos I have of my parents from that time, the main thing is they always look like they were trying. Like they were trying so fucking hard.

6

Dad liked to tell me the story of how I was born. He said I was two weeks overdue, and breech. The doctors did a cesarean section and botched the stitching. Then they sent us all home.

"The minute you came out, you were just taking everything in," he said. "It was amazing how alert you were."

After we got home, Mom was out of commission for days with a rising fever as an infection took hold in the incision from the cesarean. Then, after about a week, her stitches burst.

"It happened at night," Dad said. "The incision just burst wide open. Pus came pouring out. About a pint of it. It was horrible. It was green and yellow, and a little red where there was some blood in it. But there wasn't a lot of blood. The smell was unbelievable."

They rushed Mom back to the hospital and kept her there for most of another week on a course of industrial-strength antibiotics. They stitched her back up, and did it right this time. And while all of that was happening, Dad took care of me himself. Mom wasn't breastfeeding, so I had barely any contact with her for the first fourteen days of my life.

"Those first few weeks are critical," Dad would say, over and over again. "That's when you bond with your parents. Their face. Their scent. It's called imprinting. Only your mom couldn't be with you, because she was so sick. So you bonded with me. Never so much with her."

That was his theory about why things happened the way they did, and why he was the better choice to raise me. He was a big believer in the idea of behavioralism—of positive and negative reinforcement, and psychological conditioning. He seemed to take a lot of comfort in the idea that I loved him because I had no choice. That I obeyed him because I was programmed to.

I took it less seriously as I got older.

* * *

I turned four a few months after I got back to Eugene, and about a month after that my mom moved to San Francisco. It should have been a smaller deal than it was. She hadn't wanted me to live with her while Dad was in jail. Instead she sent a letter to my grandparents explaining that I was better off with them and that she had other priorities. "The only thing that keeps me going is my art," she wrote. "I believe in my heart that art is God's great gift to humanity . . . It's the only thing in my life I haven't botched miserably. When I give with art people take gladly. I've had so much locked up so tight inside me for so long, and now some of it is finally flowing out." I didn't know about the letter for another twenty years, but I didn't need to. Even a four-year-old could see that parenting wasn't at the top of my mom's to-do list.

Not to say she didn't raise a huge stink when she decided to move to San Francisco. For weeks, she and my father raged at each other. Sometimes over the phone, sometimes in our living room. Sometimes out in the yard. One day they stood at opposite ends of the dining room table in the Hayes Street house, legs apart like a couple of gunfighters, and screamed at each other for what seemed like an hour—Dad saying Mom was too irresponsible and selfish to ever take care of me, Mom saying she had a right to raise me. Everything came into the argument: Dad's arrest, their mutual drug use, Mom's drinking, stuff from when they were still together; times he'd been out for days without so much as a phone call; times he'd come home to find the sink full of dishes, me screaming in a dirty diaper, and her hiding in the upstairs bedroom, too overwhelmed to deal with any of it. Then they'd argue about who loved me more. There was a lot of swearing.

I found it strangely thrilling to watch them while they did this. I got light-headed. Euphoric. It was like their voices just sucked all the air out of the room.

When Mom finally gave up and went to California, I felt strangely bereft. Not about her moving, but because I didn't get to watch them fight anymore. I needn't have worried. She called once a month or so and they jumped right back into it over the phone. I only got Dad's half, but he'd always done most of the talking anyway.

7

One advantage of having my parents fighting over me was that they periodically tried to buy my affection, or my forgiveness, with presents. The regret and guilt they felt was transitory, but the swag just kept accumulating, so I had a slightly ridiculous stock of really nice toys.

My favorite was an old cap gun that was designed to look like an old cowboy six-shooter. It had a hammer that I could either cock back with my thumb, or cock and fire in one motion by just pulling the trigger. The barrel and the frame of the gun were cast out of some kind of cheap steel alloy, with elaborate scrollwork etched into the barrel and a cylinder that slid open to reveal a bunch of metal spools and gears where I could insert a roll of paper caps. Every time I pulled the trigger, the gun would feed a fresh paper cap into the space between the hammer and the striker, drop the hammer, and the toy would make a noise like a real gun. Sometimes the caps would even throw some sparks. Most of the gun was built to last a million years, except for the cheap plastic handle that broke off after I'd had the toy for less than a month. It could be taped back on, but the tape would inevitably get loose and the handle would come off again.

One morning, while I was playing by myself before my dad got out of bed, the handle fell off. The tape was in my dad's room to keep me from playing with it, but he was asleep. He usually stayed up late and slept in, and the rule was that I had to leave him alone until he woke up on his own. So maybe I forgot, or maybe I was just four years old and wanted what I wanted, but I knocked very gently on his bedroom door and poked my head inside his room.

"Dad?" I said.

He was under the covers on his bed and he didn't move, but I could tell he was awake.

"Yeah?" he said after a minute.

"Dad, can I have the tape? My cap gun's broken."

"Let me see it," he said, holding out his hand.

I walked over and handed the toy to him, hoping he'd have some magic fix that only grownups knew. He looked it over for a second, then threw it against his bedroom wall as hard as he could. It was a quick, startling motion and I jumped back away from the bed. The gun exploded into pieces and loose parts that rained down on his bookshelves and dresser. There was an enormous dent in the wall where it had struck. I was too surprised to react for a second.

"I've told you once," he said in an even, measured tone. "I've told you a million fucking times. Do not wake me up in the fucking morning unless it's a fucking emergency."

I started to cry. Partly from surprise, but mostly from disappointment. I was still processing the fact that he wasn't going to help me fix my toy.

"Stop that fucking sniveling or I'll give you something to cry about!" he roared.

I scurried out of the room, but I stopped to close the door carefully behind me. Because slamming the door was something else I wasn't supposed to do in the morning, and I was in enough trouble as it was.

Supposedly, this was all part of Dad's master plan.

Whenever he told me to do something and I refused, I got to the count of three to comply or there'd be a spanking. Usually a set number of swats with his bare hand while he held me over his knee. That was his version of obedience training. But there were other kinds of spankings, where maybe I got to the count of three or maybe I didn't. Maybe we were fighting, or maybe I did something that just pushed him over the edge. Those were the ones where I screamed and tried to get away and he'd hold me down while I was thrashing and hit me anywhere he could get a piece of me—ass, back, legs, neck, head. There were the kind where he'd use a spatula or a belt. And all of that fell into his general philosophy of parenting. He was always telling people—sometimes right in front of me—that parenting was all about positive and negative reinforcement. He said that even if he wasn't consistent about punishment, there was an over- arching consistency to his moods, and subtle cues that I could learn over time if the stakes were high enough. So sometimes there were spankings and sometimes there were beatings, and one time when I was four he picked me up and threw me against my bedroom wall.

He was telling me to do something and I was saying no, I wouldn't do it—and he just charged. I dropped to the ground and curled up, even though I knew it was a bad idea. Any time I tried to protect myself it always made him madder: running, hiding, trying to cover my head or face. That was all forbidden. Once he started coming, I was supposed to hold still and take it. So I knew when I dropped to the ground that I was only making it worse. But instead of flailing away at my back like he sometimes did, he hissed "Motherfucker" under his breath, grabbed me by my leg and shoulder, hoisted me into the air, and threw me at the wall, above my bed.

At first I didn't even understand what had happened. I was dazed and my ears were ringing, but nothing was broken except something inside the wall. I'd heard something under the plaster crack when I hit, but the wall looked fine. I didn't know what to do, so I just lay there on the bed. And Dad was gone. He'd run out of the room as soon as he did it.

When I made some reference to it later, he told me never to talk about it again.

"Anyway," he said, "it was an accident. I was aiming for the bed."

* * *

Over the course of a year, John told me the whole story of *The Hobbit* and *The Lord of the Rings*. He may not have read me the books in their entirety, but if he didn't read every word, he certainly read from them while he worked his way through the epic. He used different voices for a lot of the main characters. He sang the songs and chanted the poems. Sometimes he'd compare one or another of the characters in the book to some of his lead figures, to show me what chain mail or a long sword looked like. John particularly liked doing the voice of Gollum, the wretched creature that follows the heroes through most of the story, and nearly destroys the world because of his sycophantic obsession with a stolen magic ring. I let John do the voice as long as I could stand it because I knew he liked doing it, but one day as we neared the end of the story, I just snapped.

"Stop it," I said. "I hate that voice."

"Why?" he asked. He was clearly surprised by the criticism.

I thought about it before I answered.

"I hate Gollum," I said. "He's the worst person in the book."

"Why's that?" John asked.

"He's weak. He can't even fight. He just lies and cheats and steals. Anyone could kill him—should kill him—but he begs and whines and they let him live. And then he does bad things to them after they were nice to him."

"Well," John said. "That's true, I suppose. But that's the thing about Gollum. He knows what the right thing is. He can see it. And he wants to be good. But he had some bad luck. Right? He found the ring. And once he found it, he needed it. The ring made him that way."

"Because he's weak."

"Maybe," John said. "But remember—nobody else could carry it besides Frodo and, for a little while, Sam. None of the other good guys even wanted to touch it. Gollum just didn't know how dangerous it was. Isildur, the first human to carry it, was a good guy before he got the ring. But once he had it, it corrupted him."

"Then he shouldn't have messed with it."

"How could he have known? You might say, Jason, that the most evil thing the ring does is take people who were good, or who wanted to use the ring to do good, and change them. And that once they're changed, they can't go back. Not all the way. Gollum had that ring for hundreds of years."

"I'd never let it change me," I said.

"A lot of people think that. Boromir thought it. But you can't know until you go up against the power of the ring, and most people lose that fight. Everyone except Frodo and Sam, in fact."

I didn't know what to say to that one.

I still hated Gollum.

* * *

We spent almost exactly a year on Hayes Street, and I was bored out of my mind for most of it. There were six other kids my age within walking distance: two straights who lived on our block, two hippie kids who lived at the end of the street, and two kids from our crew who lived a few blocks away. The two straights, a girl named Mickey and a boy named Kurty, made me nervous. The girl was a year older than I was, and the boy a year younger, and they both had "narc" written all over them. Their father, Mr. Wagner, was a grumpy older guy with a day job, who wore plaid pants and short-sleeved sweaters and kept his hair short. Their mom was a tense middle-aged woman who wore more makeup than any woman I knew besides my grandma, and dressed like Mrs. Jetson. Mr. and Mrs. Wagner clearly didn't like me or my dad or our housemates; they seemed to want us all to go away. Possibly Mr. Wagner worked in lumber, or farming or textiles. The kids didn't seem to feel as strongly about me as their parents did but they were eager to please, and I could easily imagine them running straight to their parents if I let something slip about Dad smoking pot or having gone to jail or any of that.

The hippies at the end of the block, Geoff and Sarah, were okay except that their parents were the real deal; honest-to-god house-building guitar-playing ex–Peace Corps vegetarian pacifists. In some ways this made them as dangerous as Mickey and Kurty. My people looked like hippies: they dressed like hippies, listened to hippie music, and said "man" a lot. But we were basically white trash rednecks in hippie clothing. Most of the adults I knew loved meat and many of them got in fights all the time and had decent gun collections. To say nothing of all the crime. Besides dealing drugs, my dad and his friends engaged in fraud, theft, and vandalism on a regular basis. Geoff and Sarah's parents might be willing to occupy an ROTC building or march without a permit—they might even smoke some grass every so often. But if they knew half of what went on in our house, or in our social circles, they'd call the cops on us as sure as Mickey and Kurty's parents. They'd probably agonize over it more, but they'd do it.

The two kids from our crew were Ezeriah and Edward. Ezeriah was one year older than I was, Edward two years older. Their mom, Emmy, was a friend of my dad's, though she didn't have much to do with the rest of Dad's social circle. She was tall and thin, which was what Dad liked in women, and he could never shut up about how beautiful he thought she was. I didn't have much of an opinion about her one way or the other, and as nice as it was not to have to worry about what I might let slip around her kids, I didn't like playing with them. Edward was just a little too old, and Ezeriah was just a little too butch. I liked make-believe games based on the stories John read to me. Ezeriah liked sports—as in games that grownups played, with bats and balls. And math. Lots of math. He constantly talked about his favorite players and their batting averages and errors and—Jesus. I didn't even know what a batting average was. He talked about football. He talked about the Ducks. I had no idea. I didn't even know the University of Oregon had a football team. Once we both got chickenpox at the same time and spent a week in my living room watching *Dialing for Dollars* and *Sci-Fi Theater*, and we got along pretty well that week because we had a shared love of war movies

41

and Godzilla and we happened to get sick between seasons for his favorite sports. But most of the rest of the time he just confused me.

And that was about it for my social outlets. There were some other kids in our crew who I got along with pretty well. Calliope and Miles were my favorites. But they didn't live nearby and I only saw them once or twice every couple of weeks. The rest of the time I played by myself or watched TV or hung out with John.

When my dad got tired of listening to me complain about how bored I was, he'd give me a serrated steak knife and tell me to mow the lawn with it. I'd spend hours out in the front yard, cutting clumps of grass loose from the dirt, trying to make them all a nice uniform height. Sometimes it was the high point of my week.

8

My dad's Grandma Brown died sometime during the summer of 1976, and she left us about $4,000. She was Dad's mother's mother, and the last of Dad's grandparents to die. Dad spent the money on a new car, a new TV, and two Beaver State Indian blankets from the Pendleton Woolen Mills, Pendleton, Oregon. Personally, I wanted to spend it on groceries— Beth had recently pointed out to me that not only were the little black things I kept finding in my powdered milk not supposed to be there, but that they were actually mouse shit. So my vote would have been for milk that came in liquid form, and maybe some fresh fruit. But Dad said we had to cash the check and get rid of the money immediately or the welfare people would take it all. So we got a new Vega and I kept eating USDA cornflakes and mouse poop-flavored powdered milk for breakfast.

* * *

Dad started classes at Lane County Community College the month after I turned four, which meant I was eligible to start going to their Montessori day care. I'd been to day care before, in Los Angeles, where my grandparents had sent me to something called a Town & Country preschool, but I hadn't done very well there. I had a problem with authority. I had a problem with other kids. Basically, I just had a lot of problems. Things didn't go much better at Lane Montessori. I only made two friends the whole time I was there: a teacher named Dee Dee, who took a special liking to me, and my chicken, Charlie.

Charlie was the product of a school science project. The teachers had designed and built an egg incubator out of stuff they got at the hardware store and told us all about how it worked. Then they brought in some fertilized eggs and put them in the incubator, under a bank of warm lights. We all watched the eggs obsessively and when the teachers passed around permission slips that would allow students to take the chickens home with us, I talked my dad into signing one.

"We don't have any place to put it," he said at first.

"We've got the whole backyard!" I said.

"It's not fenced."

"We can build something."

By which I obviously meant that he could build something. He sighed.

"Fine," he said. "But it's your problem."

Keeping in mind here that I was four.

43

When the chickens hatched, all us kids were ecstatic. We watched the birds poke their way out of their shells, and we talked about how long it took them to be born. Sometimes a chick would spend a couple of hours working its way to freedom, sometimes the process would last overnight. And once they were out, the entire school got to play with them for a few days before they started getting sent home with the kids who'd talked their parents into signing permission slips. My dad balked again when he came to pick me up and actually saw—and smelled—the baby chickens in the incubator, but I whined until he let me bring Charlie home.

It started out well enough. I kept Charlie in a cardboard box in the living room. He was small. He didn't eat much or make much noise. But as he grew, it started to become obvious we'd need to take him outside. Dad stalled as long as he could on building me a chicken coop, but then one day he found an old playpen in an alley and brought it home for me to put Charlie in. He unfolded it proudly and stood back to show how the vinyl-padded metal frame supported the pink polyester mesh walls that would keep Charlie safe and sound in the backyard.

"It's got holes in it," I said. "He'll get out."

"No problem," Dad said. He went into the house and came out with a darning needle and a roll of dental floss. A few minutes later he'd patched all the largest holes with dental floss, in such a way that it looked like a giant spider had been making half-assed webs in the gaps.

"Won't he peck through?" I asked.

"Of course not," Dad said.

And the playpen worked pretty well for a few weeks, until Charlie started to crow. By this time he'd gone from a little yellow fuzzball to a medium-size white rooster with a bright red crest, and he wanted to let the world know he was in our backyard. Eugene was still rural enough that the neighbors didn't give us any grief about the crowing, but the sound drove Dad batshit.

"Jason," he said one day. "We can't keep Charlie. He's too noisy."

"What do you want to do with him?" I asked.

"Give him to Sean," Dad said, referring to a friend of ours who owned a farmhouse out near Dexter, some twenty-five miles from the center of town.

"Sean eats his chickens, Dad."

"Well—okay. But he won't eat Charlie if we ask him not to."

Sean was a car mechanic from Georgia who was best known in our circles for getting so jacked up on speed that he once blew all the windows out of his house with a shotgun. That, and beating a murder rap for supposedly killing a woman he'd picked up in a bar one night. He was one of the least child- and animal-friendly people I'd ever met, and I had absolutely no faith in any promise he might make not to eat my chicken. I could already imagine him saying, "Charlie? Oh yeah, that's him, right there. What's that? Charlie was white and that one's orange? Well shit. I don't know what to tell you, kid."

Something on my face conveyed all this to my dad, and he sighed dramatically.

"What if I get you another pet?" he asked.

"Like what?" I said.

"Something quiet. Like a gerbil. That way you can keep it in the house. And play with it."

I had to admit that second part sounded nice. As much as I loved Charlie, he wasn't much fun to play with. He didn't really learn tricks, and he tended to peck at me when I tried to pick him up. Sometimes, when my friends were over, we'd make little mazes in the front yard by flattening the tall grass with our feet or cutting it with a steak knife, and then we'd run Charlie through the maze. But mostly he just ate, crowed—and pecked holes in the playpen.

"I'll try a gerbil," I said.

"So I can call Sean about Charlie?"

"No!"

"Well. I guess Miles and his mom might take Charlie out at their place."

Miles and his mom, Laurie, were part of our extended social network. They lived in a house that was situated on an actual farm just east of Springfield. The land around their house wasn't being cultivated anymore, but they had a lot of space and a long dirt driveway and an abandoned barn next to it. The whole setup was perfect for a chicken, and I figured they might be willing to give Charlie a patch of yard or something.

"Okay," I said. "If I like the gerbil."

The next day, when Dad brought me home from day care, I found a brown gerbil in a shoebox in my room. I took him out and tried to play with him, but he didn't seem to like being held any better than Charlie did and when he bit me, it hurt a lot worse than getting pecked. I played around with him for an hour or so before I put him back in his box and went to ask my dad where the gerbil's permanent home would be.

"Can't we just use the shoebox?" he asked.

"Won't he chew his way out?"

"I don't think so," he said. "The sides of the box are too smooth. His teeth can't get a grip."

I could feel something warm and soft on the bottom of the box.

"I think he peed in there, Dad."

Dad opened the box and wrinkled his nose.

"Hold on," he said. He went to the kitchen and came back a minute later with a paper bag.

"We can keep him in here while I line his shoebox with

newspaper," Dad said. We moved the whole operation out to the kitchen table and Dad tried to grab the gerbil out of the box. He seemed reluctant to touch the little brown creature, and I didn't offer to help because I sort of enjoyed watching him squirm. Finally he gave up trying to pick it up in his hand and just hoisted it out by its tail.

"That looks like it hurts him," I said as the gerbil gyrated around and tried to get a grip on my dad's fingers with his little pink paws.

"No," Dad said. "It's fine. They—"

Then the gerbil dropped back down into the shoebox.

At first I thought Dad had just lost his grip on the tail, but when I looked I saw he was still clutching it in his hand like a little scrap of ragged brown string. Dad and I both looked at the tail in his hand, then at each other—then down into the box.

The gerbil was on his back, legs flailing in the air, making little gasping movements with his mouth. There was surprisingly little blood from the stump of his tail, but it was clear the rodent was fucked.

"Shit," I said.

Dad didn't say anything back.

"What's wrong with him?" I asked.

"I think it's in shock," Dad said.

"In shock?" I asked.

"Yeah. I've heard it happens to rabbits and stuff, when they get really scared. It usually kills them. Like, from a heart attack."

"Is there anything we can do?" I asked.

"Nope."

Suddenly Dad got up and went out the back door of the house. I had no idea where he'd gone, but I didn't want to leave the gerbil alone. Not because I had a lot of love for the animal, but because I was afraid he'd jump out of the box and start running around the kitchen, like one of Sean's chickens with its head cut off.

When Dad came back a few minutes later he had a shovel.

"Is that so we can bury him after he dies?" I asked.

"Why wait?" he said, scooping up the box and walking toward the front door.

I couldn't really believe he was going to do what he said he was going to do, so I followed him out the front door. He put the box down on the stairs and used the shovel to dig a deep hole behind the iris bulbs, near the foundation of the house. It was still daylight outside and I looked around to see if anyone was watching, but, as usual, nobody was out on the street or in their yard. When Dad had a hole about the right size, he put the box in the bottom of the hole and put the lid on it. As the lid came down I could see the gerbil was still twitching, but it did seem to be winding down. I hoped that meant it was actually dying.

"Hold on," Dad said, going back into the house. When he came back he dropped the gerbil's tail on top of the box, then started shoveling dirt in on it.

"Is it going to . . . hurt?" I asked.

"Nope," Dad said. "Just like going to sleep."

"Jesus," I said, revising my opinion of sleep on the spot. "Are you gonna say something?"

"What do you want me to say, Jason? A gerbil's pretty much a rat. We put out mousetraps. When we catch one we just throw it in the garbage. At least this one's getting buried."

"Okay," I said, as he finished up.

When he was done he paused with the tip of the shovel resting on the fresh-turned earth and looked down at what he'd done. We exchanged a look and he sighed dramatically.

"Dear Mr. Gerbil," he said. "I'm very sorry that things didn't work out. Better luck in your next life. Jason?"

"Sorry, Mr. Gerbil," I said to the garden.

"All right," Dad said. He left the shovel leaning against the house and led me inside to the kitchen table. After he sat me down he went to the refrigerator and poured some of Beth's milk into a Mason jar. Then he went to the cupboard and stole one of her cookies. He set both things down in front of me, then went to his room and came back with his stash box. While I ate the cookie, he rolled himself a big fat joint and lit up. He took the first hit with a shaking hand and leaned back in his chair and closed his eyes.

"So," I said after a few minutes. "I can keep Charlie, right?"

He put his free hand over his eyes and made a noise, partway between a sob and a laugh.

"Yeah," he said. "You can keep the fucking chicken."

"Thank you," I said.

"Yeah—fine. Okay. Could you be quiet for a little while, please?"

"All right," I said. It was getting dark outside, and I knew Beth might be home soon. I finished the milk and cookie, rinsed out the Mason jar and wiped the crumbs off the table, so hopefully she wouldn't notice we'd been into her food.

* * *

Dad still didn't build a coop for Charlie, but he moved the rooster to the garage, where the sound of his crowing wasn't quite as loud. I felt bad about it—I knew it was dark out there and that the garage was full of broken glass and other old junk that the bird could hurt himself on. I thought about what I might be able to do to get Charlie out of there. But nothing I could think of—short of getting my dad to build a coop, which had been impossible so far—would improve Charlie's situation much.

Then, a few months later, John solved the problem for me when he accidentally left a candle going in his room and halfway burned the house down. After that there was no question of staying on Hayes Street. We'd all have to move, including Charlie.

9

In a way, we were lucky about how John caught the house on fire. The fire happened in the middle of the day and Dad was the only one home. John was actually out of town. He'd left the day before, to take a shipment of kefir and whole-grain bread down to San Francisco. Which gives you an idea of how big that goddamn candle was. I was out playing with Mickey and Kurty, the straight kids down the street, and I didn't realize anything was wrong until I saw the smoke and heard the fire trucks.

"Hey," Mickey said, walking out to the street so she could look down the block. "I think your house is on fire."

"No," I said. "That can't . . ." I walked out and stood next to her and looked at where the fire trucks were gathered.

"Well fuck," I said.

"Jason!" Mickey said.

"Sorry."

I walked down the block to my house and saw my dad carrying loads of our stuff out of the house one armful at a time: TV, stereo, record collection, and then various antiques. He stacked it all as neatly as he could, off on one side of the yard, while firefighters wearing dirty yellow bunker gear went in and out past him. They'd already blasted one of their giant hoses through John's bedroom window. The attic was smoking fitfully, but the fire was mostly out. Dad was just trying to get as much of our stuff out as possible before the water started to make its way through the ceilings and into the lower part of the house.

Right as I got there, one of the firefighters called out the window for everyone to get clear, then tossed John's scorched mattress and box spring from the second floor onto the front lawn. I looked at the exposed metal springs and wondered if this was what had happened to the mattress Marianne had told me to be careful on, back at our house on 15th.

"Step back, kid," one of the firemen on the street said to me as I tried to get into the yard to help Dad move our stuff.

"That's my house," I said.

"Jason!" Dad called to me. "Stay back there. I'll be with you in a minute."

So I stood and watched while the firefighters threw more of John's stuff out the window onto the lawn, and Dad kept hauling our stuff to safety. Once he was done with our things, he started bringing Beth's belongings out and putting them in another pile. I kept looking over my shoulder, expecting Mickey and Kurty to come and watch the whole thing, but they didn't even come back to the street to wave at me. Either this was a lot less interesting than I thought it was, or their parents had told them to come inside.

After a while my dad seemed satisfied that he'd saved as much from the house as he could, and walked over to where I was standing. He looked sweaty and annoyed, but not nearly as angry as I would have expected.

"We can't stay here tonight," he said. "I'll have to find us a place."

"Okay," I said.

"I'll need to move our stuff, too," he said. "We can't just

leave it out here on the lawn. It'd be easier if I could leave you with someone. What about those kids you were playing with? Could you stay there for a few hours?"

"I don't know," I said. "They don't like me that much."

"What about their parents?"

"I was talking about their parents."

"Oh," he said. "Come on. I'll talk to them."

So I walked down the street to Mickey and Kurty's house in the afternoon twilight, and my dad knocked on their door. When Mr. Wagner answered I got the same feeling of vertigo I usually experienced when Dad talked to straight people. Seeing him standing there in his flamboyant hippie clothes while Mr. Wagner stood in front of him in a Lycra polo shirt and plaid slacks, arms crossed, biceps flexed—it was like matter and antimatter were about to collide. I didn't hear much of the conversation but Mr. Wagner seemed to appreciate that our house had caught on fire, and I went inside while Dad ran off to make arrangements for us and our stuff.

I'd never actually been inside Mickey and Kurty's house before. It seemed not to have enough windows, and the dining room table was directly beyond the front door. The whole family was sitting there looking at me—the kids and Mrs. Wagner.

"Won't you join us?" Mrs. Wagner asked.

"Uh," I said. Then I looked at the table and felt my pulse quicken. It was covered in pretty much my favorite foods ever: fried chicken, mashed potatoes, broccoli, carrots, and peas. I'd never seen that much fried chicken in one place in my life. Everyone was still staring at me, and I remembered I'd been invited to share this bounty.

"Sure!" I said. I started for the table, but Mrs. Wagner looked horrified and I paused again.

"The bathroom's through here," Mr. Wagner said, guiding

me to a small room off the dining room that had a toilet and a sink in it. I went in, because he seemed to expect me to, but after he closed the door I just stood there until I remembered that Grandma had sometimes told me to wash my hands before eating. So I rinsed my hands quickly under some cold water, toweled them off, and went back out. By then they'd made a place for me at the table.

"This looks great," I said, sitting down and reaching for the nearby platter of chicken. "You guys eat like this all the time?"

Mickey and Kurty exchanged an embarrassed look. Mr. and Mrs. Wagner were giving each other looks, too, but I couldn't read them. I paused and looked at everyone else's plates. They'd all been eating, so I knew they weren't waiting to say grace—the other weird ritual I'd learned from my grandparents. I couldn't figure out what I was doing wrong, but all that good food was calling to me so I piled on the chicken, served up a heap of mashed potatoes and gravy, and dug in.

"Man," I said, "this is delicious."

"I'm glad you like it," said Mrs. Wagner. Then they all started eating, but with a lot of sidelong glances at me and secret looks between each other.

Finally everyone else was done, and the kids got up to watch TV in the other room. I was basically full so I started to get up, too, but Mr. Wagner shook his head and said, "Uh-uh," while he was looking at my plate.

"What?" I asked, looking around to see what I was missing.

"You have to clean your plate first," he said.

"Oh," I said. "Okay."

I started to scrape the remaining pieces of chicken back onto the chicken plate, but he stopped me again.

"No," said Mr. Wagner. "You can't put it back. You've touched it. It's been on your plate. You have to eat it."

And I finally realized what all those looks were about.

"But you all made me wash my hands before dinner," I said. "They're clean!"

I held out my hands so the Wagners could see how clean they were.

"You've been eating with them since then," said Mrs. Wagner. "We don't share germs in this house."

"But . . ." I couldn't even formulate a reply to that one. In my house we ate each other's leftovers all the time. When our crew went out skinny-dipping in Fall Creek, ten or fifteen of us would eat watermelon and whatever else by passing it around and taking big sloppy bites out of it. We all drank out of the same jugs. Me and my dad even shared bathwater to save money on hot water; he'd take his bath first because he liked his water hot, and I'd take mine after when it was just warm.

I looked at the pile of food on my plate. Looked at Mr. and Mrs. Wagner. I could hear the TV playing in the other room, where Mickey and Kurty had gone. The Wagners looked at me. I looked at them. Then Mr. Wagner went in the other room to watch TV and Mrs. Wagner started cleaning up. And I just sat there while she took everything else off the table except my plate. Sat there while she did dishes in the kitchen. Sat there when she went into the TV room with the rest of her family, until finally, after an hour or so, the doorbell rang. When Mrs. Wagner answered it I heard my dad's voice.

He'd found a place for us to stay. He was there to pick me up.

"He's in here," Mrs. Wagner said, stepping aside to let Dad see me at the table.

Dad just poked his head through the doorway and said, "C'mon, Jason. I got all our stuff in a storage unit. Got your chicken out at Laurie's, with Miles. We'll crash out at Sean's place for a while."

I looked at Mrs. Wagner. "Can I be excused now?"

"I suppose," she said.

I hopped down off the chair and grabbed Dad's hand. He thanked the Wagners for keeping an eye on me and we left out the front door. It was dark outside.

"What the hell was that all about?" Dad wanted to know.

When I told him what had happened, he started cursing the Wagners and said that if they had house rules they should've told me what they were before I got a pile of food on my plate. I thought he was right about that, but I couldn't shake the feeling that most people, most of the time, would agree with what the Wagners had done. Most people would think I needed to be taught a lesson in civilized behavior. And I wondered, not for the last time, what being right gets you if everybody else thinks you're wrong.

10

Forensic fire investigation was evidently still in its infancy in 1977, because not only did nobody figure out it was John who'd burned our house down, but somehow the thing was ruled an accident from faulty wiring. This was good news for John, who couldn't afford to pay for the damages, but it didn't mean much to me and my dad. Dad left all our stuff in storage and we couch-surfed with friends for a couple of weeks until he found us a place to live.

We ended up in a comfortable little apartment in downtown Eugene. My father had historically expressed his dislike of apartments—he didn't like sharing walls with strangers—but he said this one reminded him of Los Angeles. Which he apparently thought of as a good thing. After we'd been there less than a month he decided to make me some fried chicken of my own—only once he got the chicken going he realized he was out of rolling papers, so he took me down to the liquor store a few blocks away. By the time we got back, the fire department was there and all our neighbors were out on the street. Dad stood on the sidewalk and looked through the open front door into the blackened, gutted interior. As I stood next to him, I was mostly struck by what a huge difference a few minutes of uncontrolled burning could make in the atmosphere of a charming mid-century modern. Older houses stood up to this kind of thing better, I decided.

One of the firefighters noticed us and said, "Is this your apartment?"

Dad looked at the firefighter, looked back through the open front door, and said, "Nope."

Then he put his hand on my shoulder and started guiding me down the street toward the Vega. When I started to turn around to look back at the firefighters, Dad squeezed my shoulder. Hard.

"Don't do that," he said.

It wasn't a huge loss for us. All we had in the apartment was a bunch of junk we'd picked up on the cheap at Goodwill. I felt kind of bad about the other people who lived in the building, but I hadn't known any of them by name and it was an easy thing to put behind me.

* * *

After the unfortunate burning-down-the-apartment incident, we moved into a small house on Fillmore Street with a woman named Marcy and her three kids, Crystal, Faith, and Isaac. The house only had two bedrooms and space was tight, but the price was right. Marcy got her own room because it was her house, and Crystal and Faith shared the other bedroom because they were older, and girls. Isaac and I bunked in the laundry room. Dad slept in the unheated storage area behind the garage. Dad and I left most of our stuff in the long-term storage locker at the edge of town since there was no place to put it in Marcy's house.

Pretty much the only member of my family who got a better situation at the new house was Charlie—though he may have considered it a step down from the accommodations he'd enjoyed at Miles and Laurie's place. The way the backyard was set up, Dad was able to string some chicken wire between the garage and the neighbor's fence and create a little safe space for Charlie. Or so we thought. He died a few months after we moved, and while Dad wouldn't let me see the body, I got a glimpse of a mangled mass of white feathers. Dad's theory was that Charlie died of natural causes, and that something—a cat or a raccoon, maybe—ate him afterward. I didn't see any evidence to support that idea, but I was happy to believe the fiction.

11

Dad had toned down his drug business considerably after his arrest, but every so often a deal came up that seemed relatively safe and offered a good rate of return and he'd be tempted out of his semiretired status. Not long after we moved in with Marcy, he was offered a chance to make a few hundred dollars delivering a shipment of pot from Eugene to Portland. It fit his criteria of low risk and high profit, so he agreed to make the run and left me in Eugene with Marcy while he headed north. He wasn't heard from again for three days, but when he came home he had a story to tell.

He was supposed to move the shipment in a dozen thirty-five-gallon black garbage bags, full of bud and loose leaves. Dad preferred to transport large quantities of pot in garbage bags; he said that if he got stopped, he could just tell the cops he was taking a bunch of yard clippings to the dump. Even if he did end up getting searched, he could claim someone else had given him the bags and paid him a couple of dollars to get rid of them. It wasn't much of a defense, but it had the advantage of being plausible and easy to remember.

The dozen garbage bags completely filled the hatchback of the Vega, so Dad drove the whole 110 miles north using his side-view mirrors to change lanes. When he got to Portland he had some trouble finding the address where he was supposed to make the drop, but eventually he made his way to a small house on the west side of the city. He parked the Vega on the street and went to the door to make sure he had the right place. When he pressed the doorbell, another young male hippie answered.

"I've got a delivery here," Dad said.

"From Eugene?" the man asked.

"Yeah," Dad said. "I—"

But the dealer interrupted him and asked, "Is that your car?"

What happened next is probably owed to the fact that most of Oregon is comparatively flat. Not Midwest-flat, but Eugene and Portland are both in the Willamette River Valley, and most of the development is on the low, level ground near the river. The problem here was that Dad's connection didn't live in the Portland basin. He lived in Portland Heights, an upper-class residential neighborhood on the slopes of the Tualatin Mountains, west of Downtown Portland. The Heights have good schools and great views. And they also have steeper hills than any urban residential neighborhood in the state.

Afterward, Dad always claimed he'd set the parking brake when he got out of the car—that it was broken, and he'd just never noticed because Eugene is so flat. But he also neglected to turn his front wheels toward the curb.

When Dad looked over his shoulder to see what the connection was staring at, the Vega was just beginning to roll. Dad lunged after the car. For a few frantic seconds, as he chased it down the street, his fingers brushed futilely at the driver's side door handle, but gravity had sunk its teeth in by then and the car was accelerating. It inched ahead, then really took off, almost like it wanted to get away from him. By the time it slammed into the galvanized steel utility pole at the bottom of the hill, he figured it was going a good sixty miles an hour.

The pole took the car dead center and sliced halfway through the engine compartment. The entire front of the car just puckered up like a horrified face. The headlights were pointed, more or less, at each other.

Dad stopped and stared, but only for a second. The sound of the impact was still echoing through the hills when he ran back up to his connection's house. The door was closed. Dad pounded frantically until the guy looked out past his security chain.

"Help me get that shit out of the back of the car!" Dad shouted.

"No fucking way," the connection said. "Get it up here and dump it in my backyard, I'll keep it. But I'm not going down there."

Dad just turned around and ran. He couldn't blame the dealer. It was exactly what Dad would have done under the circumstances.

Surprisingly, there was still nobody around when Dad got back down to the car. He used his key to pop the hatchback, grabbed four garbage bags, and ran back up the hill. Then down and back, two more times. He threw the last set of bags over the fence and came back down the hill to check on the car. A few of the neighbors came out on the street to see what was happening. Then, just as Dad got to the bottom of the hill, a police car pulled up.

Dad said later that the cops knew something was up but they couldn't prove anything, so they arrested him for leaving the scene of an accident. Dad explained that he hadn't left the scene of the accident—that he'd just arrived when the police showed up. That excuse worked, but not before he'd spent two days in jail and squandered his phone call trying to reach Sean. Sean was Dad's go-to guy when it came to getting bailed out of weird situations. But while he was a great guy to have on your side in almost any situation, he didn't yet own one of the new-fangled answering machines that were just coming out on the market. After Dad got home, he got paid for the delivery, but most of the money went to cover the cost of having the eviscerated corpse of the Vega towed back to Eugene.

* * *

After the Vega was totaled, Dad finally quit community college, took an actual break from dealing drugs, and found a semi-straight job working under the table with an anarchist tree-planting collective called the Hodads. The job took him out of town for days at a time, sleeping in the converted school bus the Hodads used as a mobile bunkhouse and planting saplings in the wreckage of clear-cut forests.

Dad quitting school meant I couldn't go to day care there anymore, but the theory was that Marcy would cover child care while Dad was gone. In practice, she wasn't around much either, and all four of us kids spent a lot of time on our own. We didn't mind. There were a lot of other kids in our neighborhood, and Eugene still had enough small town innocence that even Isaac and I, who were only five, could wander around relatively freely.

The nearest busy street was West 11th Avenue, just to the south of us, which we weren't supposed to cross. But we could go as far as we wanted to the east or west, and that meant we could play in the alleys behind the businesses on our side of West 11th. Whenever the weather was good, Isaac and I would traverse the whole area, Dumpster-diving and rooting through junk, looking for old machine parts or packing material that we could turn into toys. We could tell just by looking at a Dumpster whether it would be worth opening. Most were too gross to mess with, but some of them belonged to warehouses or auto parts stores. The outsides of those Dumpsters were always clean. When we opened them, they were usually full of broken-down cardboard boxes.

On a hot day, the smell of dry cardboard wafting out of a clean Dumpster was enough to make me want to crawl inside it and go to sleep. Except that when I mentioned something about it to my dad he told me a story about a kid getting emptied into the back of a garbage truck and crushed by the truck's big hydraulic compactor. It didn't keep me out of Dumpsters, but it took all the romance out of the idea of sleeping in one.

Mostly Isaac and I just played with the boxes. If we could find empty ones, we'd fold them back into cube-shapes and pretend we were superheroes, throwing giant empty boxes at each other like Superman and Captain Marvel hurling Styrofoam boulders. But every once in a while we'd find something interesting—like the time we found dozens of small white cardboard boxes with individually wrapped chandelier crystals inside. We assumed someone had accidentally thrown out several pounds of diamonds, and we brought as many of them home as we could fit into our pockets.

12

My grandpa had a heart attack while we were living on Fillmore. It was his first one. Dad, all of twenty-seven years old, still felt enough of a connection to his father to drop everything, get special permission from his probation officer, buy some overpriced plane tickets, and fly us down to L.A. to visit Grandpa in the hospital. I didn't really know what a heart attack was, and I didn't know why Grandpa having one meant we had to go to Los Angeles, but I didn't mind making the trip. I had my own reasons for wanting to go.

Like most five-year-old boys, I was crazy for dinosaurs. At some point my dad had read me a book about dinosaurs and prehistoric mammals that included a few paragraphs about tar pits, and how tar pits sucked dinosaurs down into them and dissolved the flesh off their bones over a period of centuries. The book said that the skeletons left over from this process were some of the best-preserved specimens in the world. The book said there were tar pits that had been around for millions of years, like the La Brea Tar Pits, in Los Angeles, which were surrounded by chain-link fences to keep people from getting sucked into them.

The book had pictures of lots of dinosaurs in it, but no pictures of the tar pits. So my five-year-old brain conjured a picture of a kind of prehistoric monster called a tarpit that basically just sat there on the ground like a giant Venus flytrap and waited for something to step on it. Then it would pull its victim down into its gaping maw and spend a few centuries digesting it before pooping the cleaned skeleton out into the desert where humans would later stumble across it and put it in a museum. I was fascinated by the idea that there were living specimens of these things in Los Angeles—and that I'd missed my chance to see one while I was living in Torrance.

When Dad told me that Grandpa's heart attack meant we had to go to L.A., I knew the universe was conspiring to give me another chance to see the tarpits.

* * *

Dad's cousin Dave met us at the airport in L.A. Dave was related to Dad on his mom's side, and he didn't look anything like us—he had wavy blond hair and fair skin that tanned a kind of ruddy brown. He was a hippie, but Dad had warned me that Dave was one of those clean-living hippies like I saw on TV and I shouldn't say anything about our family business around him.

We threw our stuff in Dave's van and he drove us straight out to the hospital. I was glad we were going to get this part out of the way, but we ended up in a traffic jam. I'd never seen one before, and I couldn't believe how many cars there were all around us, or how wide the freeways were. I couldn't understand why the cars were all stopped or why the ones up front didn't just go. But every time I asked about it, Dad told me to be quiet. Eventually I gave up and lay down on the floor in the dark back compartment of the van—until Dad and Dave both jumped in their seats.

"Holy shit!" Dave said.

I sat up and looked to see what they were staring at and at first I didn't see anything. Then I spotted something a few hundred yards ahead. Some kind of bird or . . .

"What is that?" I asked.

"It's a tire," Dad said.

That didn't make any sense, but he was right. It was a tire, bouncing down the shoulder of the freeway toward us. On each bounce, it seemed to go fifty or sixty feet into the air. I wondered where it could possibly have been dropped from to make it go that high.

"Why's it bouncing like that?" I asked, as we watched it lope down the freeway toward us.

"It's a spare," Dad said. "It's still got a rim and a tube in it. Jason, come here."

He reached behind him and pulled me onto his lap, then opened the passenger side door a crack. Dave did the same on his side. Neither one of them took their eyes off the tire.

I realized the tire was moving down the freeway toward us much faster than I'd first thought. I leaned forward and watched it sail into the air, hesitate for a second, and start to come back down.

"It'll land in front of us," Dad said.

"Yeah," Dave agreed.

Watching it come down, I started to get scared. When it hit the concrete shoulder of the freeway I felt the impact as much as I heard it, and then the tire flashed back up into the sky again, so fast I could barely see it. Dave tilted his head and watched in his rearview mirror.

"Wow," he said.

Slowly but surely, the traffic started to move again.

"Was that it?" Dad asked. "How many miles could that thing have bounced down the freeway without going off?"

"I don't know," Dave said.

Ten minutes later we saw a delivery van on the left shoulder of the freeway with a police car parked behind it.

"Mark," Dave said.

"Hey, Jason," Dad said, pointing at an imaginary object on the right side of the van. "What's that?"

"What's what?" I asked, looking where he was pointing,

expecting to see another tire. But he wasn't looking where he was pointing, and neither was Dave. They were looking at the van. When I tried to look where they were looking, we'd already passed it.

"What was that?" I asked.

"That van got hit by the tire," Dad said. "The cab was crushed and the driver was killed."

"How could you tell?" I asked.

"It was obvious," Dad said.

"Wow," I said. "He was just driving along and—splat."

"Yeah," Dad said. "Sometimes that's how it happens."

Dave gave Dad a look, like Dad had said something wrong, but I wasn't sure why.

* * *

When we finally got to the hospital and went up to Grandpa's room, I couldn't understand what the big deal had been. Grandpa looked fine, I thought. There was a machine next to his bed: a white metal box on a wheeled stand, with four or five unmarked switches and a few red lights. A clear plastic tube ran out of it and up under Grandpa's hospital gown. I had no idea what it did. I couldn't even tell if it was on. Lying in his large, comfortable-looking bed, watching baseball on the cable TV on the wall, Grandpa looked like he always had: big, strong, and totally humorless. He was wearing his usual large-framed yellow-tinted sunglasses. His ridiculous pompadour toupee was on straight, his face was fresh-shaved. His dark skin was a little yellow, but otherwise he seemed healthy and lucid.

"Hi, Dad," my dad said when we came in.

Grandpa looked at Dad, but his expression didn't change much.

"Mark," he said.

Dad sort of looked like he wanted to hug Grandpa, but Grandpa didn't move or respond to Dad's movements, so Dad just stood next to the bed, holding on to the metal railing. Grandpa's eyes drifted down to me.

"How's it going, pardner?" he growled. He was always calling me stuff like that. He always said it in that raspy growl, like he was making an effort to sound extra-tough when he was talking to me.

"Okay," I said.

"All right," Grandpa said, and went back to looking at the TV.

Dave was standing in the doorway behind us. I looked at him, but he was watching Dad and Grandpa.

"I'm glad you could make it," Grandpa said. His eyes flicked away from the TV, then back.

"Of course," Dad said. He sounded surprised.

Dad and I stood there for a while. Eventually I noticed a chair up against one wall and sat down. Dad stared at Grandpa. Grandpa looked at the TV.

"All right," Dad said after about twenty minutes. "We'll head out. We're staying at Aunt Gin's. I'll be back."

"Okay," Grandpa said. He held up his left hand. Dad squeezed it once, then headed for the door. I got up and followed him.

Dave's van was in a multistory parking structure next to the hospital. This had been another revelation to me—I'd never seen a whole apartment building just for cars. In Eugene, people parked on the street, in single-car garages, or in parking lots. Between the freeway, the traffic jam, the killer tire, and the parking garage, I was getting a picture of L.A. as a place where cars had made a world for themselves. They had their own roads, where people weren't allowed to walk or ride bikes; they committed acts of violence against each other, and had special buildings to sleep in. People were just along for the ride.

When we got to the van, Dad's mouth was a straight line, and his face had a dark purple cast to it. Most people with our complexion, we didn't blush, but Dad's face always got darker when he was upset. I felt bad for him. He didn't like people to see him get rattled. Grandpa had just surprised him, was all. As a rule, Dad weathered other people's cruelty pretty well as long as he could see it coming.

* * *

We spent the night in the guest bedroom at Aunt Gin's place. Aunt Gin was one of my dad's mom's two siblings. The other one was Uncle Bud. I'd liked Aunt Gin when I'd stayed with Grandma and Grandpa before. She was friendly and she could cook, which distinguished her from Grandma. And while I understood that Aunt Gin was a Christian of some sort, she never once quoted the Bible at me or tried to convert me.

Aunt Gin's husband, Uncle Bert, was hard of hearing. Or, really, he was mostly deaf. I never saw Uncle Bert move, even to go to the bathroom. He sat in the living room, watching sports or news programs on his small black-and-white TV. Sometimes he watched it with the volume down. Other times he ran an earpiece from a wire that plugged into the front of the TV and blasted the commentators' voices into his good ear at a volume he could hear. Aunt Gin brought him food and glasses of ice water. When she wanted to talk to him, she shouted. He always looked surprised to find her in the room.

Aunt Gin and Uncle Bert lived in a one-story rambler about three times the size of any house I'd ever lived in. There was a guest bedroom, where Dad and I slept, next to the bathroom. The backyard had a tree that grew edible pink and white flowers. The back fence was a tall cinder-block wall. Lizards liked to climb on the wall, to bask in the sun. I spent hours trying to catch one.

I was glad we were staying there instead of at Grandma and Grandpa's house.

* * *

On our second day in L.A., Dave came to ask Dad if he wanted to come to the park for a game of touch football. When Dad said yes, I assumed touch football had to be a euphemism for something. We went out and got into Dave's van and drove to a park a few miles away. There were a bunch of other guys about my dad and Dave's age waiting for us at the park. Dad seemed to know most of them. They exchanged greetings. Some of the men took their shirts off. Then, to my utter amazement, they actually started playing football.

I watched in stunned fascination. I'd never seen my dad engage in any kind of sports activity. Ever. But there he was, running and jumping and catching the ball. The weirdest thing, from my perspective, was that he seemed to be taking the game absolutely seriously.

When the game was over, Dad and the other guys chatted for a while before everyone started leaving.

"Go ahead," Dad told Dave. "Me and Jason are going to stay here for a bit."

"You sure?" Dave asked.

"Yeah," Dad said. "We can get a bus."

"Okay," Dave said. "I'll see you soon."

They waved their goodbyes, and Dad came over to where I was sitting on the grass.

"Come on," he said.

I got up and followed him across the park.

"We used to come to this park a lot when I was a kid," he said. "Me and my brothers—your uncles—would play football right here. I went to church with a lot of those guys when we were kids."

I looked around the park. It was nice. Surprisingly green, for Southern California. It had hedges and a rose garden, big trees, and green grass rather than the dried-up brown stuff I'd seen in most L.A. parks.

"There's a duck pond down this way," Dad said, gesturing toward a wooded area up ahead of us. One of my favorite things to do in Eugene was when Dad would take me to the mill pond, next to the pulp mill on the east side of town, to feed the ducks. The pulp mill smelled like God's own fart gas, but I loved the ducks and their soft quacking. There were very few lakes or ponds in Eugene—our water was generally on its way somewhere else—so ducks were a special treat for me.

When we got to the pond I saw a small lake, with cattails and reeds near the shore, and a little house next to the water for the ducks to roost in. I could tell by the way the shoreline dropped suddenly into the water that the lake was man-made, but it had a nice feel to it. I climbed on top of the house and looked down at a flock of mallards, who came over to check me out. Dad stood nearby and smoked a cigarette.

"Hey, Jason," he called after a few minutes. "Look at this."

I hopped down off the duck house and went over to where Dad was standing, reading a sign posted near the trees. I wasn't a great reader, but I recognized KEEP OUT easily enough. There was a bunch of other stuff underneath that part.

"What's it say?" I asked.

"Says the swans are roosting," Dad said. "They're laying eggs back in the underbrush here."

"And they don't want people to step on the eggs?" I asked.

"I guess," Dad said. "It says they're easily upset when roosting. Come on. I want to see a swan egg."

"But . . ." I pointed at the sign.

"They'll get over it," Dad said.

"I'd feel bad," I said, "if I stepped on an egg."

"Okay," Dad said. "You don't have to come."

I went over to the duck house and climbed back on top. Dad crept quietly into the trees and disappeared from view. Everything was quiet for a few minutes before I heard branches breaking. And hissing. And screaming.

Dad came staggering out of the bushes, pursued by an incredibly pissed-off swan. I'd only seen a few swans before, and I'd never fully appreciated how big they were. Maybe because I'd never seen one next to a person, where I could get a good sense of scale. This one had its wings spread and raised, and it looked bigger than Dad. Dad, for his part, wasn't moving quite fast enough to stay clear of the bird, because he was running backwards. If he'd just turned around and really tried to sprint, he probably could have gotten away pretty easily. But he didn't seem willing to admit defeat and run away from a bird—even a thirty-pound bird that was chasing him and hissing at him like a demon from hell.

The swan snapped its wings down and forward, scissoring Dad's calf between its beautiful white limbs. The impact made a sound like a two-by-four snapping in half. I jumped. Dad screamed again and staggered back. The swan hissed and kept chasing him, hitting him over and over again. The sound was horrifying. Finally Dad just gave up, turned tail, and ran.

The swan stood triumphantly in place for a minute, hissing and coughing and snapping at the air. Then it turned and waddled angrily back into the trees. I stayed on top of the duck house until Dad came and got me.

"Are you okay?" I asked.

"No, I'm not okay!" he said. "Look what that fucking thing did to me!"

He rolled up his pants and showed me one of his shins, which was now covered in angry red welts. I climbed down off the duck house for a closer look. I could see right away that the bruises, when they formed, would be totally black.

"Let's get the fuck out of here," he said.

I followed him out of the park, and we caught a bus back toward Aunt Gin's house.

"Not a word about this to anyone," he said as we sat on the bus.

"Okay," I said.

"I'm serious," he said.

"I know."

I knew I wouldn't need to keep the promise. Dad would tell everyone we knew, sooner or later. He liked a good story too much to keep this one to himself, even if it was kind of embarrassing. Besides, I didn't need to tell anyone else. Until that day, I'd never seen anyone or anything get the better of my dad. Never even known it was possible. But nobody would ever enjoy hearing about my dad getting his ass kicked by a bird half as much as I'd enjoyed watching it happen, and trying to prolong my satisfaction by telling other people about it would just be greedy.

* * *

Dad went out to the hospital the next day and came back looking frustrated and angry.

"We're going home tomorrow," he told me. "Aunt Gin says I can borrow her car to take us to the tar pits. Get your shoes on."

He drove us a few miles north in Aunt Gin's old Buick. When we finally stopped we pulled into a parking lot in what looked to me like a park. Which I supposed made sense. They wouldn't just leave one of these things sitting in the middle of an intersection. They'd want a clear area around it, both to keep people from falling into it and so they'd be able to collect any dinosaur bones it pooped out. I followed Dad across the parking lot and into a sort of nondescript building in the middle of the park.

71

The building turned out to be a museum, full of all the bones people had found in the tar pits. There were saber-toothed tigers and giant sloths and lots of other interesting things. There was a weird trick with mirrors that turned a human skeleton into a half-naked cavewoman. Then Dad took me out to the pits themselves, which had a life-size fiberglass model of a mammoth being sucked down into them, and giant chain-link fences all around the whole area.

Dad walked me to the edge of the pits and stopped. At first I wasn't even sure what I was looking at; it just looked like a big oily lake. The fences hugged the shore pretty tightly. In some places the black water crept out under the fences and left sticky slime in the grass. I stood there for a few minutes, looking at the filthy water and wondering when we were going to get to the tarpits. When it seemed like we were going to stare at the black stuff for a while, I decided I'd better humor Dad by pretending I was interested, if only so we could go on to the good stuff.

"What is that?" I asked, pointing at the noxious muck.

"It's a tar pit," Dad said.

I scowled. "What, you mean, like, the tarpit's down under there or something?"

"No," Dad said. "That's it. Right there. That's the tar pit."

"What's that black stuff?" I asked, pointing at what I assumed was old motor oil floating on the surface of the water.

"That's the tar."

I stared at the pit for a long time. Looked at him. Looked at the pit.

"That's tar?" I asked, pointing at the pit.

"Yes," Dad said, clearly starting to get annoyed.

"So it's a pit," I concluded. "A pit full of tar. That's a tarpit?"

"Yeah," Dad said. "That's tar. That's a tar pit. Animals get stuck in it, and they drown. What the hell's wrong with you?"

I stared at the tar pit for a while, readjusting my worldview.

Then I asked if we could go home now. Dad gave me some "But you've been begging to see this for days!" static about it, but he relented pretty quickly. I think he could tell how disappointed I was, though he didn't seem to understand what was actually bothering me.

The next day, Dave drove us out to the airport and we went back home to Eugene, our bodies mostly intact—our illusions somewhat less so.

13

As often as my dad was out of town working with the Ho-dads, I spent surprisingly little time with Marcy. She didn't seem to like me much. I just found her confusing. She was an overcooked redhead who always seemed slightly greasy to me, like her features would smear if I touched her. She had big blue eyes and wore a lot of makeup, tight clothes, and high-heeled shoes. My instincts told me that I had to be careful with her; she was absolutely the kind of grownup who would hold a grudge against a five-year-old. In spite of all of this, Marcy had a lot of friends, including John, our old housemate from Hayes Street, and Kris and Jimmy. Kris was a friend of John's from when he was in high school, in Arizona, and Jimmy was Kris's man—a tree planter who'd hooked Dad up with his job at the Hodads.

John and Kris both liked kids, so they came by the Fillmore Street house a lot and hung out with me and Isaac and the girls. Sometimes they took us to the park or to Fall Creek. Other times they took us out to the movies—and not just Disney movies.

They took us to epic fantasy movies, like the postapocalyptic cartoon feature *Wizards* or the animated version of *Lord of the Rings*. And *Star Wars*. John invited me to *Star Wars* a dozen times, and I begged off every time because it wasn't animated and I didn't like grownup movies. But eventually he talked me into going, and sometime in early 1978, my mind was thoroughly blown.

John took me, Isaac, and Miles to see it. Miles had already seen it, but he was happy to go again. We sat in the dark, joking and pushing each other, until the curtain parted and the 20th Century Fox fanfare came up. We slowed down and stared. Then the startling jolt of brass instruments as the score kicked up, and a stream of words I couldn't read rolled up the screen and into the distance. All of that stood out clearly in my mind afterward. Then, comprehension ended, and I spent the next two hours being blasted into my seat by a pure adrenaline rush of emotion. Because sure, there were spaceships and sword fights and special effects and all that. But mainly, it was the first time I could remember seeing people like me—people who looked like me and my dad and our friends—portrayed on-screen as heroes.

The protagonists were two guys with shaggy haircuts, an alien who basically was a shaggy haircut, two gay robots, and a sarcastic hippie in a muumuu, and they were noble and selfless and brave. George Lucas's "used future" looked a lot like the houses and communes my people lived in. His main characters bought stolen junk machinery from shady Jawas, jumped into Dumpsters, worked for mobsters, smuggled contraband, and fought against the police—and they were the goddamn good guys. I'd never seen anything like it.

When the movie was over I rode back to the Fillmore Street house with John, Isaac, and Miles. Isaac and Miles were recounting all their favorite parts of the movie, but I was just staring out the window. John kept looking at me out of the corner of his eye until finally he couldn't stand it anymore.

"Did you like it?" he asked me. "Did you like the movie?"

He'd already seen it forty times. It was important to him that I like it, too.

"I loved it," I said. "I want to be Han Solo."

"Han—what about Luke?" John asked.

"No," I said.

Luke didn't look anything like me. He was blond. He had blue eyes. And while he could do a lot of cool things, he never seemed to have much choice. Or he never made choices. Han Solo made choices, and most of them were pretty self-serving. He was a smuggler. He shot that green guy in the bar. But when the chips were down, he made a choice to come back and join the fight. He saved Luke and sent Darth Vader spinning off into the void. Luke was fine. But I wanted to be Han Solo. I wanted to be the guy not to fuck with, who comes through at the last minute and saves his best friend's ass. I didn't care about destroying the Death Star. I wanted to be loyal. And brave.

John just kept glancing at me, like he was expecting me to say more.

"Han Solo, huh?" he finally said.

"Yeah," I said, with the sincerity of a religious convert. "I wanna be Han Solo."

"Then I'll be Luke," Isaac said.

"Sure," I said. "You can be Luke."

I was already thinking about how we could use the wreck of the Vega, sitting in our garage back on Fillmore Street, as our own *Millennium Falcon*. With the front caved in like it was, it even kind of looked like Solo's ship.

14

Dad and I lived on Fillmore Street for more than a year before Dad and Marcy started fighting. Most of their fights happened behind closed doors so I didn't hear the details, but I could feel Dad's moods the way a bird on the wing can judge the weather, and I knew we were heading for some kind of blowout. Then one day, Dad told me to stay away from Marcy's boyfriend, Kenneth. Kenneth had the distinction of being pretty much the only black person I knew, besides Dad's probation officer, Diana, and he was the front man for a local band. Otherwise he was totally unremarkable; just another tall skinny guy in bellbottoms and a loud shirt.

"What do you mean, stay away from him?" I asked.

"Don't be alone with him," Dad said.

"Alone with him?" I was never alone with Kenneth. He was always with Marcy. Or, when he was around us kids, it was all of us in a group. Like the time he and Jimmy took us all to get ice cream cones over in Springfield.

"Just do what I say," Dad said, using his serious voice.

I said I would.

About two weeks later, Dad told me we were moving. When I asked him why, he said Kenneth was messing with Faith and Crystal.

"Messing with them how?" I asked.

"Touching them in ways he shouldn't," Dad said.

Usually, when I asked Dad questions about grownup stuff, he just gave me the facts and let me sort out the reality as best I could. That was his approach to questions about drugs, sex, violence, politics—pretty much everything. But for some reason, when it came to sex crimes, he tended to resort to evasions and opaque metaphors. A few months earlier there'd been a string of rapes in Spencer Butte Park, and Dad had taken that opportunity to explain to me that a rapist was a kind of monster who attacked women and children at night and forced his penis into them. The image that conjured for me—a sort of half-bat vampire thing with an enormous erect phallus—was terrifying, but made no practical sense.

On the other hand, things I'd seen on TV and stories other kids had told me had alerted me to the existence of perverts and molesters. Here again, the exact nature of the evil was a little vague in my mind, but I understood that perverts and molesters touched children's genitals—our "underwear area" as my friends said—in ways they weren't supposed to, and that this was probably what Dad was talking about in reference to Kenneth.

"Did Marcy tell you that?" I asked finally.

"No," Dad said. "The girls did."

"Did you tell Marcy?" I asked.

"Of course I did," he said.

"What did she say?" I asked.

"She said the girls were lying. At first. Then she asked them about it. They started to tell her what they'd told me and she flipped out, and they changed their story. Told her they'd never said it. So then she said I was lying, because I'm jealous of Kenneth. And because he's black."

Another point of confusion for me: among the hippies of Eugene, people talked about Martin Luther King Jr. the same way my grandma talked about Jesus Christ. Even my dad, when I asked him questions about Dr. King, talked about what an incredible leader he was, and how moral and committed he was. But I also knew, based on things Dad had said, that he disliked black people generally. He made fun of how they spoke—or how he thought they spoke. And he thought they were dangerous. It didn't come up very often, if only because I could count the number of black people I'd met in Eugene on one hand, but I knew it was part of Dad's thinking. A few other people were aware of it, too, and Marcy was apparently one of them.

I didn't think it went as far as making something like this up about Kenneth, though. Dad tended to use words to make real things bigger or smaller, but total fabrications weren't his usual way of lying.

"What now?" I asked.

"I don't know," Dad said. "But one thing is, we might move to Seattle."

"What's in Seattle?" I asked.

"Jobs," he said. "Something. I don't know. It can't be worse than here."

* * *

We probably would have left Eugene after the Hayes Street house burned down, but the conditions of Dad's probation barred Dad from leaving Oregon for any reason. It wasn't a small problem; the economy in Oregon was a shambles, and Dad still had a couple of years on his sentence. But Diana had recently told Dad that the state was trying to save money by granting early release to nonviolent offenders, including people on probation for drug crimes. It wasn't a sure thing, but under the circumstances it was all Dad felt he had to look forward to.

So after we moved out of Marcy's house we spent most of the next nine months in a big cheap house at the edge of town, waiting for word to come down from my dad's probation officer that we could go to Washington. We left most of our stuff in the storage unit we'd been using since the Hayes Street fire, so we wouldn't have to move it twice, and lived as simply as we could out in the boondocks of Roosevelt Boulevard.

* * *

I'd turned six that summer and started first grade that fall, when we were still living with Marcy. I went to Ida Patterson Elementary, in Mrs. Shoemaker's class. I was enrolled for almost two months before I realized that the giant field behind the school was actually the field I'd lived next to when my dad got arrested, three years earlier, and that the large low building I'd seen in the distance back then was, in fact, the school.

Ida Patterson was a short walk from the Fillmore Street house. Isaac and I used to make the walk together, cutting through the parking lot of the local National Guard detachment. The Roosevelt place was a lot farther out, and there were no school buses, so I depended on Dad to drive me in one of the loaner cars he borrowed from Sean—which meant I only made it to class about half the time. Other kids made friends and formed little groups. Then I'd show up once or twice a week and spend the day getting picked last for dodgeball, sitting alone in the lunchroom, and not understanding the lessons. The teachers talked a lot about how school was supposed to encourage kids to grow and learn, but it felt to me like everyone in that place either was out to get me or wanted nothing to do with me.

"Don't worry about it," Dad would say. "School just trains you to be a good little worker bee. A good drone. They crush your spirit and your individuality."

Which I supposed was a fair description of my experiences at school. But the alternative wasn't much better. After a couple of months sitting by myself in our big empty house on Roosevelt, I'd started to think I'd gladly let someone crush my spirit if they'd just play checkers with me.

I got passing grades that year in spite of my abysmal attendance, but I wasn't looking forward to having to go back at the end of the summer. Then, in the summer before I turned seven, my dad's probation officer told Dad that the state of Oregon had washed its hands of him; we could leave any time we wanted.

* * *

Dad and I left Eugene early that fall, right after my birthday. There were a couple of factors that contributed to the delay in leaving town. One of them was Dad's strange obsession with getting the Vega fixed up. After having it towed to Eugene from Portland, he'd had it towed from Marcy's house to the Roosevelt house. When the time came to make the move to Seattle, he insisted we were going to do it in the Vega. He never explained his reasoning, but I assumed he was just mad at himself for having totaled his first new car. Or for having screwed up the pot delivery. Or some combination thereof. It wasn't exactly surprising. Hanging on to things that would be better let go of was kind of a cultural through-line among my people.

We didn't have the money to pay a regular garage to fix the car, so Dad made a deal with Sean, the shotgun-crazy drug buddy he'd wanted to give Charlie to. Sean took Dad's $500 and the job, which he accepted as a sort of challenge against his prowess as a mechanic and a friend. The Frankenstein contraption he gave back to us a few months later was more or less Vega-shaped and capable of moving forward under its own power, if not much else.

We packed light, just some bedding and a few changes of clothes. Everything else went into the storage locker with the stuff we'd put in there after the house fire on Hayes. Dad's plan was to spend our first night camping out by Fall Creek, then head north and look for a house in Seattle.

We found a good spot that night, at a bend in the creek where the water ran over giant sheets of volcanic rock and shaped the stone into natural pools and rapids. We roasted marshmallows and drank tap water out of old milk jugs. Then we crawled into the back of the Vega, cuddled up under our Pendleton blankets, and went to sleep.

Dad woke up in the middle of the night because he was hot. He couldn't figure out what was wrong until he noticed something was off about my breathing. He put his hand on my forehead and I was burning up with fever. He woke me up, and I was lucid enough to answer his questions so he decided to wait until morning and see how things looked.

When the sun came up it was obvious that something was pretty far wrong. Every nick, cut, and scrape on my body was swollen red. When Dad touched an old cut on my arm, it immediately popped open and started discharging a mixture of pus and blood. That was bad, but the part that really freaked him out was that I didn't cry. I just stared at the gunk coming out of my arm like it was happening to somebody else.

He packed up the car and drove straight to Sacred Heart Hospital in downtown Eugene. The ER doctors said it was a staph infection. They loaded me up with antibiotics, and acetaminophen to bring my fever down. They also prescribed a special soap to use against the infection. They said Dad should check my temperature every hour, and if it got above 104, he should bring me back to the hospital.

Dad stopped at the pay phone in the hospital lobby and called everyone he could think of, looking for a place for us to stay. But most of our friends in Eugene had kids. None of them could risk having the infection spread to their family. I sat on a green vinyl chair next to the phone and watched Dad go through a pile of change. He never raised his voice. His face just got redder and redder.

"I'm thirsty," I said.

"In a minute!" he snapped.

I lapsed into silence until we were back out at the car.

"What's staph infection?" I asked.

"It's bad," he said.

"How bad?"

"Really bad."

"Oh. Okay."

We got into the car and he made sure my seat belt was locked in. Then he sat quietly with his hands on the steering wheel for what seemed like an hour before he started the car and drove us back out to Fall Creek.

I was in and out of consciousness for the next two days. I was too hot, then I was too cold, and I was always hungry in spite of being sick. We didn't have any food and Dad was afraid to move me to get any. I kept complaining about being hungry, and he just kept feeding me marshmallows and boiling creek water for me to drink. And checking my temperature; it hovered around 104, but never went over. I used the special soap twice a day and rinsed off in the creek. By the time my fever started to drop, my skin was also clearing up. The infected cuts dried out and started to heal. The inflammations went down. By the third day, my temperature was close to normal.

Dad left me alone at the campsite and went into town to get food. I spent the day swimming in the creek and trying to catch crayfish with a washcloth. Dad was back well before dark. There was a cardboard box full of food in the back of the car. I ate almost an entire box of graham crackers by myself.

Dad said we couldn't go to Seattle for at least another two weeks; that was how long I was supposed to keep using the soap, and Dad didn't want to get caught out on the road if I had a relapse. So we stayed at our campsite on Fall Creek. I spent most days off by myself, swimming and chasing wildlife. Dad sat by the car and read science fiction paperbacks.

The banks of the creek were steep and rocky. On sunny days, the exposed granite and basalt turned the valley around us into a kind of tropical hothouse. There were shallow caves to be explored, and mossy old trees to climb on. I usually swam in my underwear or naked, and I spent most of that two weeks imagining I was the only person in the world. At one point I noticed that I'd gone a whole day without speaking. I couldn't recall ever having done that before. Even in the isolation of the Roosevelt house I'd talked to myself, just to hear a human voice.

Then one day Dad announced that it was time to go.

"Go?" I asked.

"To Seattle," he said.

"Oh. Right."

"Listen," he said. "I've been thinking. How would you feel about spending a couple of weeks with your grandparents up on Camano Island?"

My dad's two brothers and their families had all moved up to the Stanwood–Camano Island area over the last couple of years, and his parents had joined them after Grandpa's heart attack. The island was about eighty miles north of Seattle, and Dad and I had snuck up there once to visit my uncle John and his family, in spite of Dad's probation. It had been a quick overnight trip, driving up in a solid eight-hour stretch, then back home the same way the next day. I'd seen my grandparents and my cousins, but mostly I remembered the steep cutback trail that ran down a cliff behind Uncle John's house to a thin strip of rocky beach. I'd seen the ocean before, in Los Angeles, but the waves there had been too large for me to swim. The water around Uncle John's place was calm, almost like a lake, so I waded in fully clothed and swam around during the dead of winter. In the process, I drank enough salt water to make myself violently ill the next morning and for the whole trip back. Uncle John had been stoic and quietly judgmental, like Grandpa. Dad had done his best to emulate his older brother.

Dad had talked a lot afterward about how beautiful Camano Island was, but this was the first I'd heard about staying with Grandma and Grandpa. My mind flashed to Grandma's awful cooking, and her hateful little dog.

"Why?" I asked. I wondered if I was being punished for getting sick.

"Well," Dad said. "We're pretty much out of money. I didn't save as much as I'd hoped to before we left town, and that soap was expensive. So was the doctor. So we don't have enough for first and last on a new place. I was thinking I could leave you with Grandma and Grandpa, just for a couple of weeks. Get a job. Get us a place to stay in Seattle. Then I could come get you."

I realized we were up against it, and that Dad didn't like the idea of sending me up there any more than I liked the idea of being sent.

"I guess that'd be okay," I said. "Just for a couple of weeks?"

"Yeah."

"Okay. Sure. That sounds like fun."

* * *

Two days later, Dad pulled up in front of Grandma and Grandpa's house. The four of us had an awkward lunch together. Dad stayed the night in a room in the basement, and I slept in the guest room upstairs. The next day he got back in the Vega and headed down to Seattle.

I ended up staying with Grandma and Grandpa for about three months.

I was enrolled in second grade at Stanwood Elementary, which meant a forty-five-minute bus ride into town every morning, and a forty-five-minute ride home in the afternoon. I tried to make friends, but the other kids confused me. Every place I'd been up to then, there were rules about not swearing and not telling dirty jokes, but they were teachers' rules. Flouting them was usually the easiest way to get other kids on my side and make friends. Instead, the kids I met on the bus and at school seemed genuinely upset when I told jokes about poop, or called one of them a cocksucker.

Their attitude toward violence was also strange. When I pushed one of them, instead of pushing me back or beating the stuffing out of me, or even running away, they'd go and tell the teacher. At first I interpreted their curiously nonconfrontational behavior to mean that they were all just exceptionally nice, but that didn't turn out to be true either. Most of them were really forthcoming about telling me they didn't like me, and telling everyone else what a jerk I was (evidently "jerk" was the strongest word most of them felt comfortable with, which I also found confusing). Meanwhile, the houses on the island were so far apart that there were no kids close enough to want to play with me just because I was convenient. After a month or so I pretty much gave up on my classmates and resigned myself to playing alone until I could get out of there.

Then, to my complete surprise, I started having a lot of fun at church.

Grandma and Grandpa took me to church every Sunday, and I barely tolerated the services. I disliked the singing and the sermons. I hated getting dressed up and having to hold still for an hour. Most Sundays, I felt like the only kid in a congregation of geriatrics. Then, after a few weeks, the youth pastor sent me a letter inviting me to their youth groups on Wednesday and Saturday. I went reluctantly, but it turned out to be more fun than regular church. There was some Bible stuff that I was basically indifferent to, but there were also a lot of activities and, finally, at the end of each youth group, a chance to vent some aggression.

They played a game at youth group that was a little bit like tag. We'd get a bunch of boys on a field, someone would throw a ball out in the field, and we'd all try to get it. Whoever got it then had to run while everyone else tried to clobber him and get the ball. When the runner was tackled, he'd throw the ball up in the air and someone else would pick it up. Officially there were no points, but we compared the number of times we'd possessed the ball, and bragging rights were given for more possessions. I'd never played a game quite like it before. It was called "smear the queer."

Dad came up every week or two and stayed overnight in the basement room, smoking (in spite of Grandma's frequent admonitions), sleeping late, and refusing to go to church. When I told him about smear the queer he got very quiet for a while, then said, "Jason, remember when we talked about Jesus?"

"The alien thing?" I asked.

"Yeah."

"Sure."

"Well, this is still that same church. That game they've got you playing is about teaching you to hate and persecute people who are different than they are. They're teaching you to single someone out, gang up on him, and beat the shit out of him because he's different."

"Well, but, anyone can get the ball," I said.

"Sure," he said. "But you know what 'queer' means?"

I realized I didn't. I had sort of an idea that it was something undesirable, but I didn't know the exact meaning.

"It means 'different,'" he said. "It means odd, or strange. If you heard a noise in the middle of the night, you might call it a queer sound. If your food tasted wrong, you might say it tasted queer. Spoiled milk would taste queer. And if there was someone you knew that just didn't seem to fit in, you might say that person was queer. They're teaching you to smear—to beat—the outsider. That's what that game means."

I might have dismissed Dad's analysis of smear the queer out of hand except that, like his Jesus-was-an-alien kick, it answered so many of the questions I had about what I'd seen and heard since being at my grandparents' place. I thought about the way kids at school were, and how they'd all reacted to me. They didn't just dislike me—they talked about it. They created consensus: pizza is our favorite lunch, celery's the worst vegetable, and Jason's a jerk. They didn't give second chances. There was no romantic after-school-special idea about finding out that the weird kid was cooler than you thought he was. That wasn't even part of their thinking.

And what did it mean that the only place where any kind of violent physical play was allowed was at church during smear the queer?

After Dad went back to Seattle, I spent a few days thinking about what he'd said. When youth group came around again on Wednesday, I just went through the motions while I watched people, and thought about the things they did in terms of the positive and negative reinforcement stuff my dad was always talking about. What kinds of behaviors did kids receive praise for? What kinds of behaviors were they criticized for or ignored for? What were the incentives? Which kids were considered leaders? By the end of the night I felt sort of sick to my stomach. Because it wasn't just smear the queer. Everything they did seemed designed to teach the kids in the group how to identify, isolate, and attack outsiders. People they disagreed with. All the little Bible stories they read basically boiled down to one thing: do what we tell you, or else. How had I not noticed this before? Why was Grandma sending me to these people?

Of course, I knew the answer to that one. She was the one who'd had me invite Jesus into my heart, back in L.A. Dad had told me once that, when she was young, Grandma had been a missionary in Japan—a career path the youth group people at her church talked about all the time. Kids who had done missionary work with their families were considered the rock stars of the group. And Grandma was a charter member of this goddamn freak show.

The more I thought about it, the angrier I got. When I went to youth group that Saturday I got put in the "penalty box" during smear the queer for mauling one of the missionary kids after he'd already given up the ball. Everyone glared at me for the rest of the night. When Wednesday rolled around I told Grandma I wanted to just stay home and watch sports with Grandpa.

About a month later, Dad and Grandma got into a huge fight about how him coming up to visit me was "disruptive." He called her a fucking cunt, told me to pack my shit, and took me back to Seattle that same night.

"Do we have a house yet?" I asked, once we were safely in the car and moving. I hadn't wanted to say anything that might make him change his mind until we were past the point of no return.

"No," he said.

"Then where are we going to stay?"

"With my boyfriend," Dad said.

15

Once, during a party in the Hayes Street house, John's friend Kris and her boyfriend Jimmy had snuck off to have sex in my bedroom. It was the kind of thing people did at big parties in that house, but I was home at the time so at some point I went into my room and found them naked on my bed, Jimmy on top of Kris, and Kris screaming her head off. In my four-year-old's mind, it seemed obvious that Jimmy was hurting Kris, so I did what I had to do: I jumped onto Jimmy's back and bit him as hard as I could. Hard enough to draw blood. Jimmy screamed. Kris screamed. Then I shouted something like "Stop hurting her!" and Kris started laughing. I was embarrassed that she was laughing at me, but I got the idea that she wasn't actually in danger, so I shifted down out of attack mode.

Once Jimmy got over his perfectly understandable anger at being attacked and savagely bitten in the middle of sex, he and Kris went back to what they were doing—only this time with an instructive narrative component: "See, Jimmy's penis goes in here. This feels good. Then he moves, like so. Men and women enjoy this." Eventually they finished up, got dressed, and left me in my room. By the next morning, every one of our friends knew about me biting the shit out of Jimmy mid-thrust, and the teaching moment that followed. It was regarded as both a funny story and an illustration of how much better our people were than the straights, who lied to their kids about sex.

It was as clear and unambiguous a lesson in human sexuality as any child could ask for. The only problem was that I didn't take a single useful fact away from it. If anything, my experience with Jimmy and Kris left me more confused than I had been before.

Sex didn't make sense to me. And not just because I was four when I got my first lesson.

My friends—my kid-aged friends—talked about sex as something both gross and aggressive. "Humping" was something you could be accused of doing in various contexts. Any kind of accidental up-and-down motion of the body near anything—such as during a clumsy attempt to climb a tree or an unsuccessful attempt to lift one's friend off the ground—could be construed as an attempted hump. On the other hand, some kids I knew humped each other like dogs in a pack, to assert dominance—"Haha! I just humped you!"

Playing with oneself was also frequently mocked, though that idea made even less sense to me than humping.

Then, of course, there was TV. On TV, there was a lot of emphasis on romance, and lots of kissing, but no clear connection between romance, kissing, and what Kris and Jimmy had been doing. It didn't help that, on TV and in movies, pretty much everyone got married when they were in love. Where I came from, hardly anyone got married. Or they did, but then they got divorced almost immediately and ended up hating whoever they'd been married to. Among my people it was considered axiomatic that the best way to totally ruin a relationship was for two people to get married. Jimmy and Kris weren't married. Jimmy had been married to someone named Janet and had a kid with her, but they'd divorced and now they hated each other.

My people tended to "be together." And then later, they'd "stop being together." These terms were rarely explained. Jimmy and Kris were together. Dad and Marcy had been together, briefly, but then they stopped being together and were friends until Marcy and Kenneth got together.

How did screwing fit into all this? Humping? And fucking. What was fucking? Calling someone a fucker was bad, but fucking was good? I had no idea.

And, of course, in a totally separate file from all this was the idea of reproduction. I'd spent enough time around farm animals to understand that a male of virtually any species could put his penis in a female of the same species and leave some sperm there. Then she'd either give birth or lay an egg, as her anatomy dictated. I didn't give the idea much thought, but I assumed that this ritual occurred when the individuals involved wanted to reproduce, and probably at no other time.

I didn't understand any of it. And while I knew that it was extremely important to other people—mostly adults—I didn't worry very much about not understanding it because there were just so many other things in the world that I knew were important but that I didn't understand at all; things like drugs, and jobs, and the difference between a city and a state. I didn't understand why we had to stand in line to leave or enter the classroom at school. I didn't understand why girls got to wear pants but boys didn't get to wear skirts. Life was full of things I didn't understand. The only way I'd figured out to cope with all of it was to play along. Stand in line? Okay. Raise my hand to go to the bathroom? If you say so. Hop on one foot and crow like a rooster? Sure, why not. Overthinking it was the path to madness.

And that was my entire approach to the question of sex, and who was having sex with who, and why, and what it all meant: just say what seems expected of you and don't think about it too much. Which was why I didn't really understand, when my dad introduced me to his boyfriend, Phillip, in Seattle in October of 1979, that something important had happened.

* * *

Phillip was a small, fit man about the same height and build as my dad, though he usually dressed more conservatively due to his professional status as a registered nurse. He had an angular face, dark brown skin, a pencil mustache, and an enormous mane of black hair that could only be intended to frighten predators and impress potential mates. Dad told me that Phillip's family was from the Philippines and that this meant Phillip was a Filipino. When I asked him the obvious question, Dad said there was no connection between Phillip's name and his ethnicity, but I found that idea difficult to credit.

When we got to Seattle, Dad and I spent about a month in Phillip's tiny one-bedroom apartment on Boren Avenue. Phillip was a surprisingly good sport about it, all things considered, and he went out of his way to engage with me. He was a decent artist, so he drew cartoons for me on the fly, and he liked to tell jokes and play games. I found the obviousness of his efforts a little unnerving, if only because the last person who'd tried so hard to get along with me was my grandmother. But he was patient and friendly, and he mostly won me over.

All the same, I didn't like being in Phillip's apartment alone, so Dad took me to work with him at a place called Seattle Counseling Service. Dad was nonspecific about what Seattle Counseling Service did exactly. I spent most of my days in their employee lounge, watching TV and drawing dinosaurs and dragons on the backs of typed documents that Dad retrieved from the office scrap bin. The office was housed in a two-story brick building at the intersection of two busy streets; the main doors were on the corner of the building, rather than off to one side or the other, and there was a concrete eagle above the door with a large clock set into its stomach. The eagle and the clock fit with my idea of what buildings in cities were supposed to look like, ideas based almost entirely on Bugs Bunny cartoons and Humphrey Bogart movies.

At the end of our first month in Phillip's apartment, Dad found us a house on Aloha Street, on the east slope of Capitol

Hill. He took me to see it as soon as the landlord gave him a key. It was a small one-bedroom that had been abandoned for several years. Or at least it smelled like it had been. The walls were covered in thick layers of wallpaper, and the whole house was just . . . moist. There was a gas stove in the kitchen, and a gas heater in the living room, and an entire extra house in the backyard that we were getting for free.

"Can I live back there?" I wanted to know as we stood in the back doorway and looked at the extra house. The current plan was for me to sleep in the "dining room" half of the living room in the main house. Dad would have to go back and forth past my bed at night to go to the bathroom.

"No," Dad said. "It doesn't have gas or electricity, and parts of the ceiling have collapsed from water coming in through the roof."

I didn't think that made it significantly worse than the main house, but it didn't seem wise to say so. Dad was really proud of having found a place we could afford, even if the backyard was a giant mud pit and the ceilings were eight feet high and covered in an underlayer of foam popcorn to give them "texture." The front yard was dark, wet, and skewed sideways by the incredibly steep hill we lived on. The west side of the property was bordered by a fifteen-foot concrete retaining wall that loomed over the house like a death threat, and the east side was bordered by another retaining wall that dropped down into a vacant lot full of illegally disposed-of construction material. That eastern exposure should have given us a nice view of Lake Washington, but someone had thoughtfully planted a giant salal hedge on that side of the yard, lest any sunlight touch the house. Ever.

We moved into the Aloha Street house with no beds, very few clothes, and no cooking implements. All our stuff was still in a storage unit in Eugene. We spent December sleeping on the floor in improvised bedrolls made of stacks of electric blankets—sans power sources and controls—that we bought at Goodwill for a dollar each. The lumps caused by the wires and heating elements in the blankets could be annoying, but they were incredibly warm and soft.

Dad was in no hurry to register me for school. He had a low opinion of public education. So I spent weekdays hanging out in the break room at his office and weeknights and weekends working on the house; peeling off the wallpaper with a rented steamer, repainting, and cleaning. The process of steaming the wallpaper off and sanding the plaster walls smooth filled the house with mildew and mold spores. The steamer was at least eighty years old, operated by burning kerosene under an ancient cast-iron boiler, with the exhaust vented right into the interior of the house. The latex paint was old-school high-solvent white. Somehow we managed not to asphyxiate or blow ourselves to smithereens, but the memory of the smell inside that house was burned into my memory forever after.

* * *

Paying two months' rent and a deposit on the Aloha Street house pretty much wiped us out financially, but it was December so Dad decided we were getting a Christmas tree, whether we could afford one or not.

"We won't be able to put much under it," he said, "but you're going to have a tree."

"How can we pay for it?" I asked. Normally I didn't pay much attention to our cash flow situation, but we were sleeping with the heat off, in December, because we couldn't afford to heat the house. So the idea that we were broke was closer to my thinking than it otherwise might have been.

"It's no problem," he said.

I didn't realize what he meant until he woke me up late that night and told me to get my shoes on. He didn't need to tell me to get dressed; I slept in two pairs of jeans, two pairs of socks, two T-shirts, and a sweatshirt.

"What's happening?" I asked.

"We're going to get a Christmas tree," he said.

I looked out the window. It was pitch-black outside.

"What?" I asked.

"Just get your shoes on," he said.

We locked up the house and climbed into the Vega. Dad took us south on 23rd, the big main road near our house. I had no idea where we were going, but the streets were completely empty so I could tell it was really late at night. No business would be open at this hour.

"Once we're there," Dad said, "you just wait in the car. Don't get out for any reason. But if we run into any trouble—if we get busted or if the cops come—I want you to cry."

Dad had given me a lot of "if we get caught . . ." directions in my life, but they were usually "Just tell them you lost your ticket" or "Throw it in the bushes and no matter what happens, don't admit it's yours." Telling me to cry was a new one.

"What's that going to do?" I asked.

"It's Christmas," Dad said. "Who's gonna throw a single father in jail for trying to get a Christmas tree for his crying kid?"

We drove for another ten minutes or so. The houses on either side of the road disappeared. They were replaced by big parking lots and a series of strip malls, car dealerships, and warehouses. Finally Dad slowed down and drove up onto the sidewalk next to a tall chain-link fence. It had started to rain while we were driving, and once we stopped I could see that the rain was falling at a sharp angle. This was how it had been since we got to Seattle: raining constantly, almost freezing, but never actually snowing. It was miserable, and all Dad had on for outside clothes was a thin navy blue windbreaker. It was his best coat, but it wasn't much good in this kind of weather.

"Stay here," he said, as he got out of the car and went around to the fence. I looked out the window and saw there were Christmas trees on the other side of the fence, but it wasn't a regular Christmas tree lot. It was some kind of store that sold Christmas trees out front. A sign in the corner of the lot said CHUBBY AND TUBBY.

Dad looked up and down the wide street we were parked on, but the road was deserted. When he seemed satisfied that there were no witnesses, he put his fingers in the fence, braced his toes, and scrambled up the chain links. When he got to the top he grabbed the triple row of barbed wire, swung over it, and hung from it for a second before dropping down onto the other side of the fence.

I watched the whole operation in mute fascination. My dad went through periods of being physically active, but I would never have accused him of being agile. This fence-climbing Dad was an interesting new side of him that I hadn't seen before.

He walked around between rows of trees for a minute before he found one he liked. A few cars passed on the street, but nobody slowed down. Probably they didn't even notice us. Suddenly I heard a thump and looked over to see that Dad had thrown a tree over the fence, onto the ground next to the car. Then he came over the fence himself—until he got tangled in the barbed wire at the top. It was angled in, so getting into the enclosure was a lot easier than getting out. I watched him trying to straddle the barbed wire strands while he got his clothes loose, then watched him nearly fall off the fence as he tried to climb down.

That was closer to the Dad I knew.

He ran around behind the car, opened the hatch, and threw the Christmas tree in. Then he came back to the driver's side, climbed in, and fastened his seat belt.

"Tore my fucking coat," he hissed as he got the car started and turned around to head back to our house.

I could see a ragged hole in the right sleeve, near his elbow. There was a little bit of white cotton batting poking out, from the jacket's minimal padding. I knew then the tree-stealing thing had been a bad idea. That coat was the one he wore to job interviews and other official functions. It was worth a hell of a lot more to us than some stupid Christmas tree. When we got home he used a match to seal the edges of the torn polyester, but I knew the coat was basically ruined and I felt like it was my fault.

A few days later we celebrated a small Christmas, with our tree nailed to a piece of plywood to keep it upright and decorations we made out of pieces of tinfoil and cut-up aluminum cans. When Dad got his next paycheck, at the beginning of the month, we took a long weekend and he drove us to our storage unit in Eugene. We loaded all our stuff into a U-Haul trailer and drove it back to Seattle, then spent a week or so unpacking.

It was the first time in almost three years I'd slept in my own bed.

16

We never really settled in at the Aloha Street house. It was dark and cold and smelled like dirt. We couldn't figure out where the dirt smell was coming from until Dad opened up the storm door that led into the basement crawl space and we discovered that there was no foundation under the house. Most of the structure's weight rested on posts that were set into concrete pads. Otherwise it was just a wooden box built on top of an enormous hole in the ground. As wet as the climate in Seattle was, water evaporated up through the house like an oversize chimney, bringing mold and the smell of dirt with it.

"I bet I could grow pot down here," Dad said, as he looked at the dirt basement with a flashlight.

It was interesting to me how rarely Dad and I had the same reaction to a given situation.

* * *

I'd been asking my dad for a dog for years, mostly because I imagined it would give me someone to play with, but we'd never been able to swing it. Because we had roommates, or because we'd be moving soon and we weren't sure where we'd end up. Because we didn't have a yard. Because the yard wasn't fenced. The reasons changed, but the answer was almost always no.

Dad had relented once, back on Roosevelt Boulevard. I'd been so depressed and bored while we were there that he'd gone to the pound and picked up a cute little beagle/hound mix to cheer me up. I named the dog Charlie, in honor of—well, nothing really. I just liked the name Charlie. Besides Charlie rooster and Charlie dog, I'd also owned (briefly) a rabbit and a crow, both named Charlie. I probably would have named the gerbil Charlie if he'd lived long enough to name. But the rabbit escaped and the crow healed up its broken wing and went back to being a wild crow. So when the new dog came along I had a Charlie vacancy that he filled nicely.

Unfortunately he was about as cheerful as a coma patient. All he did was lie around and eat and shit. He never wanted to play or fetch. We never tied him up because he never went more than ten feet from his food bowl. He didn't even like to be petted. When Dad got off probation and it was clear we'd be leaving the state soon, Charlie mysteriously ran away. That was what Dad told me, that Charlie just ran away. The idea of Charlie running anywhere was ludicrous, but I sensed that examining Dad's story too closely was only going to bum me out.

When we got to Aloha Street, Dad said I could get another dog. But that wasn't what ended up happening. Instead, Dad got a dog and tried to convince me it was mine so I'd clean up after it.

"I wanted the black Lab," I said, after we got the new dog home. "You wanted the collie."

"He's a Border collie," Dad said. "And you named him."

That part was true. I'd made up my mind before we went dog shopping at the pound that I was done with Charlies. This pet was going to be named something distinctive. Authoritative. This one was going to usher in a new era of pet naming. So I named him Thunder. Thunder the Border collie. He was small-ish, with a brown and black body, a puff of white fur on his chest, and a slightly curled tail with a jaunty white tip. Pointy ears. Intelligent eyes. Smart. Sneaky. Cleverer than a dog should be. And definitely not mine.

Whenever Dad left the house, Thunder would howl at the door and jump and bark. Sometimes he went on for ten or fifteen minutes. Whenever I left the house? Nothing. Crickets chirping.

A few months after we got Thunder, we went to Arizona to visit Kris and Jimmy, the couple John had introduced us to in Eugene. As the seventies were winding down, most of our people had moved out of Oregon, and Kris and Jimmy had ended up in Kris's hometown of Tucson. We were going down there partly because we'd just heard that Kris was expecting a baby and we wanted to give our blessings—and partly because there were rumors that Mount Saint Helens was going to explode and bury the entire region under three feet of lava. Dad had always been a better-safe-than-sorry kind of guy when it came to apocalyptic natural disasters.

So we got Phillip to check up on Thunder and headed to Tucson on a Greyhound bus. And, sure enough, the mountain did explode while we were down there, but Seattle survived. So Phillip dutifully fed and watered Thunder and let him out to go to the bathroom twice a day. But he didn't go into the house much.

Dad thought we might come home to the reek of dog pee. I worried about dog poop. Neither thing turned out to be an issue. The problem was that Thunder had had access to the entire house, except we accidentally left the bathroom door closed. Assuming we must be in there—or, to my reading, that Dad must be in there—Thunder had dug a hole through the kitchen wall, into the bathroom.

Dad cursed under his breath for two days while he repaired the wall, but I think he found that level of devotion kind of touching. He and I were growing apart.

17

Dad registered me for second grade early in 1980, and I said my goodbyes to the employee lounge at Seattle Counseling Service. Our local school was Isaac I. Stevens Elementary, which Dad told me was named after a government stooge who had become famous for massacring Indians and stealing their land back during pioneer times. Because Dad felt I was too smart for normal classes and that I was averse to structure and rules, he got me into an experimental learning program called the Garfield Area Option Program, or GAOP—pronounced "gay-op." The GAOP program was housed in a couple of double-wide trailers next to the main school building. This gave me the feeling that I wasn't so much a student at Indian-Killer Elementary as I was a squatter, camped out in their driveway.

I didn't exactly thrive at GAOP any more than I had in Stanwood Elementary or Ida Patterson Elementary. Dad said it was because I wasn't a cog in their machine, but I knew there was something else going on. I didn't have a name for it, but I could feel it: a kind of static that filled my head whenever I was around groups of kids my own age. Or groups of people generally. Or more than two people. Or one person I really liked. It wasn't exactly excitement, and it wasn't exactly fear. There didn't seem to be a word for it in the language other people spoke. But when it was happening, I had a hard time controlling the volume of my voice. Or what happened on my face. It made me rowdy. When I got wound up, I wanted to knock other kids down and jump up and down on them. It wasn't out of any conscious desire to do violence. It was more of a full-body nervous tic. I would have been just as happy for them to knock me down and jump up and down on me, but nobody else seemed to feel the urge to do this.

Kids in my class were always asking me what was wrong with me. The question confused me, made me angry, and embarrassed me. I didn't know what the answer was, but I was starting to suspect it wasn't a circumstantial problem. It wasn't just about being new to Seattle, or new to Stanwood, or new to elementary school or day care or whatever. It had been happening for a while.

I felt like I didn't have any friends. And the more I thought about it, the more I realized that I really never had. My dad got mad at me when I said that. He accused me of feeling sorry for myself, but it was sort of true. I had acquaintances: I'd meet a kid, we'd hit it off, we'd spend a few days playing together. But then they'd always start trying to get away, like they'd turned over some stone in my personality and found a poisonous snake.

Back in Eugene, most of my friends had been family friends— the kids of my dad's friends. We hung out because we had to, and we got along. But most of them had other kids they hung out with in their neighborhood or at their school. I was the only one who didn't have friends outside our network. On Hayes Street, Mickey and Kurty had played with me, but only when they had absolutely nothing else to do.

The idea was hard to hang on to. I had to work my way around to it, going over all my interactions with people, remembering each kid I'd thought of as my friend and how they seemed to feel about me. What their faces looked like when they saw me show up at their house, or what they said to me when we played together. If I added it all up, I could start to get a clear picture of how much most kids my own age seemed to dislike me. But it wasn't like other conclusions I arrived at through my own reasoning; proving it once didn't make it true in my mind. As soon as I relaxed my grip on the facts, the whole idea started to seem ridiculous. It implied questions I didn't have answers for, like what did it mean if I was just some irredeemable prick that nobody liked? Was I just supposed to hate myself? That couldn't be right. There had to be another explanation. Because, for one thing, even irredeemable pricks had friends. Some of them were actually quite popular. I'd seen kids—really awful kids—who had lots of friends.

Like, for example, Dickie Seever.

* * *

Dickie Seever was a kid in my class at GAOP. He wasn't exactly a bully. He didn't beat up on little kids or kids who won against him in tetherball or whatever. He didn't seem to act out of insecurity or physical opportunism, and he didn't really have that kind of reputation. Dickie was more calculating than that; a sociopath looking for a target for his predations—a target who wouldn't create too many collateral problems for him. Someone he could injure with impunity. Someone like me. Because within a month of starting at GAOP I'd alienated the teachers, the students—everybody. And I was big for my age. I was the biggest kid in my class. I was bigger than most of the kids one grade up. People would always give Dickie, an average-size white boy with a tight, puckered face, the benefit of the doubt.

I felt him circling, but I didn't do what I should have done: I didn't go quiet and try to avoid him. Later, I had to admit to myself that I may have let his ridiculous-sounding name lead me to a deeply mistaken estimate of how dangerous he wasn't.

Our first run-in was a month or two before the end of my second grade year. We were lining up to go back into class at the end of recess and he cut in front of me. I stepped around him to get my place back in line, and he shoved me.

"The fuck is your problem?" I asked. I cursed easily when I was upset.

"The fuck is your problem?" he mimicked, shoving me again.

"Don't shove me!" I yelled, shoving him back.

We locked into the traditional kid-shoving stance, arms on each other's shoulders, trying to throw one another off balance and onto the ground. But after just a few seconds of this grappling behavior, Dickie did something that took me completely by surprise: he jerked back and, as I stumbled forward, he kicked me in the nuts. Hard.

I collapsed onto the ground. Once, back in Eugene, Isaac's older sister, Crystal, had kicked me like this and gotten in a lot of trouble for it. I'd never done it to anyone. I couldn't imagine making a choice to inflict this kind of pain on another human being.

Dickie stood over me for a second, then kicked me in the ribs and went inside. Other kids just walked around me while I cried on the ground. After a few minutes, I was alone. When I got my breath back I got up and limped inside.

* * *

When Dad came home from work that night I told him about what had happened. His response surprised me.

"Just punch him in the nose, Jason," he said. "You punch him in the nose once, he'll decide you're more trouble than you're worth and leave you alone."

"How do you . . . do that?" I asked.

"Do what?" Dad asked.

"Punch a person in the nose," I said.

I wasn't trying to be cute. I'd always liked to roughhouse, and sometimes I injured other kids by accident when I got too wound up. But the idea of intentionally hurting another person outside the context of an action movie or a comic book just wasn't part of my emotional anatomy. Dad may as well have told me to swing from a tree by my nonexistent tail.

"I don't understand," I said.

Dad chose to interpret my confusion as a technical problem. He gave me a little seminar about how to make a fist and which part of the nose to aim for. He talked about how I should only use the first two knuckles of my fist. He showed me a guard position that was supposed to keep me safe while I threw my punches.

"You can't let them push you around," he said. "You have to establish dominance."

"What's that mean?" I asked.

"Like dogs," Dad said. "There's a top dog and a bottom dog. You have to fight back."

None of this made any sense to me. I didn't understand the mechanism involved. How would hitting someone in the nose with my hand show them that I was a top dog? How would being a top dog keep them from hitting me back?

"If you beat this Dickie kid up, he'll be too scared to mess with you again," Dad said.

"But . . . he already beat me up," I said. "Now I'm scared of him."

"You have to get past that!" Dad said.

"I don't understand," I whined. "If I can get past him beating me up, why can't he do the same if I beat him up?"

"Because he's not as smart as you are," Dad said.

Dad said stuff like this a lot. I had yet to see any objective evidence of this massive intellect he thought I had, but I appreciated his vote of confidence. Unless it meant I had to commit suicide-by-bully.

"Can't I just tell the teachers?" I asked.

"Nobody likes a narc, Jason," Dad said.

* * *

The next week Dickie cut in front of me in line again. I shoved my way in front of him again. He seemed genuinely confused by my response.

"What the hell are you doing?" he asked.

I made a fist, reared back, and said, "Hiiii-ya!" as I threw a gigantic cartoonish haymaker . . . at a spot about a foot to Dickie's left.

Dad's explanation about top dogs and nose punching had made sense in theory, but when it came to cases, I just couldn't bring myself to do it. Not even to Dickie. Just thinking about it made something in my brain recoil in horror. I hoped I could get away with fudging it. Maybe if I pretended a willingness to punch him in the face, Dickie would get scared and leave me alone. Later in my life, when someone explained the puff-up-to-look-bigger trick employed by certain animals as a defense strategy, I grasped the idea immediately.

Dickie leaned to his right and watched as I sailed past him. When I turned to face him, curious to see what effect my posturing might have had, he frowned, shrugged, and punched me in the mouth hard enough to split my lips.

When I told my dad about it that night, he sighed and shook his head.

"I've done all I can," he said. "You have to deal with this."

* * *

A few weeks later, Dad asked me how I'd feel about the idea of having his friend Olive and her daughter Calliope come to live with us. Calliope was ten years old, two years older than I was, kind of ill-tempered and a girl into the bargain, but she was one of my two favorite kids from our Eugene years.

"Where would they stay?" I asked.

"The house out back," Dad said.

"But . . . there's no power. No heat. The roof leaks, you told me."

"You remember their house in Charleston?" Dad asked.

He had a point. Olive and Calliope had moved from Eugene to a fishing town on the coast of Oregon, a few miles south of Coos Bay. Charleston had about two hundred people in it. The town's fishing fleet docked in a slough next to the ocean and processed their catches through a packing plant that dumped its waste into the same slough. Whenever Dad and I went to visit, we could always smell Charleston before we could see it.

My strongest memory of visiting there was playing barefoot on the docks with Calliope and getting a splinter the size of a pencil that went in through my heel and ran the length of my foot. Dad and Olive had to use a razor blade and a pair of pliers to get it out, then flushed the open gash with rubbing alcohol. My whole leg swelled up from the fish guts and creosote in the wound.

The house Olive and Calliope had been living in there was a shack next to the water, with a decent-size yard and a fence made out of street signs. It had a certain piratical authenticity, if you went in for the whole fishing-nets-and-glass-floats aesthetic. And, contrary to Dad's suggestion, it had been weathertight when we stayed there. But nobody could say it was many steps up from the extra house we had in our backyard.

"When are they getting here?" I asked.

"Tomorrow," Dad said.

18

Olive and Calliope had come north to get away from Olive's boyfriend, Mike; Mike the fisherman, also known as "Crazy Mike." The only surprising part about their move was that Olive had finally gotten wise and made a run for it. In our circles in Oregon, in spite of all the crime, there were really only two people that everyone was genuinely afraid of: Sean and Mike. And Sean was considered the saner of the two by a wide margin. He'd had that one murder rap, and he'd snuck up and put a .44 Magnum up against the head of a surveyor once—"Guy crawling around my land, in the bushes, with a telescope on a stand. How the fuck was I supposed to know he worked for the Department of Transportation?" But Mike was a whole other thing.

While Sean had the sort of quaint story about how he'd blown all the windows out of his farmhouse with a shotgun during a bout of meth-induced psychosis, Mike had the story about how he'd smashed all the windows and half the walls out of Olive and Calliope's house while he was trying to kill Olive with an ax. Sean had thought he was in a shootout with imaginary DEA agents. Mike was actually trying to murder Olive in the rational light of day—while Calliope was in the house. Mike was definitely fucked up on speed when he did it, but he wasn't nearly so far from himself that the incident could be regarded as a complete aberration, or even much out of his way.

I wasn't sure what Mike had done to drive Olive north. Maybe it was the ax incident, and she'd just needed a year or so to think about it and decide it was worth leaving the state over. Maybe it was something else. Whatever it was, Dad and I were happy for the company, and the help with the rent.

* * *

Olive had grown up on a pig farm in Georgia. It gave her a southern accent, and a Hobbesian worldview, like she almost didn't trust a meal that hadn't been loved by its mother. My dad admired her pragmatism and her emotional detachment; Olive didn't want to get rich, or build anything. She ran drugs because it was the easiest way to make money, and worked straight jobs because they covered her fixed costs, like rent. But if she had enough cash on hand to cover booze, smack, and a little food, she'd walk right past a million-dollar score. I always thought that, with just a little more ambition, Olive would have been a natural as a contract killer.

She was tall and rail-thin, with curly black hair that stood straight up, and a high forehead. She always wore a pair of small sunglasses with dark purple lenses. I'd only seen her actual eyes a handful of times—narrow horizontal slits in a long, oval face. Our people in Eugene called her Olive Oyl, and the nickname was dead-on physically but totally inappropriate for her personality. In spite of her cartoonish appearance, the only sign of whimsy I'd ever seen in Olive was that she named her daughter after a steam-powered pipe organ.

Calliope looked nothing like her mom—she had a broad, open face that usually wore a blank, slightly appraising expression. Her smiles were sudden and transformative, but I never understood what caused them. There was no rhyme or reason to it. She wore glasses, which was unusual among kids in our circles. They were the square-framed plastic kind that everyone on welfare wore, and she was forever having to repair them with various improvised splints and pins. Her hair was an even brown color, her skin pale. Like me, she was always dirty and scraped up. And she cursed like a sailor, which I found affirming since I didn't seem to be able to break myself of the habit. She had some of her mother's pragmatism, but in Cal I found the trait more admirable and less intimidating than I found it in her mom.

Olive and Cal came to Seattle on a Greyhound bus and caught a cab from the bus terminal to our house. We celebrated their arrival with a chicken dinner for the whole family. Dad made a good lemon chicken, cut up into sections and pan-fried; mashed potatoes and steamed spinach on the side. We all ate at the little table in the kitchen. Cal and I talked about our favorite TV shows, while Dad and Olive talked about Mike and developments back in Oregon.

When we were done I caught Olive looking at my plate. I glanced down to see what she was staring at, and she picked my chicken bones off my plate and started plucking at them with her long, calloused fingers. Within minutes she had a huge pile of meat flecks on the plate in front of her. She tossed the cleaned bones aside and looked at my dad as she took a pinch of meat and dropped it into her mouth.

"You'd have let him throw all that food away?" she asked as she chewed. "You're spoiling him, Mark."

19

Dad had a hard time with the weather in Seattle. The constant cloud cover pushed him down into a black funk. He'd hide in his room for days at a time, and when he came out he was always in a foul mood. He smacked me around and yelled at me. And if Thunder got into the garbage or chewed something up, Dad just went nuts. He screamed and kicked the little dog until Thunder curled up in a ball and made a horrifying yelping, howling noise. A noise I'd never heard a dog make before. When he was done, Dad would apologize to the dog. Give him treats. Thunder would hold his head low, wag his tail, and huddle gratefully in Dad's lap. The pattern was eerily familiar.

Dad's depression hit him in other ways. Back in Eugene, his nickname had been Fatty. It was meant to be ironic. At five foot ten his speed- and cocaine-fueled metabolism kept him at a svelte 120 pounds. But by the end of our first six months in Seattle he'd gone up to 180—the heaviest he'd ever be.

He fought back against this lethargy by working various angles to get money. He got us on the wait list for subsidized housing and welfare. He got us food stamps. He kept working as a secretary for Seattle Counseling Service, but he also started working at a methadone clinic, and breaking into empty buildings to find furniture he could fix up and sell.

White flight had left huge blocks of central Seattle totally abandoned. Dad would go out with the Vega, climb through a window or break in with a crowbar, and look for old desks or chairs. Once or twice a month he'd come home with a rolltop desk or a credenza. He'd take it down in our dirt basement and strip it, and replace any parts that were too badly warped or broken to be repaired. Then he'd sell it with an ad in the *Little Nickel*, a weekly listing of classified ads that worked as sort of an early print edition of craigslist.

His furniture raids also yielded things we could use around the house, including an old Speed Queen washer from the thirties. It was a giant metal tub on three legs, with an agitator in the bucket, and a set of wringers on the side for wringing water out of clothes. He had to rewire it to make it work, but the engine was in good shape and the wringers were dangerously powerful.

"You get your hand caught in these, you hit this emergency

bar here," he said, showing me the silver bar that would pop the ringers apart.

"What happens if I can't?" I asked, looking skeptically at the arrangement.

"It'll crush every bone in your hand and your wrist, then pull the skin off and spit the pieces out on the other side."

That seemed like an awful lot of risk to take on just to get your clothes halfway dry, but I didn't say anything. The washing machine would save us five or six dollars a month, and on our budget that was real money. We kept the machine in our fenced-off backyard, and dried our clothes in the kitchen over the stove.

* * *

Olive found a gig working at a clothing store in Pike Place Market, a kind of farmers' market located in downtown Seattle. It had been built at the top of a cliff in 1907, and in later decades it spilled over the edge, down toward the waterfront. The original market up at the top still sold lots of fresh fruits and vegetables, local meats and fish. The buildings that backed up against the cliff under the main market were a chaotic warren of stairways, ramps, and bridges connecting a few enormous market halls. The halls were lined with small stalls that sold everything from used books to exotic pets and stage magicians' equipment. Calliope and I could spend a whole day down there, looking at Mexican amethysts, Brazilian pythons, and dried apple cores from Wenatchee being sold as shrunken heads from Papua New Guinea.

Olive made friends in the Market, like Tillie, who owned a little toy store called Pippin. She would let Cal and me hang out in her store for hours at a time, but most of the toys she sold were "craftsman" toys, like wooden tops and popguns with actual corks in them. It was entertaining for a while, but we were used to toys with more flashing lights and clever gimmicks, so we got bored with the good stuff pretty quickly. We ended up spending most of the summer of 1980 at home by ourselves, trying to keep each other entertained.

Finding things we both liked to do was always a challenge. Calliope didn't like to watch TV as much as I did, so we did a lot of projects. I had a toy bow and arrow set I'd bought in a novelty shop in Tucson, during my avoid-the-volcano vacation earlier that year. It was designed to be pretty low-power, but Calliope and I figured out that if we shortened the string and reinforced the bow with duct tape and pieces of bamboo, we could increase its power significantly. It didn't take us long to shatter the cheap arrow that had come with the bow, so we got some better ones from the sporting goods section of the Fred Meyer department store on the other side of the hill and spent a couple of weeks knocking holes in the big piece of plywood that fenced the front yard off from the backyard, until the overworked bow finally gave up the ghost entirely.

We also put together some puppet shows for our parents, and a jitterbug routine we'd dance to an old Andrews Sisters record my dad had in his collection—"The Boogie Woogie Bugle Boy of Company B." We drew comics, and told stories, and had little sketch routines we'd perform based on *Star Blazers*, a Japanese cartoon that came on early weekday mornings.

I got a Daisy lever-action BB gun for my eighth birthday that summer. Once I had that, it was pretty much all Calliope and I played with. We could spend hours at a time in the backyard, shooting paper targets. By the end of the first month, we could walk BB holes across a piece of paper from thirty feet away, putting each shot within millimeters of the last.

The other thing we did was, we fought like crazy. I always

got the worst of those encounters. Calliope and I were exactly the same size, but she was twice as mean. While I fought to dominate—I'd try to push her down and pin her—Calliope fought to kill. She'd pull hair, bite, scratch, gouge. When all else failed, she'd resort to trying to strangle me. I knew I had to do the same if I ever wanted to win. But if I couldn't bring myself to take a swing at Dickie, I certainly couldn't hit Calliope. So I got my ass kicked a lot and took my revenge in other ways— like locking Calliope out when she needed to use the bathroom, or unplugging the extension cord that ran across the backyard to bring power to her house. I knew Han Solo would approve. After all, he'd been happy enough to use a disguise to sneak into the prison and then just start blasting away at the guards. Sometimes you had to take your shots when you could get them.

20

I developed a *Star Wars* action figure habit over our first summer in Seattle. Marcy's son, Isaac, had owned a few back in Eugene, but we didn't play with them much. In Seattle I got really into them and funneled all my allowance money into buying them. I could afford to get one about once every three weeks, and I went to the toy section at Fred Meyer every week to see if they had any new figures in. I had a few *Battlestar Galactica* figures, too, but the *Star Wars* collection was my pride and joy. When *The Empire Strikes Back* came out that year, half of my excitement was that there'd be new action figures issued because of it.

I started third grade at Stevens that fall, and one day, in spite of the no-toys policy at GAOP, I brought my brand-new Bossk bounty-hunter action figure to school with me. None of my classmates were very impressed, and my teacher confiscated it immediately. When the final bell rang I went and asked her for it. She went to her desk and looked around for a minute. Then she said it was gone.

"You threw it away?" I asked.

"No," she said with a shrug. "It's just gone. It was right here on top of my desk."

"But . . . that's not fair. You took it and you lost it!"

"That's a risk you run when you bring toys to school," she said.

I noticed then that some of the other kids in class—Dickie and a new kid named Virgil—were whispering and laughing to each other. And suddenly I knew exactly what had happened. I walked over and held out my hand.

"Give it back," I said.

"Give what back?" Virgil said.

"My action figure," I said. "You took it off her desk. Give it back."

Virgil and Dickie exchanged a smirk, and Virgil turned back to me, grinning.

"I don't know what you're talking about," he said.

"Lynne," I said to our teacher. "Virgil took my action figure off your desk!"

Other kids had to call their teachers Mister or Miss whatever, but GAOP was supposed to be too progressive for that, so we called our teachers by their first names. Suzie and Lynne.

"Virgil," Lynne called from her desk. "Do you have Jason's action figure?"

"I don't know what he's talking about," Virgil said.

I looked at Lynne and she just shrugged again. By now some

other kids had come over to see what the fuss was about, and half the class was standing behind Virgil and Dickie. I looked Virgil over and saw the unmistakable shape of an action figure in the front pocket of his jeans.

"It's right there!" I said, pointing.

"Right where?" Virgil asked, looking down.

"Right there," I said, poking at the plastic toy through his pants.

"Get your hand off my dick!" he said, slapping my hand away.

Dickie and the other kids laughed.

"Lynne!" I said. "I can see it. It's right there in his pocket!"

"I can't search him if he says he doesn't have it," Lynne said.

"So you can take my stuff and let him steal it, but you can't come over here and look and see that he's got my action figure?" I asked.

I couldn't believe this was really happening. Lynne and Suzie had never liked me much. Suzie had even gone so far as to tell me she didn't like me once, when I awkwardly asked permission to leave the classroom to go to the bathroom. She listened to me stammer out my request, including a lot of phrases like "I need to . . ." and "To the you-know . . ." followed by obscure hand gestures. Because having to ask to take a leak was one of the many conventions of public school life that always seemed totally uncivilized to me. When I was done with my little mime routine she looked me right in the eye and said, "You know, stuff like that—that's exactly the reason nobody likes you."

I'd walked across the playground to the bathroom feeling like I'd swallowed a bowling ball.

So maybe this behavior from Lynne wasn't so surprising. But it seemed to me that colluding with other students to rip me off was crossing some kind of line.

"Jason," she said. "You knew you weren't supposed to bring it to class. It's not my responsibility if you can't follow the rules."

I thought about the weeks I'd saved to get that action figure, and how happy I'd been to get it. I thought about the weeks I'd have to save to get another one, and the possibility that Fred Meyer might be sold out of Bossks by the time I'd saved up enough to buy one. And my face got red. And then I started crying.

"Oh, he's crying!" Dickie said. "Like a little baby!"

"Fuck you!" I screamed, rounding on him. "Fuck you! And fuck you!" I shouted at Virgil. "Fuck every single fucking one of you fucking motherfuckers! And fuck you, Lynne! Fuck you fuck you fuck you!"

Nobody seemed to know quite what to do with that one. Lynne looked totally shocked. Other kids giggled nervously. Dickie smiled triumphantly, and Virgil's face just went totally blank. I stormed over to the coat hooks next to the door, grabbed my jacket, and ran out of the building.

For most of the walk home I was just plain mad. It wasn't until I was a few blocks from my house that I started to wonder what was going to happen next. What would Lynne do? What would the school do? What would my dad do when he found out? By the time I got home, I was in a panic. When Calliope came home a few hours later, she found me curled up on my bed, in my bedroom/dining room.

"Hey," she said. "I heard you went nuts today."

I groaned and covered my face. Cal was in fifth grade, in the main building. If she'd heard about it, that meant the whole school knew. And Lynne would have to do something. She couldn't let it slide if the whole school knew about it. Not that she would have anyway.

"What happened?" Calliope asked.

When I told her the story she just shook her head.

"You've gotta learn to rein that shit in," she said.

"They ripped me off!" I protested.

"Of course they did," she said. "What did you expect?"

"But all they talk about—they're always talking about not stealing and telling the truth," I said, trying to figure out how to explain what bothered me about it so much.

Calliope got it immediately.

"You mean because they're straight?" she asked.

I nodded.

"That's what they do," she said. "They lie. They steal. And they never admit it, so they're a thousand times worse than us. I don't know why you can't get that through your head."

"So I can't trust anyone?" I asked. "Ever?"

I was being sarcastic. What she was saying sounded ridiculous to me, but she didn't get it.

"Nope," she said. "Nobody. But at least here, with our own, we know what the rules are and nobody lies about them."

When Dad got home, his reaction to the story was pretty much the same as Calliope's: that it was my own fault. Partly it was my fault for bringing the toy, but mostly it was my fault for not having protected it, and for being surprised when a bunch of straights fucked me over, and for letting that push me into losing control.

"Cops are the worst thieves," he said. "Politicians and lawyers the worst liars. Priests and teachers molest children. The only reason those people have so many rules is so they can break them to fuck people like us over."

That didn't sound like it could possibly be true. The implications were just too horrifying. But I wasn't really in a position to argue the point.

* * *

I didn't go to school the rest of that week. When I finally went back the following Monday, Lynne was rude and brusque with me all day. I was ready for that. I was ready for the note she gave me at the end of the day, too, to take home to my dad.

"I'll need him to sign this, and you bring it back," she said.

"Fine," I said, taking the paper and walking home.

The note told Dad he needed to come in for a conference. Later that week, he met with Lynne, Suzie, the school principal, and Booker, the fourth grade teacher who sort of ran the GAOP program. The meeting was after school, so I had to go home and wait for him. When Dad finally got back, he looked tired.

"They wanted to put you in special ed," he said.

"Like, for retarded kids?" I asked.

"Yeah," he said. "I mean, not exactly for retarded kids. They said you need too much attention, and you take time away from other students. They said that, in special ed, teachers would have more time to spend on you. So it's not so much that they think you're stupid, as that they just can't handle how smart you are."

"Okay," I said. I didn't really buy that interpretation, but it was one of my dad's necessary fictions. "What did you say?"

"I told them you're smarter than they are, and that the only reason you're acting out is because you're bored. I told them I'd sue if they tried to put you in special ed. That there's a stigma attached to it."

"What's a stigma?" I asked. "Like, when you can't see?"

"That's an astigmatism. Kind of the reverse idea. An astigmatism means you can't see things. Lack of the ability to identify a mark. A stigma is a mark that doesn't come off. It means even if you're plenty smart, people will assume you're retarded because you're in special ed."

"What did they say to that?"

"They didn't care. Educating children isn't much of a priority for them, really. So I asked to talk to Booker privately and we came to an arrangement."

"What did you tell him?"

"The facts of life," Dad said. I assumed this was a euphemism for some kind of threat, though I wasn't sure what Dad could have threatened Booker with that would stick.

"So now what?" I asked.

"Now you go to counseling at Seattle Mental Health every other week, to deal with your anger issues. And you keep going to GAOP."

"What's Seattle Mental Health?" I asked.

"It's a shrink. You're supposed to go to a shrink."

I wasn't sure how being crazy was less of a stigma than being retarded, but nobody was asking my opinion.

* * *

Dad and Phillip were still dating, but they usually went out instead of staying home, so I didn't see as much of Phillip as I used to. He was still working as a nurse, but he was getting a more advanced nursing degree from Seattle University. This only mattered to me because SU had a swimming pool, and SU students were allowed to use it and to bring guests. Once or twice a month Phillip loaned Dad his student identification so Dad could take me to the SU pool.

This was how Dad and I met Dr. Epstein.

The SU pool had a high dive that I liked to walk to the end of. Then I'd gird my loins and jump off. It was only about fifteen feet to the water, but standing on the end of the thing gave me vertigo. The problem was that most of the people who used the SU pool liked to swim laps. So, before I could jump into the pool, I had to look under the diving board and make sure there weren't any lap swimmers under me. I couldn't do this from the end of the board because I was too dizzy and I was afraid I'd fall off. The fifth or sixth time Dad took me to the pool, I leaned over the railing above the ladder to see if there was a lap swimmer under me and just flipped right over the rail.

Dad was sitting on the edge of the pool a few yards away, and he watched helplessly while I fell fifteen feet and landed flat on my back, on the concrete floor that surrounded the pool. He said afterward that the worst part was that I bounced. He'd never seen a person bounce like that before. Didn't even know it was possible.

When he got to me, my eyes were rolled completely back in my head, and he yelled at the lifeguard to call 911, but the lifeguard was already running over to me so Dad got up and ran into the office and started punching frantically at the phone, but nothing happened.

"How the fuck do you get an outside line on this thing?" he shouted at the lifeguard. But she was bent over me running through her first aid checklist: airway, breathing, circulation.

"The phone's not working!" Dad screamed at her. "How do I make the fucking phone work?"

"Dial 9!" she shouted back at him.

He dialed 9. Nothing happened.

"It's not working!"

"Dial 9, then dial 911!" she yelled back.

Dad punched in the number and finally got through to an emergency operator and ordered an ambulance.

That was Dad's story of the incident forever after: me bouncing, my eyes rolled back in my head, not being able to get the phones to work, and not being able to get the lifeguard to answer his questions.

I woke up as they were taping me to a backboard. Being

taped down hurt. The tape on my forehead hurt. When I tried to move my head, the tape pulled at my skin. That hurt. My head hurt. Everything hurt. I started to panic. Suddenly Dad was in my field of vision.

"What happened?" I asked.

"You fell off the high dive," he said.

"Mr. Schmidt," one of the ambulance guys said. "Why don't you follow behind us in your car? We'll meet you at Harborview."

They rolled me out to the ambulance and drove me to a hospital. At the hospital I got rolled down various hallways and left sitting like a piece of abandoned furniture outside the doors of various offices while I waited to be X-rayed, poked, and prodded. The outcome was as surprising to me as it was to everyone else: there was nothing wrong with me at all. No fractures, no sprains. Once they were sure my spine was okay they cut me loose from the backboard, and I realized that most of the pain I'd been experiencing was from being taped to a piece of wood. When they rolled me onto my belly there wasn't even a bruise on my back where I'd landed. I'd been knocked unconscious, but I didn't have so much as a goose egg where my head smacked into the concrete.

After what seemed like a couple of hours of exams, I was taken to an overnight bed, wired up to some machines, and given an IV drip that hurt like hell. The nurse told me it would only hurt when she put the needle in, but for some reason it just kept throbbing.

Dad was ushered in a few minutes later and sat down in a chair next to my bed.

"You're okay," he said.

"I know," I said.

As we sat there in awkward silence, a young guy in a lab coat came in. He was immediately interesting to me: he had dark, curly hair and he was wearing a tiny little hat on top of it, held in place with a bobby pin. He had an oversize metal clipboard in his hand. It was the bobby pin that got my attention, for some reason. He had enormous features, and a slightly stooped posture that may have been explained, at least in part, by his efforts to keep a cup of coffee he was carrying in his other hand from spilling. He was smiling when he came in, and he kept smiling the whole time he was in the room.

"Hiya," he said, as he set his coffee cup down on a counter next to the door. "I'm Dr. Epstein. How you doing? You're Jason? And Mark. Nice to meet you. So I'll just get right to the good news—you're fine. Remarkable, really. You fell fifteen feet? Onto concrete? Knocked unconscious? No bumps, no bruises, nothing. Never seen anything like it. Kids! They bounce, huh? Amazing. I guess you're not one of those kids who bruises easily, huh? Amazing. Really. So I'd like to keep you around overnight, just for observation, but I'm pretty sure you're a-okay. You got any questions? Anything you're wondering about?"

"Huh?" I said.

"How do we pay for it?" Dad asked.

"You got no insurance?" Dr. Epstein asked.

"No," Dad said. "And no money."

"Don't worry about it," Dr. Epstein said. "We got a program, no sweat. Probably why they brought you here. Swedish was closer. But we do all the free work. We got some paperwork you'll need to fill out, but don't sweat it. Hey, you want a free bus pass?"

Now it was Dad's turn to say, "Huh?"

"There's a program with Metro, you get a bus pass if you're disabled. Fifteen bucks a month, unlimited rides."

"I'm not . . ." Dad said.

"You broke?" he asked.

"Pretty much," Dad admitted.

"You're disabled. The kid, too. You need a note from your doctor. That's me. I'll leave it with the kid's discharge papers tomorrow. How you doing, kid? You doing okay?"

"Sure," I said.

"Head hurt?"

"No," I said.

"Back hurt?"

"No."

"All right. Hold on."

He took a little flashlight out of his pocket and walked over to my bed.

"Look at the light," he said. He flicked it into my eyes; flick-flick, flick-flick. Then he moved it side to side in front of me, and I tracked it back and forth, up and down. He put his light away and held my chin up so I had to look him in the eyes. He frowned contemplatively, like he was evaluating me for something.

"Knock knock," he muttered.

"Who's there?" I asked.

"Interrupting cow," he said.

"Interrupting c—"

"Moo!" he shouted.

I giggled and he let go of my chin.

"He's fine. You're fine, kid. Mark. Mark, is it? Right? You want a cup of coffee?"

"It's a little late . . ." Dad said.

"Come on, we'll talk," Dr. Epstein said, making a few notes on his metal clipboard, then picking up his cup of coffee and holding the door open while he waited for my dad, who gave me a quick kiss on the head before he followed the doctor out into the hallway.

"You on AFDC?" Dr. Epstein asked as Dad followed him out.

"We're on the wait list," Dad said.

"Yeah," Dr. Epstein said. "I can move that along for you. Come on. Bye, kid! You're looking great."

And then they were gone. I lay there alone for a couple of minutes before I realized there was a TV mounted on the wall near the door, and that I had a remote sitting on the table next to my bed.

21

I started at Seattle Mental Health. My therapist's name was Grace. She was nice enough, but definitely more of a them than an us. Her dry brown hair was cut to shoulder-length with bangs. She wore light makeup, no jewelry, and one layer of clothing on each part of her body: a sweater and a skirt. Slacks and a tunic shirt. Always solid colors. No textures. Her shoes were simple flats. Her face was smooth and unlined. If someone had asked me to draw her I could have done a good likeness without having to take my pen off the paper more than two or three times.

Seattle Mental Health turned out to be a complex of new buildings about a half mile from our house, near 15th Avenue. The buildings were laid out like a series of small houses, connected by hallways and covered walkways. It was all very 1970s urban renewal, with high, sloping roofs and wood exterior siding. Grace's office looked out onto a small courtyard with a covered patio and a few young maple trees. There wasn't much in her office itself: a desk, three government-issue chairs, a box of toys, and a bookshelf full of children's books. When I came in for my first appointment, Grace told me we were just supposed to talk. We could talk about whatever I wanted.

"Can I play with those while we talk?" I asked, gesturing at the toys.

"Sure," she said. "As long as you keep talking to me while you play with them."

That seemed fair, so I got down on the floor and started sorting through the box. Somewhat to my surprise, Grace sat down on the floor across the room from me, leaning up against the wall near her desk and putting her writing pad on her knees.

"What do you want to talk about?" I asked.

"Anything you want," she said.

"You know why I'm here?"

"Why do you think you're here?"

"Because I yelled at my teacher," I said. "And I said a bad word. A couple of times."

"Was it fuck or shit or . . . ?" she asked.

I paused in the act of picking through the toy box.

"Fuck," I said. "And . . . motherfuckers. And fuck you."

"So I guess you were pretty mad."

"Yeah," I said.

"What were you mad about?" she asked.

I told her the whole story, from beginning to end. When I was finished, she was quiet for a while.

"Yeah," she said finally. "I guess I might have said fuck a couple of times, too. If that had happened to me."

* * *

A week later Dad and I went down to the Metro administrative office to get our bus passes. Metro was the government corporation that ran Seattle's buses and, for some reason, also ran the city's sewers and was in charge of water quality. As we approached the office, Dad kept coaching me on how to act.

"Remember," he said. "You're supposed to be retarded."

"So are you," I said defensively.

The bus passes Dr. Epstein had set us up with were for people with disabilities. The easiest disability to fake, we figured, was being developmentally disabled, but in 1981 the term in common usage was "retarded."

"Sure," Dad said. "The point is, you don't want to seem too smart. And that goes for when you're using the pass, too. You don't want some driver to figure out we're scamming the things and take it away from you. Dr. Epstein's going out on a limb for us with this."

"What's a retarded person act like?" I asked.

"I don't know. Don't worry about that. Don't actually try to act retarded. Don't make a thing of it. Just don't go reciting the Gettysburg Address while you're on the bus or anything."

"The what?"

"That's my boy!" he said, slapping me on the back as we walked into the office.

The process of getting the passes turned out not to take very long. We got our pictures taken, and they stuck the pictures onto cards that had our names and other information on them. Then they laminated the whole thing and put a sticker on it to show it was valid, and told Dad how to renew the stickers by mail. And just like that, we had new super-cheap bus passes. As we were leaving the building, Dad noticed something and grabbed my shoulder.

"Come here," he said. "And don't say anything. You got it? Don't say a word while we're in here."

"Okay," I said. I looked up as he guided me into a large room with a counter up near the door and a bunch of metal shelves behind it. The sign above the door said LOST AND FOUND.

"Hi," Dad said to the guy behind the counter. "This is lost and found?"

"Sure is," said the man, looking up from a book.

"We left a couple of things on the bus about three weeks ago. I didn't know you all had a lost and found, or I'd have come to get them sooner."

"What'd you lose?" the man asked.

"A jacket," Dad said. "A dark blue nylon windbreaker. And an umbrella. Black. One of those kinds that folds up."

"What size was the windbreaker?" the man behind the counter asked.

"I got it at Sears," Dad said. "And I can't remember if it was sized in numbers or letters. It's either a medium, or about a 34."

"Hold on," the man said. Then he disappeared into his shelves for a while and came back with a large plastic box. "This is what I got."

Dad picked through four or five windbreakers before he found one like the one he'd ripped the year before, during our Christmas-tree-stealing expedition. It took him less time to pick out an umbrella he liked.

"You get a lot of stuff through here?" he asked.

"You wouldn't believe," said the man.

"People usually come claim it?" Dad asked.

"Not even a tenth of it," said the man.

"What happens to the rest?"

The man shrugged. "We throw it all out every couple of months. Or donate it, depending."

Dad looked at me. I was wearing a Goodwill ski jacket I'd picked up a few seasons back. It was already too small for me, and the arm was covered with duct tape to keep the stuffing in.

"You got anything that's about to expire?" Dad asked. "Like that ski jacket?"

"Hold on," said the guy behind the counter. He went back

into his shelves and came back a minute later with a brown ski jacket in my size.

"You lose this on the bus?" he asked me, holding it up. I looked at Dad, who nodded.

"I sure did," I said.

"Here you go, kid," he said, handing me the jacket.

"Thanks," I said.

"Yeah, thanks," Dad said. "Let's go, Jason."

As we turned to go, the guy behind the counter cleared his throat, and Dad turned back to look at him.

"Not for nothing," said the man. "But you wouldn't want to lose things on the bus too often. Not more than once or twice a year. You know what I'm saying?"

"Sure," Dad said, nodding. "And thanks."

"You have a good day now," said the man.

When we got outside we sat down in a bus shelter. Ironically, Metro's administrative offices were sort of off the beaten path, and bus access to them wasn't very good. We had a good wait ahead of us.

"I guess I should fall off high dives more often," I said.

"No," Dad said. "You shouldn't."

* * *

We got onto Aid for Dependent Children that fall. Dr. Epstein may or may not have had something to do with it. Dad didn't want to tell me. But AFDC included medical coupons, which meant free doctors and dentists. One of Dad's bottom teeth had disintegrated the year before, and I'd never actually been to a dentist, so the coupons came in handy. Dad got some gold crowns on the backs of his bottom teeth, and I went to Odessa Brown Children's Dental Clinic to have some folks poke around in my mouth a bit.

"You're going to need braces later," said the nice lady dentist who did the exam. Then she shot my mouth full of Novocain and pulled out two of my incisors.

Generally, our second year in Seattle was going better than our first. With AFDC, we were able to keep our heads above water financially. But also, we were re-creating the same type of network we'd had in Eugene. A better one, really; the one we'd had in Eugene hadn't included any doctors. And Dad was meeting people through Seattle Counseling Service who helped us out in various ways. Dad had a regular drug dealer named Scotty, who gave him a good deal on pot. And Phillip was introducing Dad to people around town. Dad was doing small deals, selling pot a few ounces at a time, and going to some parties, which was how people like us built support systems.

School still sucked, and Olive announced that she and Calliope would be moving out at the end of the school year because, evidently, that whole no-power-or-running-water thing was becoming kind of inconvenient. But even that worked out for the best. Our subsidized housing finally came through that summer, and Dad started shopping for rentals on the north end of town.

"We can get a place with two bedrooms," he said. "And a better yard. And a better neighborhood."

I would have settled for a house that didn't smell like mushrooms, but a bedroom of my own sounded nice, too.

22

In the summer of '81, the summer I turned nine, we moved into a two-bedroom house in a north Seattle neighborhood called Ballard. The house was almost perfect. It had a huge yard, it was a half block from an elementary school, and it had a good-size living room and dining room. There was even a third bedroom in the basement, but the basement could only be reached through an external side door, so it wasn't convenient to use as an actual sleeping space. And Ballard was a historically Scandinavian neighborhood with a lot of kids in it.

Our new landlord was a scruffy-looking young guy named Tim, who came from a rich family. He had a slim, muscular build, curly brown hair, blue eyes, and the kind of tan that pale people get when they spend too much time in the sun: part tan, part permanent sunburn. Tim had gotten himself semi-disowned by his rich parents after dropping out of college and going off to fish for crab in the Gulf of Alaska, but not before he used his trust fund to buy the house in Ballard.

"I used to stay here between crabbing seasons," he said, when he showed us around the house. "But that meant it was vacant so much of the year, I just figured fuck it. Someone should get some use out of it."

"We'll definitely get use out of it," Dad said.

"Yeah," Tim said. He led us out on the front porch and took a cigarette out of a crumpled pack he was carrying in his back pocket. "The only thing I guess I should mention is Carmella Johnson, the bitch who lives next door."

He leaned over the porch railing and pointed at the neighbor's house as he said it. I looked to see what he was pointing at, but there was nobody there. Just a squat little house behind a thicket of old plum trees. There was plenty of yard and trees and bushes, but whoever owned the place was too old or too lazy to take care of it. The grass was three feet high, and the trees pushed in over the patio to hide the house in shadows.

"What's her deal?" Dad asked.

"She's just a bitch on wheels," Tim said. "This driveway that lies between the properties, technically we've got an easement on it. So we can get to our parking space down at the back of the lot there. But Carmella, a couple of years ago, started parking her car to block the driveway so I couldn't get in there. She does it long enough, I might lose the easement. So we've been back and forth over that for years. But the main thing, I have to admit, is mostly my fault."

"What's the main thing?" Dad asked.

"Well, she's got these two little rat dogs," Tim said. "And I guess . . . well, it doesn't make me proud to admit this, but there used to be three of them."

"No," Dad said, sounding slightly horrified. Or like he was pretending to be horrified. Ironically horrified.

"Yeah," Tim said, skipping over the irony. "About a year ago I was walking home and those little rat dogs were out in the front yard, barking at me. And I just picked a rock up and winged it at them. Like, not thinking I was gonna hit anything. Just to scare them? And I tagged one right in the head, by accident. It kept barking, but it started running in circles. And then it just kind of . . . slowed down. Like a clock winding down. Yap-yap-yap yap yap yap, yap, yap, yap . . . yap. Yap. Boom. Dead."

"Jesus," Dad said.

"Yeah," Tim said. "Like I said, it was an accident. I hate those little dogs, but it isn't their fault Carmella's the goddamn Antichrist. Dog's just a dog, right? Anyway, she's had it in for me big-time since then, and I guess she might bestow some of that hatred on whoever moves in here as my tenants."

"Well," Dad said. "We'll try to steer clear of her."

I made a little noise that was almost a laugh.

* * *

I kept on meeting with Grace every other week for a few months after we moved to Ballard. Apparently whatever deal Dad had worked out with Booker and the other GAOP teachers was with the district, more than with anyone in particular at Stevens, so even though I changed schools, I still had to finish out my sentence. As it were. Grace acknowledged that we were going to be done soon and seemed to want to ask me a lot of big-picture questions to wrap things up.

"What's the most important thing to you?" she asked.

"I want to be good," I said, without pausing to think about it. That was part of what I used her toys for. By focusing on the toys, I found I could answer her questions without having to concentrate on them very hard.

"What's that mean to you?" she asked.

"Like Han Solo," I said. "You know Han Solo? From *Star Wars*?"

"I know Han Solo," she said. "But I'm surprised. What about Luke?"

I wondered why people kept asking me that.

"Luke doesn't do anything," I said. "Like, not really. He didn't do anything much in the first movie. And in the second one, he went to Yoda, and Yoda told him what he needed to do, and he couldn't even do that. He just ran off to save Han and Leia, even though Yoda told him not to. But Han—he could leave at any time. He had a whole life before he met Luke and Leia. He sticks around because he wants to. He asks questions. He thinks about stuff, and makes fun of people for being stupid. But when it comes right down to it, he does the right thing. And I think it means more when he does it. Him and Leia both, really. Luke wants to be a hero because he's got some stupid idea about being the good guy just to be the good guy. Han and Leia do it because they know why it's important. They understand what's at stake. Luke never even seems to think about that part of it. How many Bothans died to bring us the plans to the Death Star, or whatever. He could give a shit. He just wants to be the guy with the blaster who everyone says 'thank you' to."

"But you said you wanted to be good," Grace said. "Isn't that what Luke wants?"

"Luke doesn't want to be good. He wants everyone else to think he's good. It's different. That's why he's vulnerable to the dark side. He's full of pride."

I kept playing with the toys from Grace's box, but at some point I realized she hadn't said anything in a while and I glanced up. She was sitting on the floor with her writing pad, same as she always did, but she was giving me a weird look, like something I'd said, or the way I said it, made her uncomfortable.

"What?" I asked.

She shook her head and looked at the clock.

"We're done for today," she said.

23

Olive and Calliope had found a place over in the Eastlake neighborhood, a few miles away from our new place in Ballard. Like our new digs, their house was half a block away from a school and had two bedrooms. Otherwise it was a completely different vibe. They lived in a triplex instead of a single-family house, and the backyard was an overgrown mess. The neighborhood was an industrial nightmare, pinned between Interstate 5 and the shipyards of Lake Union. The playground for the school near their house was pretty good. It had a wooden play structure, a zip line, and a big field. But the rest of the neighborhood was full of shattered blue-collar retirees, scraping by on workers' comp and Social Security. Even the lake was a ruin. The shipyards had turned it into a giant oil slick full of solvents, and during heavy rains, raw sewage would blow right into the water from the combined sewer outfalls that emptied out every five or six blocks along the shoreline.

On hot days we swam in the lake anyway, figuring the chemicals from the shipyards would kill whatever was leaking out of the sewers. We just tried not to get any in our mouths.

Whatever setup Olive had to pay her bills, she spent most of her time drinking and shooting smack at the Eastlake Zoo, a bar a couple of blocks from their house. Some of her friends from Oregon had made their way to Seattle by this time, and most kept plying their trade as fishermen in the Alaskan fleet that launched out of Salmon Bay every year. But that meant they had most of the year to sit and drink with Olive, who would bring one of them home every so often. There was Paulie, with his giant early-model Suburban, the Blue Beast. And Will, who seemed like a decent enough guy except Calliope told me that once she woke up in the middle of the night to find Will on his knees next to her bed, jerking off and crying.

Between the masturbating, the crying, the drinking, and the smack, Calliope chose to spend a lot of nights and weekends at our house in Ballard. Also, we had cable, and MTV had just come on the air. Calliope was obsessed with MTV.

* * *

Ballard was as much like the 1950s—as much like how my dad described his childhood—as any place I'd been up to that point. Ballard had been its own town until it was swallowed up by Seattle in 1907, and it still had its little downtown, with a movie theater, a pet store, the Scandinavian Shoppe, and an old Carnegie free library that had been boarded up and abandoned years before. Block after block of single-family housing: five-thousand-square-foot lots, compact brick houses, lawns, kids, old people.

Big chunks of Ballard were still semirural. There were areas without sidewalks or storm sewers; places where there were still just ditches next to gravel roads. Some of the houses still had barns behind them, from when they'd been farms, and there were properties in the neighborhood that ran to a couple of acres, sometimes taking up an entire city block. The topography of Ballard also meant that some areas just couldn't be developed. The street grid was interrupted by unstable cliffs, or greenbelts that cut across places where the grade was too steep to build on. Ballard was part of the City of Seattle, and had been for seventy-five years, but there were still wild deer in the northern reaches of the neighborhood, and every once in a while a cougar would wander down the railroad tracks from the north and eat a few house pets before Animal Control could catch it and relocate it.

Ballard's big attraction was the Ballard Locks, which included a fish ladder. The locks allowed boats to move between Puget Sound and the inland lake system, including the tug boats that took half-mile-long log booms from all over the Puget Sound basin upstream to the lumber mills of Lake Washington and Lake Sammamish, a few hundred logs at a time. The fish ladder was equipped with rows of windows in an underground viewing room, where tourists could watch giant schools of thirty-pound salmon making their way upstream twice a year. The neighborhood also boasted dozens of factories, a steel mill, sheet metal fabricators, car dealerships, a decent hospital, and one of the largest commercial fishing fleets on the West Coast. It was a prosperous blue-collar neighborhood with an economy that included everyone from the paperboy to the plant manager. People lived their whole lives without leaving Ballard more than once or twice a year.

There was a lot of desperation underneath all that prosperity. Bars where young single moms would go to try to pick up a Navy husband, and crackerbox apartments and multiplexes where they could raise their kids on a shoestring budget while their deadbeat ex-husbands started new families a thousand miles away. And however many layers beneath that, 15th Avenue was three straight miles of used car dealerships, no-tell motels, and junkyards. The meth labs and maintenance alcoholics were in the old boarding houses, nestled between small-scale factories that were one insurance-fraud fire away from closing up for good.

The school where I started fourth grade that year was a 1930s brick building with an asphalt playground. Most of the teachers in it were men in their late fifties or early sixties; Korean War veterans with thick glasses in plastic frames, polyester slacks, button-down polyester shirts. Pocket protectors. They called boys by our last names. If we acted out in class, we got paddled. Each teacher had his own paddle; a long, flat slab of plywood with holes drilled in it and a handle. The paddles didn't look improvised in any way. I sometimes wondered if there was a woodshop teacher somewhere who'd made them, or if they could be ordered in a catalog.

Most of the kids I met in school came from the basement apartments and multiplexes—the land of the single mother. Or maybe those were the only kids who invited me over to their houses.

* * *

A lot of things changed when we moved to Ballard. Dad and Phillip broke up, though they remained friends. We stopped using our old Speed Queen and started doing laundry in the new washer and dryer that Tim put in our basement. And Dad quit working for Seattle Counseling Service and started working under the table for a rich child psychologist named Carol.

I had no idea how Dad and Carol had met each other, but she needed a personal assistant on the cheap and Dad needed an under-the-table gig that wouldn't cut into our welfare benefits, so he went to work for her about thirty hours a week at seven dollars an hour. That was huge money to us at the time, and between that and welfare, Section Eight Housing, and food stamps, we were almost fifty percent above the poverty line. It was hard not to get a little giddy at first. Of course Dad had a good use for that surplus income; he increased his pot consumption so he was getting high about eight times a day, every day. He smoked weed about as often as he smoked cigarettes. Meanwhile, he spent most days out at Carol's house, cleaning garbage out of her basement, mowing her lawn, or organizing her patient files. Whatever she needed him to do.

Dad's agenda changed around this time, too. He started

talking about staying in Ballard for a long time and trying to keep things stable for me. The Ballard time warp seemed to make him sentimental, and he started talking a lot about trying to provide me with everything he'd had when he was growing up. Mainly he mentioned food, housing, and clothes; all the things we'd always had kind of a spotty relationship with. He took me to the JCPenney in downtown Ballard before school started and bought me my second new pair of shoes and a bag of new tube socks. Then we went to Goodwill, loaded up on used clothes, and grabbed a few more pairs of shoes. Used shoes, but still: multiple pairs of shoes was a new thing. And a load of *Star Wars* toys for my birthday that year.

"I can't believe how spoiled you are," Calliope would say every time she walked into my room and looked at all my toys. I couldn't argue. Calliope actually had almost no toys, and hadn't for as long as I'd known her. She had a pretty good comic book collection, a few Barbie dolls that she committed various cosmetic atrocities against, and a few other special things that had been given to her or made by the various adults who looked out for her while her mom was asleep at the wheel. But compared to the ridiculous haul of swag I had in my room, she was absolutely right: I was spoiled as hell.

One other thing that changed when we first moved to Ballard was our pet ownership situation. We still had Thunder. Dad mostly took care of him—insofar as leaving him outside at night and letting him back in the next morning was "taking care" of him. But shortly after we moved to Ballard we also got cats. Nine cats. Or, it started out as nine cats.

* * *

We had a friend named Elise, whom Dad had met at Seattle Counseling Service. Elise lived in West Seattle, and I thought she was great. She was a tall, big-boned, incredibly overweight woman who told a lot of jokes, laughed easily, and always gave me ice cream.

"He doesn't need ice cream," Dad would say. "He's getting fat."

"Mark!" Elise would bark. "What a thing to say about a kid. Jesus. Let him eat his ice cream."

Elise gave me a portable record player and a transistor radio as house-warming gifts when we moved to Ballard. I had a bunch of Disney records Dad had picked out of Carol's trash when he was cleaning out her basement for her that I listened to on the record player all the time. At night, if I was having trouble sleeping, I listened to the AM radio. Elise was an unqualified good in my mind.

Right after we moved to Ballard, Elise's neighbor, who owned nine cats, had to move. And she couldn't take the cats with her. Elise was bummed that the cats might have to go to the pound, so Dad and I took them to our new house with its fabulous new yard.

"They have to be outside cats," Dad said.

"Sure," I said. "No problem."

When we got them home, Dad put an old steamer trunk with the lid open under the back porch and lined it with an army blanket. And that was pretty much that. The cats lived in the trunk. We put food out on the back porch for them every day or two. And water. And otherwise, Calliope and I just played with them whenever we wanted to. Sometimes we brought them down in the basement room, where Dad had set up a bunch of bookshelves and a bed. We'd pile the cats on top of us and read and color all day while we were covered in a heap of purring happiness.

At some point we noticed that the cats were multiplying. Dad said we could give them away, but he never got around to putting up a sign. By the end of the school year, nine cats had turned into twenty-one cats, and Carmella Johnson started to give us a hard time about it.

24

It had taken Dad about two months to start getting into it with Carmella. If anything, I was surprised by his restraint. Between his battle with Marcy back at the Fillmore Street house, his fights with Grandma, and his interactions with my teachers on Aloha Street, I'd started to get the idea that Dad sort of thrived on conflict. Having been warned that we were moving in next to another pathological shit-disturber, I was surprised by how long it took them to find each other.

It started, as Tim had warned us it would, with the driveway.

The driveway ran along the border between Carmella's property and ours, then branched at the bottom. The left branch was Carmella's and the right branch was on our property. The actual parking space, on our side, was a massive wooden deck that had been the floor of a garage, once upon a time. It was clear from the state of the remaining timbers that the people who lived in our house had been using the driveway to reach that parking space since at least the 1940s.

The Vega was barely running by this time. The cobblestone streets of Capitol Hill had been a real challenge for a car that had suffered the kind of trauma the Vega had experienced back in Portland. At one point, when Dad was driving me to school, the alternator had actually just fallen out of the car and landed on the street underneath us. Dad heard it hit the ground, stopped the car, got out, and took a look. Once he realized what had happened, he took a loose piece of two-by-four out of the back of the car, wedged the alternator into position against the firewall, started the car back up, and kept on driving. A year later, when we were in Ballard, the alternator was still being held in place by a piece of wood.

All this car drama meant that getting the Vega in and out of the driveway could be kind of a production. Sometimes Dad had to push the car up the driveway, out onto the street, and get it rolling so he could compression-start it. So when Carmella blocked the driveway with her silver Cadillac half-ragtop, it really added insult to injury. Eventually she did it on a day when Dad had an errand to run.

"I'm gonna go next door and ask Carmella if she can move her car," he said to me.

I was sitting at the table in our dining room, eating a bowl of Raisin Bran. He was standing by the front door, dressed for work. I looked up at him with a mouthful of cereal and shrugged.

"I'm just gonna be really polite about it," he said.

I swallowed.

"Sure," I said.

"It shouldn't be a problem," he said.

I raised my eyebrows. "Okay."

"So I'll be right back," he said.

"Okay. See you in a minute."

He took a deep breath and patted his pockets to make sure he had his keys and his wallet. Then he waved at me again and stepped onto the porch, letting the door close behind him. I watched out the window as he went around the side of the house, walking down the disputed driveway to Carmella's house. Once he was out of sight I went back to eating my cereal.

I had time to finish up, get dressed for school, and be ready to leave before he came back.

"That fucking bitch is crazy!" he said, stepping inside and slamming the door closed behind him.

"Polite didn't work?" I asked.

"She just started talking my goddamn ear off about Tim!"

Dad said. "And I listened for a while, but then I was like, 'Yeah, I don't know anything about that. I just need to get my car out.' And she just kept talking! About how he's trespassing, and how it's her land and how there's no reason we should be able to access our parking spot, even if it is on our land, and—Jesus. So finally she gets down to it, and says she'll move her car but I just need to understand it's her driveway. Hers. And I said I didn't know anything about that. That's between her and Tim. I just rent. No, she says. It's her driveway. I can drive across it. But I have to ask permission, like, every time."

"That's when you lost it?" I asked.

"That's when I lost it," he agreed.

* * *

Things continued to escalate over the next few months. First with the driveway. It took Dad all of two weeks to decide the solution to the blocking problem was to drive over Carmella's lawn to go around her car. Then it was a thing with the dogs. She let her two little dogs run loose in her yard all day. Thunder ran loose over the whole neighborhood when Dad let him out at night. But Carmella insisted that all the dog shit in her yard came from our dog. She and Dad argued that one back and forth for about a month before I came home one day and found three police cars parked in front of our house.

One useful thing I'd learned up to that point in my life: I knew with a fair degree of confidence that if he'd killed her, there'd be more police cars around.

It turned out he'd just buried her car in dog shit.

There were three cops on our front porch, talking to Dad. Carmella was standing in her front yard, talking to two other cops. And I could see a dry white and brown crust of shit all over her silver car. The car was parked under our front porch, and even with all those cops standing on our porch, I could make out shit stains on the walls around them.

I went around to the kitchen door and let myself into the house. Then I sat down in the living room and watched afternoon cartoons until Dad came back inside.

"What happened?" I asked. Maybe a little more eagerly than was appropriate.

"I tried," he said. He said this a lot when he was starting a story about Carmella.

"What happened?" I repeated.

"Well," he said. "You know about the dog shit fight we've been having."

"Yeah," I said.

"Okay, so, I got home today and she'd taken a shovel and flung all the shit in her yard up on our porch. All over the walls. All over everything. But I decided I was going to be mature about it. I decided to be the grownup. So I got some big rubber gloves and a garbage bag and just started cleaning it up. Right?"

"Yeah," I said. "Right. Good."

"Right," he said. "So, but, the bigger the pile got, the angrier I got. And the longer it took, the angrier I got. And finally it was just this huge pile. Huge. And it was like I'd just gathered all my anger into one place, and I just—her car was right there, and I just—well. Yeah. So that's what happened. And then she called the cops."

"Uh-huh," I said. "Okay. Well. They didn't arrest you, anyway."

"No, that's the thing: they talked to her for a half hour, and then they came over to me and said, 'This bitch is fucking crazy. You just need to stay away from her. Don't engage.'"

"Okay," I said. "So they didn't arrest you for the car. But they didn't arrest her for the porch either."

"They couldn't," Dad said. "If they'd arrested one of us, they'd have had to arrest both of us."

This sounded to me like something they'd say if they'd told both Carmella and my dad the same thing about the other person being at fault, and then told them, in effect, to leave each other alone. But I let that one go by.

"So what now?" I asked.

"Now you just stay away from that crazy twat," Dad said. "She's dangerous. And watch out for those two redneck sons of hers, too."

Carmella had two grown sons who stopped by occasionally. They seemed friendly enough, in that way that suggested I might find the bones of a few missing kids if I dug around under the foundation of their houses for a while. Avoiding them would be no problem. It had been on my to-do list anyway.

25

I steered clear of Carmella, just like I'd been told to. But I did spend a lot of time in the yards of our other neighbors. Our block had been laid out with a right-of-way for an alley down the middle, but the alley had never been graded or paved and the space had grown over. Some people let their yards encroach on it, but there was still a kind of winding track of unclaimed, unmaintained land that ran down the middle of the block. Generations of cats, dogs, and kids had cut trails through the wilderness, giving it the feeling of a secret passage of some kind. I liked those kinds of hidden trails, so I used the secret path to get to and from school some days.

One day, as I was on my way home, I saw that a neighbor about two doors down from our house had a live goat in his backyard. I paused when I saw it, worried that it might charge me the way Sean's goats used to, but this goat was tied to a stake that was driven into the ground. And anyway, it didn't seem like the charging type. It had long ears and those weird frog eyes that goats have, and it was chewing placidly while it stared at me.

I looked around and walked over to where the goat was tied up. When it didn't react to my presence, I started scratching its forehead, until a man I didn't recognize came out of the back door of the house.

"Oh!" he said, when he saw me. "Hello! Who are you?"

"I live down there," I said, pointing at the back of my house. "My name's Jason."

"Ah. Jason. Good name. You like my goat?"

"Yeah," I said. "He's neat."

"Yes," said the man, coming closer and scratching the goat's neck. I noticed he had a strange accent. "He's a sweetie. Too bad he's dinner tonight."

I laughed shortly.

"Yeah," I said. "Right."

"No," said the man. "Really. I was just coming out to kill him so we can eat him tonight, for my father's birthday party. I'm going to cook him. In that roaster, right over there."

I looked where he was pointing and saw what looked like an oil drum lying sideways on a trailer in the driveway. It didn't look like a roaster of any sort, but I thought it must be nice to be able to park a trailer in your driveway without having some crazy lady throw dog shit on your front porch. Then I looked back at the man and smiled.

"Sure," I said.

"You don't believe me?"

"Not really," I said apologetically.

"Okay," he said. "Come on. I show you."

He untethered the goat and led it toward his open basement door. After he'd gone a few feet, he looked back at me expectantly.

I looked at my house, just a few hundred feet away, and back at the man with the goat. Everything about this situation was breaking some Very Important Rules that had been repeated to me for as long as I could remember: stay where lots of people can see you, don't talk to strangers, don't go into strangers' houses. And those weren't even the rules I'd get in the most trouble for breaking. The one I was really going to get busted for was the one my dad was going to say was so common sense it shouldn't need to be said out loud: when you meet a strange man who starts a conversation by telling you he's going to take a goat into a basement and kill it, *don't follow him into the basement.* How many times had I yelled that at movie screens during horror movies?

On the other hand, I was still pretty sure this was all just some elaborate hoax, and I wanted to call his bluff. I got no danger vibe of any kind from the dark-skinned bald man with the mustache. Really, he looked a lot like a shorter, older version of my dad. It was a child's conundrum: my intellectual understanding that not feeling endangered didn't mean I was safe, versus my compulsive desire not to let someone prank me.

"Sure," I said. "Let's see it."

His basement was surprisingly bright, with sunlight coming in through some windows on the south side of the house. It was also extremely clean, with a smooth concrete floor and bare wooden beams supporting the house above us. There was no dirt on the floor, no cobwebs between the joists. The ceiling was about seven feet high. I thought it would have been a good shop space. Much better than the dirt basement at the Aloha Street house, where my dad used to refinish furniture.

As I looked around, I noticed a selection of long knives hanging from nails on one of the beams.

"Here," said the man. "This is how you do it."

He took a small, sharp-looking knife from one of the nails above his head. Then he knelt and whispered in the goat's ear as he eased it down onto the floor. And down, and down. After a few seconds he had the goat lying on its side. It didn't look especially comfortable, and I thought it would get up in a second, but the man reached around underneath it and cut its throat in one small, clean movement. He cut on the side that was facing the ground, and the dark red blood poured out across the concrete, washing down the metal drain in the floor. The goat barely moved, and the man continued to pat it and whisper.

"Shhhhhh," he said. "You're okay. Good boy. You're okay."

After a few seconds, the blood slowed, and then stopped.

"That's it," he said. "Gone."

I looked at the goat. I looked at its eyes. It really didn't seem that different. Its eyes weren't any more empty. I didn't see it breathing, but I hadn't noticed it breathing before he cut its throat. What did it mean? That the difference between alive and dead might be . . . subtle.

"Now," said the man, as if he were teaching a class. "We hang it up."

Still using his small knife, he lifted one of the goat's back legs and made a single cut behind its heel tendon. The fact that the goat didn't react to that cut was as surprising as anything else I'd seen in the last three minutes—it seemed like the kind of thing that might bring an animal jolting back from the dead. Once the cut was made, the man lifted the goat by its foot and hung it from a sharp hook I hadn't noticed before. It was screwed into the same beam that his knives hung from. The goat's other back leg stuck out at an undignified angle.

"Now we take off the skin," the man said, cutting a circle around the goat's ankle just under the hook and running a long slit from the ankle to the haunch. Then he just worked his fingers in at the top of the cut and—pulled! The skin came off the leg like a tight sock. The man made a few more cuts and, within seconds, had completely skinned the goat. What was left was just a shiny, wet thing. I could see blue veins and white fat. Pink muscles.

"After this, I do the guts," the man said. "You probably don't want to see that part."

"Okay," I said quietly.

"Hey, you want to come by tonight for my father's birthday, you come. Bring your parents. We would be happy to have you."

I smiled.

"Thanks," I said. But I already knew I wouldn't come. I wouldn't ask my dad if I could come. I wouldn't invite him. He could never hear about this. He could never hear about anything that even alluded to it.

I said goodbye to the man in the basement and walked the rest of the way home in a daze, thinking about everything I'd just learned. And I didn't tell my dad, or anyone else. Not for years and years.

26

I made fewer enemies in Ballard than I had on Capitol Hill, but I was still short of friends. I played with a kid named Danny because he lived across the street from me. He and his mom lived in an apartment building that was owned by his grandparents. Danny and I were both nine years old, but he was a good five inches shorter than I was. His mom's nickname was Tiny, and Danny took after her. He was high-strung and insecure. Calliope hated him.

I met Gabe about halfway through my fourth grade year. He was the opposite of Danny; tall, pale, and big-boned, with a round face, wiry blond hair, thick lips, and sort of a potato nose. He always looked a little stoned, though I knew there was no chance of that. Gabe and I ended up standing next to each other for class pictures because we were the two tallest kids in our fourth grade class, and we got to talking about *Star Wars*, and our action figure collections. He asked if I wanted to come over to his apartment that night.

"You mean after school?" I asked.

"No," he said. "My mom doesn't get off work until later, so I have to go to day care until she's home from work. Then I can walk home."

"Oh," I said. "Okay. So what time?"

"Five-thirty," he said.

"See you then," I said.

I walked away hoping I hadn't let my surprise show. The idea that a school-age kid would be in day care had never occurred to me, ever, in my entire life. Pretty much every kid I'd ever met at school lived with one parent, and that one parent worked. After school, we all went home to empty houses, or went over to friends' houses, or did something else, until our parents got home. People on TV had taken to calling us latch-key kids, but while it was a nice change of pace to have anything on TV relate to my life in any way, I'd always carried my key on a string around my neck. When I got my new bus pass, that got added to the string so I wouldn't lose it. Dad said it would be a handy way of identifying me if I got hit by a car or something, so someone would call him and tell him to come pick up the body.

I went home after school and collected my favorite action figures and *Star Wars*–compatible spaceships. Then I watched cartoons until it was time to meet Gabe outside the day care. I left a note for my dad, telling him whose house I'd gone to and that I'd call if I was going to be out past seven. Then I turned off the lights, left the house, and checked to make sure the door locked behind me.

* * *

Gabe lived in a single-story apartment building a few blocks from our school. As soon as we walked in I was struck by how weirdly uninteresting his place was. This was something I'd noticed since coming to Ballard. Most of the apartments I'd been in were more like hotel rooms. No paintings or tapestries on the walls. No antiques. Most of their furniture wasn't even made of wood. Gabe and his mom had a polyester-covered couch, a glass coffee table, and a bunch of other furniture that was made of particle board: a TV stand, and a few bookshelves. There was a picture of Gabe on the wall and a picture of Gabe and some grownups on one of the bookshelves, but that was really about it.

The smell of Gabe's place was weird, too. It smelled really

strongly of some kind of meat sauce. Or some weird mix of herbs. I couldn't pin it down, but it had things in common with the smells of the other Ballard places I'd been in.

I realized I was standing just inside the doorway, sniffing the air like a rabbit. Gabe was looking at me with raised eyebrows.

"Nice place," I said lamely.

"Hold on," Gabe said. He disappeared through a doorway and came out a few minutes later with an action figure case shaped like Darth Vader's head.

"Let's do this," he said, opening the case.

* * *

Gabe's mom came home around six. She dressed like an office worker, in a beige skirt and sweater. She had short, light brown hair, large blue eyes, and a heart-shaped face. She was extremely thin. She didn't look like a real mother. She looked like the sort of woman who would play a mother on TV. She introduced herself as Claire, rather than Ms. McAlister or Miss Anything-Else, which I thought was unusual among straights. I recognized her as one of the adults with Gabe in the bookshelf photo.

"Would you like to stay for dinner?" she asked me as she headed into the kitchenette in the corner of the living room.

I got excited, but I tried not to let it show. I'd eaten at other people's houses plenty of times back in Eugene, but I hadn't actually been invited to dinner at another kid's house since we'd been in Seattle.

"Yes, please," I said. "Thank you."

"Mm," she said. "Polite."

Claire turned on the oven and took a frozen pizza out of the freezer.

I watched her from the corner of my eye as Gabe and I played, and I wondered if this was how they ate all the time. My dad had inconsistent attitudes about instant food: he claimed not to believe in it, but he didn't take time to cook very often. He bought instant food as "emergency food," but then he'd end up cooking it six nights a week. Breakfast was always Raisin Bran, lunch was always Top Ramen, dinner was usually a homemade entrée with a side of macaroni and cheese. When he bothered to make an effort, it was usually for dinner. But he didn't make an effort very often. In spite of that, frozen pizza, pop tarts—instant food I might enjoy—all that stuff was absolutely forbidden. I could eat Top Ramen until it was coming out of my ears, but Chef Boyardee or Eggo waffles were right out.

When the pizza was done, Claire called us to sit down at the stools around the counter that divided the kitchenette from the living room. She got three plates from a cabinet, cut the pizza into what looked to me like six equal slices, put two slices on each plate, and handed a plate each to me and Gabe.

Gabe burst into tears. It happened so fast I nearly jumped off my stool.

"What?" I yelped, looking around to see what had happened.

"His slices are bigger than mine!" Gabe sobbed to his mom.

"I . . . what?" I said, looking from my plate to his. They looked the same size to me.

"Gabe," his mother said firmly. "Jason is our guest."

"Uh, you can have mine," I said, pushing my plate toward him.

He looked at his mom expectantly. She looked at me.

"Are you sure?" she asked.

"Sure," I said. "No problem. Really."

"Okay," she said. Gabe quickly switched our plates, and I waited a beat to see if anything else surprising was going to happen. Gabe picked up one of the slices and took a bite. I started eating, watching him warily as I did. I was momentarily distracted by how good the instant pizza wasn't.

"Would you like some milk?" Claire asked.

"Yes, please," Gabe said.

"Yes," I said carefully. "Please."

Other kids crying always left me rattled. My dad had kind of a reflexive hitting thing he did when I pitched a fit like that, where his hand would just leap out on its own and smack me on whatever part of my body was closest to him. It wasn't like I never cried—according to Calliope I was the biggest fucking crybaby she'd ever met—but actual temper tantrums like the one Gabe had just staged were simply not done in my house. Or at least they weren't often survived. When other kids had them in front of me, I always had a reflex to shush them before the smacking started. Then, afterward, I felt like I wanted to be farther away from them, in sort of the same way I'd want to put some physical distance between me and someone who was about to be struck by lightning.

I called my dad around seven, and Gabe and I played until eight. When his mom said I had to go home he pitched another hissy, but I was ready for it this time and tried not to let it freak me out.

We hung out on the playground the next day, talking about movies. Then I went over to his house for a sleepover that weekend. He didn't seem to think much of it one way or the other; I felt like I'd just won the Publisher's Clearinghouse.

27

My cats always landed on their feet. I was fascinated by it. I didn't understand how an object moving through the air—a cat—with nothing to push off of, could alter its own trajectory to land on its feet every time. Sometimes I would roll a cat off my lap, or pick one up and drop it from a height of a few feet, to see if I could spot how it controlled its fall. Every time, the cat would land upright. It looked like magic to me, but I knew it wasn't. There was an explanation for it. I just didn't understand what the explanation was.

One day in the late spring of my fourth grade year, during a fit of extreme boredom, I decided to try to figure it out.

We had a cat named Tom—because he was mostly black, but had a single white tuft on his chest. It looked like a tuxedo, so he started out as Tuxedo Tom. Then T-Tom. Then just Tom. He was the one I happened to lay hands on, and I started out picking him up and dropping him from shoulder height, to see if I could spot how he controlled his roll. Every time, he landed on his feet, glared at me indignantly, and waited to be picked up and dropped again.

I tried this nine or ten times before I realized it had something to do with how he could spin his body sideways. So I tried dropping him with a slight sideways spin of my own added to the equation, but he could always counter and correct.

Afterward, I could never say for sure why I did the thing I did next. Not being able to outspin him sideways, I wondered if I could spin him end over end. So I took his front paws in my hand, lifted him up, and kind of whipped him into the air.

At the exact instant that I let go of his paws, I knew I'd made a horrible mistake. I'd done it too hard. I'd done it too fast. It was a shitty thing to do to a cat in the first place, but as soon as I let go of his paws I realized he was going to go too high, and that his spin was completely uncontrolled. My first thought was to step in and catch him, but I knew that if I tried he'd tear me to pieces with his claws. That shouldn't have mattered—and if someone had given me a choice, later on, I would have taken the mauling—but it was enough to make me hesitate. So instead I watched, praying he'd just land on his stomach, as he arced eight or nine feet up in the air and came down right on his head.

I thought the grass might be soft enough to save him. It wasn't.

His body flopped onto its side, and he lay there, curled up in a ball for a second, before he started to make a noise—a low, long, throaty yowl. I went over to him and tried to pet him and see if he was okay, and the noise got louder as I got closer. My nerve broke, and I ran inside to get Dad.

I was crying hysterically when I ran into his room, and it took me a few seconds to be able to make any words at all. And then I started lying. First it was a weird freak accident—Tom jumping out of my arms and landing weirdly. Then it became me dropping him, to see how he landed on his feet. Then me tossing him up in the air. Each story came out once. Dad would be sympathetic. Then I'd tell the next one—closer to the truth. Dad would be less sympathetic. Every time I got a lie out—every time Dad seemed to believe it—I remembered what I'd done. I remembered Tom spinning in the air and hitting the ground—and something drove me another step closer to the truth.

"I threw him up in the air," I gasped. "I threw him, and I spun him so he couldn't land on his feet, and he landed on his head. I did it on purpose. It's my fault. It's all my fault."

Dad's face went completely blank.

"Why would you do that?" he asked.

"I don't know," I said.

"Why would you do that?" he screamed.

"I don't know," I whispered.

Dad looked at the ceiling and took a deep breath. He'd been hugging me a minute before, but now he kind of gently pushed me away and stared at the ceiling.

"You have to help," I said.

"What do you want me to do, Jason? You dropped him on his head."

"He's still alive," I said.

"He's what?"

"He's still alive," I said, pointing, through the wall to the spot in the side yard where I knew Tom was lying.

Dad walked past me and went outside. When I followed him out he was standing over the cat. Then he knelt down next to the curled-up animal and touched Tom's soft black fur. Tom howled.

Dad jumped back, took a few quick steps, and grabbed me by the shoulders.

"What the fuck is wrong with you?" he screamed, shaking me back and forth. I didn't mind. I wanted something worse. "What the fuck is wrong with you? What is wrong in your head that you would do this to a helpless animal?"

"I don't know," I said.

Dad went over and picked the cat up. Tom howled again and Dad carried him down into the basement.

"Come here!" he shouted over his shoulder.

Once we were in the basement he had me make a little bed for Tom in a box, with a blanket. He yelled the instructions at me. I did whatever he told me. Once I'd put the bed together, Dad shouted, "Stay here!" and left the basement.

I sat there next to Tom for a long time. I wasn't sure how long it was. After a while I worked up the courage to reach out and touch him. He was still warm and soft. His tail twitched. His eyes opened wide to get a look at me, like he wanted to turn to face me but couldn't move his head. He made a low noise in his throat. Not quite a yowl. Not quite a growl or a hiss.

Eventually his body seemed to relax a little. He wasn't dead. He just unclenched.

Dad came back in and dropped a plastic container of chicken livers on the floor next to me.

"You'll feed him those until he dies," Dad said. "If he shits or pisses in the box, you'll clean it up."

"Okay," I said.

Dad left me in the basement.

* * *

For the next couple of days, I took care of Tom whenever I wasn't sleeping or at school. I tried to feed him chicken livers, and I carried his box around with me. One day we had a freak bout of sunny weather and I took him out on the front porch and sat with him for a while in the sun. Dad called me inside for something, and when I came back out on the porch, Tom was gone.

"He probably went off to die somewhere," Dad said. "That's what cats do."

"I guess." I hadn't seen anything to suggest he could move, let alone crawl off to die somewhere.

About a week later, Calliope and I were playing in the back-yard when Tom burst out of the bushes behind the house at a dead run and came to a sudden stop about three feet from us. We stared at him in shock while he looked back and forth between us. Then he let out a loud "Meow!" and fell over onto his side.

"Holy shit!" Calliope said. "Is he . . . ?"

Tom looked up. Looked at us. Let out another "Meow!" and jumped to his feet and took off back into the bushes.

"What the holy hell was that?" Calliope asked.

I shook my head. I had no idea.

A few days further on, and Tom started showing up for afternoon feedings. Then he started hanging around on the porch with the other cats. He never was completely normal again. He went everywhere at a run, and when he ran his body tended to elongate, like his hind legs were just a little bit slower than his front legs. When they got too far behind him, his front legs would stop, wait for his hind legs to catch up, and then he'd start running again. He never let me pet his back, but sometimes he'd let me pet his stomach. Other times he'd let me put my hand on his stomach, then he'd close up on me like a trap, digging his claws into my arm and hand. Once he laid open my big toe to the bone. It took months to heal.

Not that I could blame him. I certainly didn't have any illusions that it made us even.

* * *

About six months after the thing with Tom, one of our other cats, a gray tabby named Kit-Kat, got hit by a car on the busy street out in front of our house. I didn't see the accident, but when I went out in the side yard I noticed what I thought was a piece of raw meat lying on the lawn. When I got closer I realized it was an embryonic kitten. The furry little body was part of a dried-up trail of blood and tissue that I followed across the yard until I found three more dead kittens—and then Kit-Kat, in the bushes near the back of the yard. She was

159

clearly alive, curled up and licking blood off her fur, but also clearly very badly injured.

I went inside, and into my dad's room where he was reading.

"Kit-Kat got hit by a car," I said. "I think she was pregnant. There are dead kittens all over the lawn."

Dad stared at me for a minute, then he put down his book, got up, and went outside. I was following him out when I saw him coming back toward me. His face was dark purple. He grabbed me by the arm and pulled me toward the little pile of sticks I kept next to the porch. I used them as pretend swords and spears for my make-believe medieval adventures. One of the things in the pile was an old aluminum tent pole. It was part of a larger pole that used to be connected by elastic cords that ran inside the poles. When the elastic broke loose, I'd kept a section to use as a kind of bullwhip. It was an aluminum tube, about eighteen inches long, with eight or nine inches of elastic cord, like bungee cord, hanging out of the end.

I'd been obsessed with bullwhips since seeing *Raiders of the Lost Ark* the year before. I especially liked the idea of using a bullwhip to wrap around things, like tree branches and people's legs, like a sort of prehensile weapon. Once, when we were living on Aloha Street, I'd used a rubber snake to try to catch Thunder's legs. The movies made it look easy, but I couldn't get it to work on Thunder, and Dad came into the living room to find me on my hands and knees, following the dog around, swinging my long rubber snake in big looping arcs to see if I could make it coil around his feet. Thunder, for his part, was hopping over the snake and looking annoyed. Calliope was watching from the couch, offering opinions on my technique.

"What the fuck are you doing?" Dad said, snatching the snake out of my hands. "You think it's funny to whip the dog? Do you? You think this is funny, motherfucker?"

I was still trying to figure out why I was in trouble when he hit me with the snake the first time. I yelped and started to get up to run, but he whipped me with it again and I started crawling, trying to get away from him.

"You think this is funny?" he kept yelling while he chased me with the snake. I felt one stinging blow after another, and then the snake broke apart. Dad picked up the pieces and started whipping me with those. Calliope, sitting on the couch, was laughing too hard to talk.

"Stop it!" I screamed, curling up in a ball to protect my face.

"Jesus, Mark!" Calliope finally gasped out. "He wasn't hurting the dog. He was just trying to catch his feet!"

Dad was past hearing. He stood over me, breathing hard, and dropped the last two pieces of the shredded snake on top of me while I lay on the ground whimpering.

"Don't ever let me see you doing that again," he growled. "Never again."

Now, in the backyard of the Ballard house, he shook the tent pole fragment at me, with its dangling piece of elastic.

"Is this what you used?" he asked. "You think it's fun to hurt animals? Huh? What did you do? What the fuck did you do?"

I stared at him blankly while I caught up with his line of thinking. He was using the same words he'd used before, or I might not have been able to make the connection.

"What?" I asked.

"Don't you lie to me, you little piece of shit," he said.

"I wouldn't do that," I said. "I told you. I told you about Tom. I didn't . . ."

"Where's the cat?" he said.

I pointed, and he went over to the bushes where Kit-Kat was lying and looked at her for a minute. He was still holding the tent pole. He came back over a minute later.

"I didn't do it," I said.

"Fine," he said, throwing the tent pole on the ground and going inside. I followed him in and saw he was looking for a veterinarian in the yellow pages. He stopped and looked up at me.

"Get a shovel and go clean that shit off the lawn," he said.

"Okay," I said. I went outside and down to the basement, where we kept our garden tools. I grabbed the shovel and started scooping up dead kittens and carrying them to the garbage cans we kept in the bushes next to the kitchen door. Then I used the hose to wash away the blood. When I was done, I put everything away. I went back to the kitchen door and I could hear Dad on the phone inside, talking to a vet. I noticed the tent pole on the ground next to the porch. I picked it up, broke it over my knee, and threw it in the garbage can with the dead kittens.

Kit-Kat lived, but that summer Carmella said we were breaking the law by having so many cats and threatened to call Animal Control on us. Dad finally put up a sign by the road, inviting passersby to take as many cats as they wanted. Two weeks later they were all gone, including Tom.

28

I had a good fourth grade year at my new school. Or at least it was a much less shitty year than first, second, and third grades had been, which felt like having a good year. So I went back to school for my fifth grade year with high hopes that were promptly dashed. My fourth grade teacher had done me the favor of not giving a shit about me. He barely noticed I was in class. If I messed up or did something against the rules, he punished me. But then he forgot about it.

My new teacher, Mr. Parsons, made it clear right away that I was going to be a special project of his. He yelled at me in front of the class for slouching, for putting my feet on my desk, for talking to myself; he yelled at me for drawing when he was talking. For laughing. He yelled at me once for loosening my belt. It wasn't exactly unexpected—four years of public school had taught me never to underestimate the viciousness of underpaid civil servants—but I didn't have much tolerance for it either. I started skipping school almost immediately.

Three weeks into the academic year I got a reprieve when the school was reorganized to create a mixed fifth and sixth grade class, with a new teacher named Mr. Fields. Mr. Fields was a comparatively young hippie with a shaggy haircut and an earnest personality. He taught class with puppets he'd made himself, and he was a better-than-fair ventriloquist. I was surprised it worked as well as it did. The class had a higher-than-average proportion of hardcore white trash in it—lots of feathered hair, smoking in the bathrooms, and sweatbands. But when Mr. Fields pulled out his talking worm, we all turned back into regular kids. Even at the time I thought it was remarkable.

I made a couple of new friends in Mr. Fields's class. Ryan had moved to Seattle from New York two years before, and had lived down in South Seattle before moving to Ballard and starting at my school. He was a sixth grader with an October birthday, so he was almost two years older than I was. Other than that, he didn't really stand out. He was of medium height and build—maybe a little on the chunky side—with big features, pale skin, and straight black hair, like I'd expect to see on an Indian or an Asian kid. He was perhaps a little less white trash than the rest of the class, in that he didn't go in for sports and his hair was impossible to feather, but that was his only notable feature. Then one day I noticed him fiddling with a twenty-sided die. Which meant he played Dungeons & Dragons.

Gabe, my action-figures acquaintance from fourth grade, had started a D&D group over the summer. Most of the other kids in the group were friends Gabe already had when I met him, so I jumped at the chance to invite Ryan to the group. *Look*, I wanted to say to them, *I can make friends, too!* And for about a week, Ryan was the new kid I'd invited to the group. He was "Jason's friend Ryan." By the second week, Ryan was telling me he couldn't hang out because kids in our D&D group who wouldn't give me the time of day were calling him to do stuff on weekends, so his social calendar was basically full.

* * *

I liked to believe that my relationship with my D&D friends was complicated, but the truth was actually pretty simple. To say I was at the bottom of the totem pole in that crew would have been a flight of self-aggrandizing fancy. The group was small. It was usually me, Gabe, his friends Joey and Patrick, Ryan, and three other kids who came and went depending on their inclinations and the status of their parents' interstate custody battles: Joel, Nathan, and Ben. What it lacked in size, the group more than made up for with infighting and acrimony.

Joey and Patrick were the source of most of my problems. They'd been friends with Gabe before I came to Ballard, and they weren't super happy about Gabe's decision to include me in their activities. Joey was what we used to call mixed race, meaning some mixture of African American and Caucasian. He lived in the basement of a house with his mom, an overweight blond woman who cooked pasta with red sauce for dinner six nights a week. His dad had been black—still was, for all I knew, but he never visited or came up in conversation. Culturally Joey was as white as the rest of us, and I'd known him for almost a year before I figured out that he considered himself any kind of outsider in ultra-white-bread Ballard.

Patrick was a skinny kid with light brown hair, weasel-like features, and a personality to match. His claim to fame was that he was descended from a famous pirate—Captain Kidd or Blackbeard or someone—and supposedly had a box of exotic knives and swords, stored at his grandmother's house in Canada, to be claimed on the occasion of his eighteenth birthday.

As time passed, Joey and Patrick's initial dislike for me hardened into something more frightening. They frequently hosted our D&D games because they had extra space in their homes, and once Patrick announced out of the blue that the only way I'd be allowed to stay for the game was if I paid a toll: I had to let everyone in the group punch me in the stomach, once, as hard as they could. I took the hits, and every kid in the group, including Gabe, gave it their best shot. After that there was blood in the water, and the conflict just intensified.

Sometimes when I spent the night over at Ryan's house, he'd lock me out on the porch without my shoes and make me answer trivia questions for an hour before he'd let me back in. Once he'd managed to lock me out in my underwear. Gabe's mom had finally relented on sending him to day care after school when he started fifth grade, but she'd also set a four-kid limit on the number of guests Gabe could have at their place when she was at work; whenever the limit was exceeded, I was always the one Gabe kicked out. They regularly ditched me on outings—in parks, in downtown Ballard after movies, or on our way to baseball games or events around the neighborhood. And all that was nothing compared to the abuse they heaped on my characters in various role-playing sessions: in our imaginary world of elves and goblins, my fourteenth-level assassin was castrated, immolated, sodomized, eaten alive, shat out, and magically reconstituted to go through the same ordeal all over again.

I told my dad about it once, only to end up having to talk him out of calling everyone's parents. I convinced him I'd made it sound worse than it was, and that it was really just a lot of regular teasing. The role-playing stuff particularly bothered him. He said it was borderline sexual abuse. After I talked him down I waited a few weeks, then told him it had gotten better.

He didn't seem to understand or care that these people were my best friends—they were the best friends I was capable of making, and the only thing I had to offer them was my desperation.

* * *

I made another friend in my fifth grade year, but the time I spent with him felt like some kind of dirty secret. Eddie was one of the sixth graders in Mr. Fields's class. We met during a vote-stacking campaign to set the class mascot for the fake currency Mr. Fields was giving to us. The idea was that we all had bank accounts; we earned "money" for our accounts by turning in our homework on time and doing extra credit projects. We got to spend the money during auctions for novelty items, like mechanical pencils or *Garfield the Cat* comic books. But all of it was based on the idea of a classroom currency, and there was a vote to decide whose face should go on the money. Eddie wanted it to be Jim Davis's iconic Garfield character. I liked that idea better than I liked any of the alternatives, so I helped him consolidate a voting bloc to give us a plurality. We didn't know any of those terms, we just knew the scam: during the pre-vote caucuses we hustled from table to table telling the most popular kids in each camp how the other groups were working against them. We dragged kids out into the hallway and offered them better seats in the class, or desserts from our lunch trays, if they voted the way we wanted them to. Garfield won by two votes.

When Mr. Fields announced we'd need to choose partners for a geography project a week later, Eddie came right to me.

"You know how to get shit done," he said.

It was the first time, possibly, in my life that a peer had said anything complimentary about me to my face. I wasn't sure what to make of it.

As we spent more time together, I started to realize that Eddie and I had almost nothing in common. He didn't watch TV. He didn't play with toys—he didn't even own any toys. He was small for his age, but hard as a coffin nail, with a wide face and a dry gravelly voice. He wore the standard issue headbanger uniform: denim jacket, acid-washed jeans, tight T-shirts, and basketball shoes. He feathered his hair, drew the logos for heavy metal bands on his Pee Chee folders, and said "fuck" and "dude" every other word. Eddie and his mom lived in his mom's boyfriend, Dan's, house, a block away from mine.

Eddie's room was a finished bedroom in the unfinished basement of Dan's house. He came and went through a door next to the driveway. His bedroom walls were covered in posters and tapestries printed with Iron Maiden album covers. He was fascinated with the band's mascot, Eddie the Head, who appeared in every image. His room always smelled like WD-40 and pot. When I called his house and his mom answered, she'd say, "Hi, this is Shirley; if you've got the dime, I've got the time."

In spite of all our differences, the things that bothered me about Eddie were all the ways in which his life resembled mine. Once I got a full picture of how much we had in common, I tried to shake him. Making friends was almost impossible for me most of the time, so I assumed all I had to do was not return some phone calls and Eddie would go away. But he kept calling, and kept inviting me to go with him down to the local video arcade; kept asking me to partner with him on school projects and trying to get me on his team during kickball games. Finally, I gave in and resigned myself to our friendship.

We never did anything I thought was fun; he was always forcing me to play his games, which were less like games and more like projects. He liked going for long walks around the neighborhood, ostensibly looking for things to steal. He liked shooting slingshots and BB guns at bottles and cans, and stealing lumber from construction sites to build illegal tree houses on city land, in the wild spaces between platted properties. None of it felt very kidlike to me and, unlike Eddie, I was in no hurry to grow up.

"You smoke weed?" he asked, the first time he lit up around me.

"No," I said.

"Ever try it?"

"No," I said. "I don't even take aspirin."

He took a huge toke off his pipe, held it, and nodded, like he was acknowledging some point I'd been trying to make. Then the smoke burst out of his mouth and nose and he took a deep breath of clean air.

"That's good," he said. "This shit'll fuck you up. Bother you if I do it?"

I shook my head. "Why would it?"

Eddie didn't have any other friends at our school. I wasn't sure why. From my perspective, he seemed like most of the other kids in our class. He liked the same music, wore the same clothes, and had the same haircut. It wasn't until I was older that I came to understand that most of the other disaffected pot-smoking headbangers in my school came from good middle-class homes. Some of them were even kind of rich. No matter how different we appeared on the surface, as far as the other kids in our class were concerned, Eddie and I were pretty much the same where it mattered.

He didn't like my other friends, the kids in my D&D group. I'd assumed, without thinking about the matter in much detail, that it was just because he was sort of jealous. Time I spent playing Dungeons & Dragons was time I didn't spend hanging out with him. Then one day Eddie and I happened to run into Patrick. He was just hanging around on a street corner near my house, straddling his new bike, like he was standing guard.

"What are you guys up to?" Patrick asked, after we'd exchanged our initial pleasantries.

"Eddie and I were just down at Goodwill and we found a bag of darts," I said, showing Patrick our haul: a ziplock bag full of cheap plastic darts with steel tips. "We were gonna go up to his place and mess around with them."

"Mess around with them how?" Patrick asked.

"Throw them at trees or whatever," I said.

"Wow," Patrick drawled. "That sounds like . . . fun?"

"Don't be a dick," Eddie said. He'd been quiet up to that point, staring at Patrick's bicycle. Eddie liked to do stunts on dirt bikes, and his great ambition in life was to get the money together to buy an ultra-light Diamondback aluminum stunt bike—not unlike the one Patrick happened to be sitting on. Eddie had been making kind of a show of looking at the bike, but now, suddenly, his attention was on Patrick.

"Oh, yeah, right," Patrick said. "Don't be a dick. I'll work on that."

This kind of behavior barely registered with me. This was how the D&D kids talked to me all the time. But I could see right away that Eddie wasn't going to stand for it. My first reaction was to get mad at Eddie because I didn't want him to embarrass me in front of my straight friend. Then everything just kind of happened.

"The hell is your problem?" Eddie asked Patrick.

"The hell is your problem?" Patrick repeated mockingly.

"Eddie," I said. "Don't worry about it. Come on."

"Keep that shit up," Eddie said to Patrick, ignoring me, "I'm gonna kick your goddamn ass."

"Oh yeah," Patrick said. "I'm so sure."

Patrick had three or four inches on Eddie, so maybe he honestly thought this was going to go his way. I just sighed and covered my eyes with my hand, so I wasn't watching when Eddie hauled off and punched Patrick in the ear.

Patrick went sideways and nearly tripped over his bike. When I looked again, he was getting his balance back and looking at me like it was all my fault. Which, I realized, it might be. The punch-Jason-in-the-stomach game had only happened a few weeks earlier, and I'd told Eddie about it afterward. He'd asked me what the hell was wrong with me, and said maybe I deserved to get hit if I just stood there and let them do it.

Eddie had a temper. I'd seen it before. But as events were unfolding now, it dawned on me that Eddie might have been looking for an excuse to kick Patrick's ass right from the minute we ran into him on the corner.

"Why'd you hit me?" Patrick shouted at Eddie.

"Keep talking shit, asshole," Eddie said. "See what happens."

"Fuck you!" Patrick screamed at him.

Eddie started moving toward Patrick again, but Patrick somehow managed to spin around and get his bike going. Eddie got a piece of Patrick's T-shirt as he was riding away, and I heard the neck rip. But then Eddie let go and just started chasing Patrick on foot. As Eddie was running, he slowed down and grabbed a few rocks out of the tilled earth of someone's flower garden. When Patrick got to the end of the block he stopped to see where Eddie was, and Eddie started throwing rocks at him as he ran. Patrick rode away. Eddie stayed after him. They kept going like that until they went around a corner and disappeared from sight.

I stood there for a few minutes. When Eddie didn't come back I went home and waited the rest of the day for him to call. He never did. When I called his house, nobody answered.

Eddie wasn't at school the next day either, but I ran into Patrick during lunch.

"What were you doing hanging out with that maniac?" he asked. "He chased me for, like, an hour. Every time I tried to stop he'd throw more rocks at me."

I just shrugged.

"He told you not to be a dick," I said. "Maybe you should work on that. You know—like you said you would."

Patrick shook his head in amazement—at my audacity or my obtuseness I wasn't sure—and walked away.

29

We had a lot of boat people at my school. That was the term we used for refugees from Southeast Asia. They numbered about sixty, in a school with just under four hundred students. I knew a lot of them were Vietnamese. Others were Laotian, Cambodian, and Thai. I had no idea where any of the Southeast Asian countries were, except that I knew they were somewhere in the Pacific. I was vaguely aware that a lot of the boat people had arrived in the United States on what amounted to rafts—that they'd taken rowboats and sampans and canoes and pushed them into the water on the other side of the ocean, then navigated halfway around the world to get to the United

States. I knew they were trying to get away from a war. I assumed it was the American war in Vietnam and that it had just taken them a really long time to get to the United States. I wondered, sometimes, how they carried enough food and water in a rowboat to cross the Pacific, but I didn't give any of it much serious thought. They were tiny little brown people who didn't speak my language, and I found them annoying.

Once, in fourth grade, I'd tried to bully one of them. It was a conscious decision on my part. I wanted some social status, and I knew none of the white kids would care if I bullied one of the refugees. I didn't understand the exact mechanism that would turn cruelty into social status, but it seemed to work for all the kids who'd bullied me so I decided to give it a shot. Not very Han Solo of me, but I was sick of taking shit off people. So I took a page out of Dickie Seever's book and pushed one of the refugees while we were in line to get back into the school after recess.

He was half my size. Like, actually half my size. Five or six inches shorter. Half my weight. He turned around and gave me a confused look, like he wasn't sure what had just happened.

"Get the fuck out of my way," I said. And I pushed him again.

I had an impression afterward that I'd stepped on something, like a land mine, that exploded when messed with. He screamed something in his own language and jumped on me. I couldn't work out a blow-by-blow afterward. It was just a blur of surprise and pain. He pulled hair. He bit. He scratched. He tried to jam his thumb into one of my eyes. He punched me in the head, ears, and face about a hundred times in the space of about forty-five seconds. At some point I managed to dislodge him and throw him a few feet away. He bounced up and came right back at me like something out of a bad dream. I turned around and ran fifty or sixty feet, then checked over my shoulder to see if he was following me.

He was still in line, but he was standing, looking at me, with his feet apart. Fists clenched at his sides. Breathing hard. Most of the American kids in the line were pointedly ignoring me. The refugee kids were all giving me the same blank look as the kid I'd pushed. Alert. A little expectant. The look of someone at sea, watching a storm cloud on the horizon.

I went in last after recess that day. Not surprisingly, the fight didn't garner me any additional social status. And after that I tried to stay as far away from the refugees as I could.

Except, of course, that when I got to Mr. Fields's class in the fifth grade, he started his own cultural exchange program.

The refugees weren't usually in the mainstream classrooms. They were in what were called bilingual classrooms, though usually the classes were at least trilingual. And the classes tended to cover multiple grades. There was a mixed fifth and sixth grade class like ours one floor down, and Mr. Fields worked out a deal with their teacher to have our classes spend some time together.

It started with a food exchange day. We all filed down the stairs, each of us carrying one serving of our favorite food for the other class to sample. We brought peanut butter and jelly sandwiches, hot dogs, macaroni and cheese. Some kids brought potato salad. Cold chicken. I usually went home for lunch and ate Top Ramen, so I didn't bring anything. The Southeast Asian kids brought cans of stuff I didn't recognize at all. The cans had writing on them that wasn't English. I tried some of the canned food, thinking, How bad could it be? and was surprised to discover that it could actually be horrifyingly bad. I started with a red thing that might have been a beet slice but that turned out to taste like raw potatoes and lye. The Thai kid who'd brought it looked at me expectantly.

"Is this how I'm supposed to eat it?" I asked him. "It's not usually . . . cooked? Or something?"

"No," he said. "That's how we eat it."

"It tastes . . . a lot," I said.

He smiled and nodded.

After the food exchange day, we went down to the bilingual classroom about once a week. Usually there was a project of some kind—pointing out where we were born on a globe or something—and then some socializing.

One day me and another kid from my class, a girl named Joanna, were talking to a group of kids from Cambodia. Somehow we got onto the subject of our families, and one of the Cambodians, a girl about my age, said she was staying with some other people who had come to the United States from her village because her family was dead.

We knew these kids were coming from a war zone, but we weren't really clear on what that meant. Most of us had never heard someone say that their entire family was dead, and the novelty of it surprised Joanna into asking a question she might not have asked otherwise.

"How'd they die?" she asked.

"You know big animal?" the girl asked, making some kind of weird gesture with her arm, holding it in front of her face and kind of waving it around.

Joanna and I exchanged a look and shook our heads.

"Big!" the girl said. "Big animal!"

"Oh," Joanna said, in a moment of pure inspiration. "You mean elephants?"

"Yes!" said the Cambodian girl. "Elephants. Other soldiers came at night. Shot guns." She mimed shooting into the air. "Elephants ran over my house."

Joanna and I looked at each other. Looked at the girl. And I was pretty sure I must be misunderstanding her. Because the picture I had in my head was just ridiculous. So I asked some questions to prove to myself that the thing I was thinking was just wrong.

"I'm sorry," I said. "You don't mean they shot their guns and scared the elephants? And the elephants ran over . . . your family?"

One of the other Cambodians translated. The girl looked at me and nodded.

"And that's how your family died?" I asked.

She nodded again.

"Were you there?" Joanna asked. "In the house?"

"Yes."

I laughed nervously, and Joanna glared at me. The Cambodian girls actually seemed less offended. Maybe they'd seen that reaction before.

I thought about the elephants for the rest of the day. I thought about them on my walk home, and I thought about them while I watched TV that afternoon. And, sitting there watching TV, I had what I regarded as a genuinely adult thought: I realized that this girl's family had been trampled by elephants in my lifetime. And odds were good I had been sitting somewhere watching TV when it happened. It occurred to me, right there, to wonder who else was getting trampled by elephants while I was watching TV. How many little kids were being orphaned or killed, right that minute, while I was sitting there watching TV?

I asked my dad about it that night, over dinner. He said little kids were always being orphaned and killed. He snapped his fingers when he said it.

"It's happening now." Snap!

"And now." Snap!

"And now." Snap!

"How can that be true?" I asked. "How do we . . . do stuff? While that's happening?"

Dad narrowed his eyes at me and shrugged. "That's just how it is. People can't worry about stuff like that all the time. We have to live."

I heard what he said, but his voice was full of other

things—things that had been growing between us, but that we didn't talk about. I was becoming a proxy for his anger at the rest of the world. The subtext of a lot of his stories lately had been that I was going to grow up to be straight—to be the kind of guy who told him he was gross for kissing other men, and who didn't care if little Cambodian girls got their entire family crushed to death by elephants. Maybe I already was, I thought, remembering the kid I'd pushed while we were in line after recess.

I didn't ask my dad any more questions that night. I went to bed, and I thought about the girl from school, and the elephants, and the boy I'd bullied. I fell asleep counting my sins.

30

Dad was going out a lot at night. Three or four nights a week, he'd come home around five in the evening, get into his party clothes, and head out until two or three in the morning. I was ten years old now, and I wasn't supposed to be afraid of the dark anymore, but I still followed the same routine I'd used when he was working for the Hodads, after we moved out of Marcy's house. I'd turn on the TV as soon as I got home and leave it on until I had to go to sleep. I'd collect all the knives in the house and put them under the couch. When bedtime came around, I'd check all the doors and windows. Then I'd put the knives back in the kitchen and turn the lights off, starting with the ones farthest from my room and working my way back until I climbed into bed. I had trouble falling asleep when I was home by myself. I always wanted to go back to the TV. It made me feel like there was someone there with me. Someone who'd notice if something bad happened to me. But Dad got mad if he came home after my bedtime and I was still awake, so I just had to lie there, alone in the dark, and wait for sleep to come.

What Dad was doing during these long nights was, he was learning to be gay.

Calliope had explained to me what it meant that Dad was gay the year before, when I was nine. Dad hadn't exactly been keeping it a secret, but he hadn't really gone into detail about it either. Calliope was the one who told me that being gay meant Dad was actually having sex with other men.

We were walking home after having snuck into the zoo. The Woodland Park Zoo was a mile or so from my house. On rainy days, when the low visibility gave us some cover, Calliope and I would scale a tree next to the fence, climb out on a branch, and drop down onto the path near the elk exhibit. Nobody ever went to look at the elks, so nobody ever saw us do it.

I walked a few blocks in silence while I thought about what she'd said, and tried to square it with the technical information I had about sex. But it didn't compute.

"How does that work?" I asked finally. "Men don't have vaginas."

"They stick their dicks in each other's butts," Calliope said.

I laughed. Then I looked at her and realized she was completely serious.

"At the same time?" I asked.

"No," she said. "They take turns."

I ran several possible interpretations of this scenario in my head, and each one seemed more ridiculous than the last. I knew that sex involved thrusting a penis into a woman's vagina repeatedly, so I had an idea that each man would thrust into his partner's butt once, pull out, turn around, let his partner thrust into his butt, and so on. That seemed like a lot of work. And a lot of movement. Phillip had slept over many times. Surely if he and Dad had been engaged in these kinds of acrobatics I would have heard them fall out of the bed at least once. But otherwise what did "taking turns" mean in a butt sex scenario? I decided this was one of those questions I didn't need a clear answer to. The relevant part was that Dad was having sex with people's bottoms. And they were having sex with his.

"Isn't there poop in there?" I asked.

"I'd think so," Calliope said. "I've never understood that part. And when they aren't having sex with each other's butts, they give each other blow jobs."

"Blow jobs?"

"They put each other's penises in their mouths."

"What about teeth?" I asked.

"They just don't bite down. Like this," she said, demonstrating on her finger.

"Do they blow on them?"

"No."

"Then why's it called a blow job?" I asked.

"I . . . you know, I don't know. Anyway, they suck. They don't blow."

"They take turns for that, too?"

"Actually, that one they sometimes do at the same time. I guess it depends on how tall they are, compared to each other. And they have to lie down. I guess. Unless one of them's really strong. I guess he could . . ."

She made a gesture that suggested holding something heavy in front of her, and moving it up and down.

"That seems gross," I said.

"It all seems gross, until you're doing it," she said.

She and I had talked about this quite a bit. There was a

woman named Julie who lived at the end of Calliope's block who was friends with Cal and Olive. She had a massive collection of lesbian porn for straight guys—cheerleaders with acrylic fingernails and shaved pussies having sex on motorcycles. Cal and I would go over to Julie's place sometimes and spend hours looking at her porn, critiquing it and joking about it while Julie lay comatose in her bed a few feet away. None of the women in the magazines looked like they were having much fun. They never smiled. But Cal and I understood, just by watching the antics of grownups in their relationships, that sex of one type or another pretty much made the world go around.

This had been true in Eugene, too—Dad and his friends back in Oregon were always sleeping together, breaking up, and sleeping with other people. The difference between our old scene and the new one, for my purposes, was that all the screwing that had been going on back in Oregon had occasionally produced a kid. Lots of people had at least one. So when someone threw a party, or had a get-together, everyone brought their kids so we could entertain each other while our parents got high and talked. I had a place in Dad's social circles in Oregon. With Dad's gay friends, there were no kids and, consequently, no place for me.

* * *

Dad got a new boyfriend shortly before I turned ten, an older man named Charles. Charles wasn't British, but in my mind he sort of was. His face was all lines and planes, but the main thing was that his colorless blue eyes were always partially lidded. Not like he was stoned or sleepy, but like he was considering things very carefully. He had a thin, dark blond mustache and a straight, narrow nose. He had the face of someone who could drink tea with his pinkie finger sticking up, or

179

charge a line of Russian cannons with a lance. He would have looked perfectly credible wearing a monocle.

His personal style tended toward long-sleeved button-down flannel shirts in various plaids, straight-legged jeans, and heavy leather shoes. He wore a bulky canvas coat lined with wool. It was all stuff I thought of as lumberjack gear. The idea wasn't totally incredible. We still had lumberjacks in Seattle then. But that wasn't Charles's line. He was a graphic artist. He worked for a print shop in Bellevue, and painted in his off hours.

Dad didn't have a clear plan for how he wanted me to think of Charles. Or he didn't seem to. There was some implication that Charles was going to be part of "our" life now, and I had to just get on the bus. I didn't understand where all the pressure was coming from. Phillip had just been a friend, like our friends back in Eugene. He seemed to like me. He told jokes I understood. He laughed at my jokes. He was also a raging alcoholic, but that only came up once during an ill-fated vacation weekend with my dad in Victoria, British Columbia, where Phillip had sobbed uncontrollably for ninety minutes in our hotel room before passing out on the floor. Most of the time he was my friend, and also my dad's boyfriend. With Charles, the expectations were different.

Even at the age of ten, I chalked some of this up to my dad's newfound militancy about being gay. They say there's no zealot like a convert, and Dad was definitely a convert; having grown up in the closet, then being sort of semi-closeted in Eugene, he'd found his full gay self in Seattle at the age of thirty. And thirty-two-year-old gay Dad was pretty pissed off about all those wasted years of having sex with women just to impress other people with how straight he was. Thirty-two-year-old gay Dad was pissed about a lot of things. Somewhat to my surprise, this became a bonding experience for me and Charles, even as it was driving a wedge between me and my dad.

We'd be eating breakfast and something would set Dad off. Something would remind him that straight people could kiss in public and he couldn't, and he'd just start ranting.

"Sometimes it just makes me so mad!" he'd say. "Sometimes at Green Lake or Madison Park, I just want to follow them around going, 'Eeeeew! Gross! That's disgusting!' Talk about them the way they talk about us. Show them how it feels."

And Charles, who liked to read the paper over breakfast, would lower the Arts section just enough to look at Dad over the top of it and say in his deep, cultured, and surprisingly un-British baritone, "Jesus, Mark."

Then Charles's gaze would slide over to me and we'd make eye contact. I'd smile. The skin around his eyes would wrinkle minutely. Then the paper would go back up. But it left me feeling like we'd connected in some meaningful way.

* * *

Charles lived in a duplex on Capitol Hill, near the reservoir. He lived with another mustaches-and-flannel-shirts homo named Billy and an enormous, ill-tempered basset hound named Boris. Billy was the compositional opposite of Charles: a tall, thin man with dark brown hair and a bushy red mustache, full mouth, enormous eyes, and narrow shoulders. Billy had a ridiculous sense of humor. Once, he took me to the International House of Pancakes and pretended to blow his nose on a flapjack. Then he put it down and ate it. The old couple sitting next to us got up and moved to another table.

Charles and Billy's place was a study in San Francisco classical revival homoerotic reductionism. The walls were papered in collages that featured photographs of Renaissance Italian statuary—nude men in marble—and famous opera singers. Over this were mounted framed posters for art shows and concerts, paintings by Charles and his friends (lots of suggestively framed Catholic religious iconography), wood-block prints, Asian calligraphy, and a deer's head with a studded leather belt wrapped around its antlers. Furniture tended toward the comfortable and overstuffed. Lots of thrift store purchases made presentable with a carefully placed Mexican horse blanket. Overall the place had a Canadian-logging-camp-meets-Andy-Warhol's-factory vibe that seemed to say, "Welcome to our lovely home. We like men. No, really—we *like* men."

There were three things I really enjoyed about Charles's apartment. One was Billy. Another was that Charles and Billy had built a loft in their living room. Or maybe "built" is too strong a word. At some point they'd noticed that the stairway that led up to their apartment had a lot of dead airspace above it. Never ones to let a damage deposit get between them and another ten square feet of living space, they used a sledgehammer and a power saw to tear a giant hole in the wall, exposing the hidden cavern above the stairs. Then they framed in a plywood platform to make a wooden box about six feet long, three feet deep, and three feet high in the east wall of their living room. They put a futon in the box and—ta-da!—instant sleeping loft.

The loft was awkwardly located, about five feet off the ground, and hidden by curtains in such a way that it looked like a blacked-out window until you peeked inside. If they had allowed me to move in and live in the loft, I would gladly have thrown away my bed, most of my toys, and all of my clothes. Living in a hole in the wall that I could pop out of like a preadolescent cuckoo bird was a fantasy I hadn't known I had until I got to act it out in Charles and Billy's living room.

The third thing I liked about Charles and Billy's place was that they had pirated cable that included dozens of extremely weird channels I'd never seen or even heard of before. They had a channel that showed nothing but Japanese cartoons, in Japanese, with no subtitles, twenty-four hours a day, seven days a week. There were Spanish soap operas. There were low-budget monster movies in languages I couldn't even recognize. Their TV was kind of small and the picture was crap, but the stuff they got on their pirated cable stations fascinated me. I felt like my horizons were expanded every time I went over to their house.

There was a painting above the TV that Charles had done, of a man who looked very much like Billy, naked, tied to a stump, and shot full of arrows. Sometimes I'd find myself staring at the painting instead of the TV, wondering what it was supposed to mean. One day as I was sitting on their couch watching *Ultraman*—in its original Japanese without subtitles—Billy came into the living room and sat down next to me. We watched in silence for a while before I pointed at the painting.

"Is that supposed to be a metaphor for being gay?" I asked. "Like, you're just putting yourself out there and being who you are, and everybody else shoots arrows at you and hates you for no reason?"

Billy looked up at the painting for a long time.

"That's Saint Sebastian," he said. "Some pagan kings ordered him to be shot full of arrows because he refused to renounce Christianity, and he survived because he was a saint, full of the glory of God. After he healed, he went around preaching the falseness of the pagan gods. This time an angry mob beat him to death with sticks and rocks and threw his broken body in a ditch where they used to shit. And he stayed dead. Why did God save him from the arrows, but not the mob? Those mysterious ways we're always hearing about, I guess."

He looked back to me. I looked at him.

"Yeah," he said after a minute. "It's a metaphor for being gay."

"I knew it," I said.

"Yes, you're very smart."

We returned our attention to *Ultraman*.

* * *

In the fall of 1982, when I was ten years old, Billy got a weird fever. None of us thought anything of it, except that it was making Billy totally miserable. He stayed home from work for days, sniffling, moping around the house, wrapped in quilts and blowing his nose until it was red and sore. He tried going back to work, but the fever didn't go away, and when he went to work he got sicker. He started losing weight. Charles had seen a story on the news earlier that year about GRID, Gay Related Immune Deficiency. Nobody was sure how it was spread. Most people thought it was caused by poppers, a kind of club drug that came in little crushable capsules that were "popped" to release a substance like industrial strength airplane glue. Some people used them constantly, but that wasn't really Billy's scene so we assumed he just had a persistent cold. Then, after almost two months, he seemed to get better.

A few weeks later, Dad came down with the same bug. It was January of 1983.

31

With the exception of a few drug dealers who just happened to be at the apogee of their career arc when I knew them, Carol Green, the child psychologist my dad worked for, was the richest person I had ever met. She lived in a giant house, on a double-size lot, in one of the richest neighborhoods in town. There was a golf course across the street from her place. She had a microwave, which was considered a relatively fancy piece of equipment at the time. There was a water faucet and an ice machine built into the door of her refrigerator, and she and her husband owned four cars between them. She had so many cars that she just loaned one to Dad while he was working for her—a big green '68 Rambler Rebel—so it would be easier for him to run her errands. He called it his company car. And she paid him a good wage—seven dollars an hour—right out of her own pocket, in cash.

It was important that Dad got paid in cash, so we could defraud welfare. It was important that we could defraud welfare because, as Dad often said, "the world is just a goddamn uncertain place."

Through most of the 1980s, Aid for Families with Dependent Children paid about $360 a month for a single parent with one kid; by way of comparison, rent at the Aloha Street house had been $250, and the Ballard house ran about $350. We got food stamps and subsidized housing as well, but it was effectively impossible for us to live on welfare alone, so Dad had to work. The problem was that if he got a straight job, we either had to get off welfare, or we had to take all the money that Dad made in excess of $360 a month and give it to the welfare

185

office. Dad told me that, the way the rules worked, if you were on welfare you got $360 a month to live on no matter what.

This would make getting off welfare seem like a no-brainer—certainly that was the intention of the people who designed it—except that the kind of work people like my dad could get wasn't particularly reliable. Low-end service jobs could end at any time, for any reason. For example, it was perfectly legal to fire someone for being gay. But if Dad took us off welfare and then lost his job, we'd have had to wait a couple of months—maybe as long as a year—to get back on the rolls. During which time, a family like ours could easily disappear under the surface and never be heard from again. So the smart play was to find an under-the-table job and just be really careful not to get caught. One thing Dad had to do to avoid getting caught was to never run any work income through his bank; signing a release allowing the welfare narcs to poke around in his bank account was a condition of being in the program. The easiest way to avoid a paper trail altogether was to get paid in cash.

Most employers weren't willing to go to all that trouble. The ones who were willing, for whatever reason, typically paid about thirty percent under market rate for any given job. Partly this was because the employer couldn't claim an under-the-table employee as a business expense for tax purposes, so they recouped the loss by gouging the wage they paid. Then they'd gouge a little more, to mitigate any future losses they might take as a consequence of getting caught with a bunch of undocumented workers. And there was always a small fuck-you surcharge, on top of everything else. Most under-the-table employers could take you or leave you, so they tended to act like major assholes.

As far as all this went, Carol was better than most. The wage she paid was fair, and she didn't make Dad eat too much shit to get it. Basically, he just did whatever she told him to do. He

186

handled her calendar and organized her office, but he also cleaned out her basement, picked up her dry cleaning, arranged catering for important functions, and helped her son pack for college. He worked a lot of seven-dollar hours doing this stuff, and for the better part of a year we were doing pretty well. But there were weird little side costs associated with working for Carol that made it hard to remember how lucky we were to have her.

For example, Carol did a lot of running around. But no matter where she was or what she was doing, at eight o'clock in the morning she would rush to the nearest television set, change clothes, and do the 20 Minute Workout. This was a televised aerobics routine that was popular for about as long as it took Americans to figure out that aerobics is, in fact, just as hard as any other form of exercise and that spandex was not actually going to be this year's black. If Carol happened to be in Ballard when eight o'clock rolled around, she would come to our house, pound on our door until Dad let her in, and do aerobics in our living room for twenty minutes.

In addition to being obnoxious, this routine made it pretty much impossible for me to watch morning cartoons. That was my beef. But I knew it was basically worth it for the seven dollars an hour. And the company car. And also, I got a lot of free stuff from Carol.

Carol had one child and an unhappy marriage to another medical professional. So when her son was still young, she bought him tons of stuff to compensate for all the other unhappiness in her life. And she was pretty unhappy, so her boy got a lot of great toys. Boomerangs, comic books, Erector Sets, chemistry sets. All the stuff any red-blooded American welfare kid really really wants and can never afford. But when I was ten, Carol's son was heading off to college. So she told my dad to pack up all those old toys and records and stuff and give them all to Goodwill. She'd never need any of it again. And Dad, being Dad, went through it and brought all the really good stuff home to me.

I had fun with all the new swag, but the one toy in the haul that I really connected with, on a spiritual level, was the Lego set. Like most kids, I'd always loved Legos. But they were surprisingly expensive so I never had any of my own. And I had never in my life, not even once, seen a Lego set at Goodwill or Salvation Army or any of those places. So I played with Legos at friends' houses, and dreamed my impossible dreams. But it worked out that Carol's son had a huge box of these things; what would have been two or three hundred dollars' worth of Legos, if I'd bought them new. And she told my dad to take them all to Goodwill.

I was ecstatic. I could build anything I wanted. I could spend days messing around on one project. The sky was the limit. And at an age when most toys entertained me for a few weeks at the outside, I played with those Legos constantly for a good six months. I couldn't believe my luck.

I should have known better.

Carol's job as a child psychologist meant that, every so often, she had to do something public for kids. Fund-raising. Donating time to shelters. That kind of thing. And for Christmas of 1982, she helped sponsor a toy drive for underprivileged children. But Carol was kind of scatterbrained. She didn't remember until the very last minute that she had told Dad to donate all her son's old toys to Goodwill. So, on the day of the toy drive, she got out of bed and went downstairs to get some used toys to give away—and panicked when she found them all gone. Until she remembered that the last time she was over at our house doing aerobics, I had been playing with Legos while I was waiting to get my TV back so I could watch cartoons.

When I woke up that morning I found Carol, in a Santa suit, digging through my closet. She was taking the Legos by the handful and dumping them into a red bag with white fur trim. It took me a minute to absorb what I was seeing; my mind was cycling through the millions of scenarios that would have been more plausible than what actually seemed to be happening. I glanced over and noticed my dad standing in my bedroom doorway. He looked weird. Angry and humiliated, but resigned. I hadn't seen that exact mix of emotions on his face since the night he got busted, back in Eugene. That was when I realized this wasn't a joke.

"All right," Carol said, standing up and turning around. "That's all of them?"

She was talking to me.

"All the Legos?" I asked.

"Yes," she said.

"Uh. They were . . . all in that box." I craned my neck to look behind her, and saw the box empty on the floor in the closet. "Yeah. That was all of them."

"Great," she said. "Sorry to wake you."

She paused for a second, then actually slung the bag over her shoulder, Grinch-style, before leaving my room. My Legos—the Legos—made a brittle sloshing sound in the bag as she left. Dad followed her to the front door and let her out, then came back and stood in my doorway again. I frowned at him.

"Is she bringing those back?" I asked.

"No," he said. "I'm sorry. I tried to talk her out of it."

He explained her charity toy drive to me. The longer he talked, the less likely the story sounded. If it weren't for the expression on his face, I never would have believed him.

"Why didn't she just buy some toys?" I asked. "She's got more money than God. Surely she could have just stopped at Fred Meyer and bought something new."

"They had to be used," he said. "It's part of the thing. Like, 'Don't throw those used toys away, donate them!' "

"To kids!" I added. "Who are on welfare! Like the one she just took these Legos from! Isn't she a child psychiatrist?"

"Psychologist," Dad said.

"What's the—? Never mind. She's not bringing them back?"

"No."

"And she's not replacing them," I said.

"No. When she showed up here this morning she was asking for the Legos she 'loaned' us. Jason, for what it's worth, I'm not sure she really understands . . . any of it."

"Okay," I said, rolling over and pulling my covers up around my neck. "I'm going back to sleep now."

"Jason . . ."

"I need to sleep!" I snapped.

He sighed and closed my door behind him as he left.

I didn't sleep. I just lay there for a couple of hours, hating Carol with an intensity that made me sweat, and telling myself a bunch of furious lies about how, once I grew up, I'd never have to bend over for anyone like her ever again.

32

One day when I was ten, my headbanger friend Eddie asked me if I wanted to come hang out with him and his friend Bobby. The question surprised me. I'd never met Bobby, never heard Eddie mention him, and Eddie didn't usually introduce me to his other friends, so I wasn't sure why he suddenly wanted me to meet this Bobby kid.

"Who is he?" I asked.

"A friend of mine from when I lived in Rainier," he said.

"He still live there?" I asked.

"Yeah," Eddie said.

"He white?" I asked. Rainier Valley was one of the blackest of Seattle's few black neighborhoods.

"Yeah," Eddie said. "Ask your dad if you can sleep over."

"At Bobby's house?" I asked.

"Yeah," Eddie said.

"You're not dragging me all the way down to Rainier just so I can watch you score, are you?" I asked. Eddie often wanted me along on his buys in Ballard. I wasn't sure why. I was visibly harmless. Maybe he just liked to show people he had a friend.

"Naw," Eddie said. "Nothing like that, dude. I like his sister. I want you to come along to keep Bobby busy."

I sighed dramatically.

"Fine," I said.

My dad might normally have wanted more background on a kid I was going to spend the night with, but he hadn't been feeling well lately so he didn't make a thing out of it. I went up to Eddie's house after school that day and we caught three buses to get down to Bobby's place, on the other end of town. When we got on the 48, going deep into Rainier Valley, I took my wallet out of my back pocket and stashed it up my sleeve so nobody would steal it. Not that there was anything in it. Slowly the bus filled with black people, getting off school or work. One of them was a kid about my age, who sat down near where Eddie and I were standing. He looked me over curiously.

"Hey," he said, after a minute. "You live around here?"

"Uh," I said. "No. Why?"

"The way you're carrying your wallet in your sleeve there, that's about as subtle as a heart attack, man. The hell's the matter with you?"

Eddie had been staring out the window, but he turned around to look at me now and he was scowling.

"Quit being such a goon, dude," he said.

I was too embarrassed to put my wallet back in my pocket while the other kid was watching, so I just stood there wishing I had a hole to crawl into until Eddie told me we were there.

Bobby's house was a blue-gray Craftsman with a chain-link fence around the yard. Tall grass out front, single-pane picture windows, and asbestos shingle siding about ten years past its warranty date. Dirty venetian blinds covered all the windows from the inside. We walked up a weed-choked path to a peeling front door and Eddie knocked once, hard.

The kid who answered the door was about our age, but he had the same look as Eddie: desiccated, hardened, underfed. His child's face was bony and flat, and his teeth were crooked and yellow. He had a cut on the underside of his jaw, like a skin infection. Pale complexion, hazel eyes, light brown hair under an unmarked blue baseball cap. Blue sweatshirt a few sizes too small. Jeans and sneakers.

"Eddie," he said, opening the door wide and letting us in.

"This is Jason," Eddie said.

"S'up," he said, nodding at me.

"Barb around?" Eddie asked.

"Naw," Bobby said. "She gets off work in a while. Wanna play some video games while we wait?"

"Sure," Eddie said.

The living room was typical white trash: dirty shag carpet, nothing on the walls, polyester couch, vinyl easy chair. Boxes stacked in one corner. The living room was separated from the dining room by an archway, and the dining room was dark and full of junk—an old Formica-topped table and four ugly metal-frame chairs with vinyl covers that were textured to look like cloth. The rest of the room was buried under boxes and milk crates full of machine parts, old fans, a broken vacuum cleaner, records with moldy covers, plastic flowers, and a synthetic Christmas tree covered in spray-on snow and tinsel.

In spite of all the other squalor, the TV in the living room was top-of-the-line: twenty-five inches, color, with a remote and an Intellivision game console. A few hundred dollars in game cartridges were scattered around on the floor.

Eddie and Bobby sat down and started to play. I took a seat on a chair in the corner, next to the boxes, and settled in. When Eddie asked me if I wanted next game, I just shook my head. Something about the place made me think it would be a good idea to keep my back against a wall and my hands empty.

After we'd sat there for a while, a man who looked like a much older, fatter version of Bobby, with big cheap plastic-framed glasses, came in and sat down in the easy chair. I expected him to tell Eddie and Bobby to turn off the game, but he watched them play without saying anything, and without looking at me. We all sat there quietly for an hour or so until the front door opened and a girl came in. She was young. Too young to have a job. She had shoulder-length dark brown hair, the same pale skin as her brother, but fleshier features: round cheeks, fuller lips, and a wide mouth. She was wearing old bell-bottoms and a turtleneck sweater under a long coat with fake fur trim. Her shoes were a kind of sandals made of flesh-colored vinyl. They were supposed to be worn on bare feet, but she was wearing them with thick hiking socks.

She didn't say anything when she first came in. Just looked at her dad, then at Bobby and Eddie. Eddie had been watching Bobby play, so he got up and went over to give the girl a hug.

"All right," Bobby's dad said. He got up and dug around in his front pocket for a minute before he came up with a roll of cash. He counted out $50 and gave it to the girl, who I assumed was Barb. "Don't come back until tomorrow morning."

"Okay," said the girl. "Come on, Bobby."

"I'm almost done," Bobby said, still focused on his game.

"Time to go," his dad said.

"Just a sec," Bobby said.

His dad walked over and hit him casually in the head. He didn't hurry, the dad, and he didn't seem to make a big deal out of it, but the force of the blow was enough to knock Bobby over sideways. I winced sympathetically. It was hardly the first time I'd seen another kid get hit. Danny, the kid who lived across the street from me, had recently picked up a stepfather named Garry who really liked to go to town on him. Just a few months earlier I'd watched from my front yard while Garry stood on the balcony of their apartment and kicked Danny into the railing over and over again, until part of it had broken off and fallen onto the sidewalk. But even with Garry, Danny usually got some warning. Bobby's dad just sucker punched him.

Nobody said anything while Bobby shook it off and got to his feet. He didn't look at any of us, or at his dad. Just walked over to the couch, picked up a ski jacket, then shuffled over to us and said, "Let's go." We filed out of the house behind him.

"What are we doing now?" I asked Eddie, as we walked back to the sidewalk.

"Dunno," he said. He looked at Barb. "What do you want to do?"

"Let's just go downtown," she said.

I followed them to a bus stop for a route I didn't know. When it came, the bus was pretty much empty. Bobby and I sat together on one seat, while Eddie and Barb sat behind us. Eddie was a good two inches shorter than Barb, but he put his arm over her shoulder and whispered in her ear. She smiled and leaned into him.

"How old're you?" I asked Bobby.

"Eleven," he said, without looking at me.

"What about her?" I asked, nodding toward his sister.

"Twelve," he said.

"What's her job that she was coming home from?" I asked. I'd started looking for a regular job lately. I made some money mowing lawns from time to time, and sometimes our friends had one-time gigs for me, like selling glow sticks during a concert, but Dad had started giving me a hard time recently about getting a regular job and carrying my weight in the house. I told him it was illegal to hire kids under the age of sixteen in Washington State, but he wasn't having it, so I followed any tip that might lead me to a place that would hire underage kids.

"She works at McDonald's," Bobby said.

"No shit? Which one? They hire kids?"

But Bobby was already shaking his head.

"She has a fake birth certificate and stuff, says she's sixteen," he said.

"Oh," I said.

We rode the rest of the way to downtown in silence, except for Eddie and Barb's whispering. We got off on 3rd and Pine and walked up to a video arcade on 2nd that had a pretty good selection of games. Barb gave us five dollars each to get tokens with, and we loaded up and went our separate ways, each of us looking for our favorite games and getting an idea of where the arcade had its difficulty levels set.

I played games I knew, like Galaga, and took long breaks between sets, going over to watch Eddie play Defender. We were in the arcade for a couple of hours before we ran out of tokens, and we made a strategic decision to save the other $30 for whatever we might want to do later in the night. When we left the arcade it was dark outside. The temperature hadn't been above freezing for a week, and we were all dressed for it except Eddie, who never seemed to get cold.

"What now?" I asked.

"Come on," Eddie said, leading us south, deeper into downtown.

We walked down streets that had been abandoned because of the cold. Eddie handed me two dollars and said, "Buy me some Fritos."

"Huh?" I said.

He gestured and I saw we'd stopped in front of a convenience store.

"Buy me some Fritos," he said again.

"Okay," I said with a shrug.

We all went into the store and wandered down the aisles. I found a bag of Fritos and brought it up to the cash register. Bobby and Barb came up a minute later with Hostess pies, and Eddie bought a soda. When we got out on the sidewalk I tried to hand Eddie his chips and he just waved them off.

"Keep 'em," he said. Then he held open his jacket and showed Barb that he had a can of beer in each of the inside pockets of his denim jacket.

I was surprised. I'd never seen Eddie drink beer before. He'd told me he didn't like the taste. Pot was enough for him.

After the beer raid, we went to McDonald's for dinner, and Eddie emptied a super-size soda down the sink in the bathroom, then filled the cup with his beers. He and Barb spent an hour or so trading the cup back and forth while Bobby and I talked about horror movies. It was past midnight by then, so we decided to head up to Seattle Center, just because it felt safer. There were fewer homeless people and dealers around on that end of downtown.

An older guy in a fleece-lined denim jacket was going the opposite direction on the sidewalk, but stopped when he got close to us. He was wearing a baseball cap, nylon pants, and too much bulky gold-plated jewelry. His short hair was hidden by a Mariners baseball cap.

"You kids need a place to stay?" he asked. "Get in out of this cold?"

"Fuck off," Eddie growled.

"Hey!" barked the guy. "Watch it, you little punk."

We just kept on walking and didn't make eye contact. The older guy didn't seem inclined to make a thing out of it, and we continued on our way. The walk took the better part of an hour.

Seattle Center was the leftover grounds from the 1962 World's Fair, where the Space Needle and the Pacific Science Center were located. There was also something called the Fun Forest, which was a kind of low-rent amusement park full of most of the same rides I would have expected to find in a traveling carnival. Except that, in the Fun Forest, the portable carnival rides hadn't ported anywhere for twenty years.

Of course none of that stuff was open when we got there, so we spent another hour or so walking around the abandoned grounds, looking at closed-up rides and the closed-up Space Needle and the closed-up Science Center. Sometime around three in the morning we noticed that one of the big fountains near the Arena, where the Seattle Supersonics basketball team played, had frozen more or less solid. And that was really all we needed for the rest of the night. Eddie and Barb were pretty well lit by that point, so we spent the next four hours sliding around on the frozen pond in our shoes. Barb and Eddie spent some time making out and dry humping on one of the bronze statues in the middle of the fountain. Bobby and I found a thin spot in the ice and broke some chunks out and started playing a hybrid game of hockey and soccer with them. It was a good time.

When we saw the sun coming up in the east, we decided to head over to the Denny's on Mercer, near the old Ford factory, and have some breakfast. We were glad we'd saved some of the money Bobby and Barb's dad had given us, because we were starved by then. We took our time, working our way through pancakes, sandwiches, and milk shakes before we wrapped it up and paid our bill with seven dollars to spare.

Around nine that morning, we all took the bus to Bobby and Barb's house and dropped them off. Eddie and Barb kissed clumsily but passionately on the doorstep. Then Eddie and I caught a couple of buses home and I watched TV until about seven that night, when I went to bed and slept for twelve hours.

* * *

Eddie and I never went back to Bobby and Barb's house. As far as I knew, they never came to Ballard, and he never mentioned either of them again.

33

By the time I was eleven, it was pretty obvious that I was going to be really big. I broke five feet when I was nine, and put on another four inches over the course of the following year. Dad started to get visibly nervous about it. Not just because he thought I was a psychopath who mutilated animals—that belief came and went, depending on his mood—but because he used to hit me a lot. And by the time I was eleven, after he hit me sometimes I'd ask him what he thought was going to happen when I got to be bigger than he was.

"It doesn't matter," he'd say. "I've trained you like a dog. Get a dog when it's little, show it who's boss, it doesn't matter how big it gets—it will always be afraid of you. You will always be afraid of me."

He seemed to be hoping that if he just said it often enough, it would turn out to be true. Not that he confined himself to verbal reinforcement. As I got bigger, he hit me more often, and harder.

On his thirty-third birthday I'd gone out with Eddie to a park that had sandstone cliffs overlooking the ocean. Dad had told me when I left home to be back before dark, stay off the cliffs, and stay out of the water. When I came home after dark, soaking wet, and with the Fire Department having called him after they rescued me and Eddie off the cliffs, Dad ambushed me: he was waiting next to the front door in the dark when I came in. I started to say, "Dad, I'm home!" and he punched me from behind, hard enough to knock me down. Once I was down, he started kicking me.

He did a thing when he really lost his shit, where he muttered and whined under his breath while he was working me over.

"Punk motherfucker! Fucking! Fuck! You! You! Piece of shit! Fucking!"

I was too surprised to cry. I just curled up in a ball. He tried to uncurl me and punch me in the face, but I stayed locked up so he dropped me again and went back to kicking me in the back, ass, and thighs.

As Dr. Epstein had noted when I fell off the high dive, I didn't bruise easily. But Dad wasn't wearing any shoes and he had long, hard toenails, so all the places where he kicked me were covered in little purple crescents the next morning.

He was full of fear.

But it wasn't just fear of me.

* * *

Dad got sick in January of 1983, and it happened to him just like it happened to Billy. He got a weird lingering fever.

Symptoms that didn't add up to anything. He kept going to the hospital and the doctors kept sending him home. Whatever was wrong with him, it wasn't bacterial, so they couldn't treat it with antibiotics. It wasn't cancer or flu. He just felt like shit all the time, and he never seemed to get better. But in the three months since Billy had gotten sick, more and more news stories had been coming out about GRID. Only now people were calling it AIDS, and we knew it wasn't caused by poppers. It was some kind of disease. It was contagious. And it killed people. Mostly gay men.

There was no test for it. It caused a low white cell count, but so did other kinds of illnesses. The only two symptoms that were considered more or less definitive were a kind of skin cancer, Kaposi's sarcoma, and pneumocystis pneumonia. Which was kind of like telling someone that the only way they could know for sure if they were falling was if they hit the ground at a hundred miles an hour.

Eventually Dad got better, just like Billy had. But we knew by then that getting better didn't mean you weren't still sick.

34

After the Lego incident, Dad worked for Carol less often. He didn't exactly quit his job, but he worked fewer and fewer hours. Which meant we went back to being broke and Dad went back to coming up with interesting ways to save money. I almost didn't mind. It was nice to have something to distract myself with.

When blackberry season started, we went around to all the

bushes that grew in the empty city rights-of-way between lots or next to roads and picked as many blackberries as we could carry. Then we did the same thing when apple season came in. When we got them home, Dad cooked them down and spooned them into boiled peanut butter jars. Then, while the fruit was still hot and the jars were still sterile, he'd pour molten paraffin wax into the jar, sealing the fruit in. We didn't eat any of those right away—we just packed them and stowed them in cabinets, for the winter.

I had to go back to drinking reconstituted powdered milk, pretty much for the first time since Hayes Street. And we ate a lot of generic food, food that came in white packaging with plain black lettering and simple descriptive names like "bread" or "macaroni and cheese." My personal favorite was a kind of meat-based hash that came in a can that was just marked "food." The generic stuff always cost a lot less than brand-name food, and sometimes it was available on sale at ridiculous prices. At one point Dad came home with four shopping bags full of generic chicken, turkey, and beef pot pies. Bartell Drugs had them on sale ten for a dollar. Dad stuffed the freezer full of them, then turned the refrigerator all the way up and stacked the rest in there. For weeks afterward, my reconstituted milk had chunks of ice in it and all I ate, three meals a day, was chicken, turkey, and beef pot pies.

We went back to sharing bathwater to save money on our utilities. When the house next door got a new roof, the roofers threw enormous piles of old cedar shingles into a Dumpster they'd parked on the front lawn. Dad would go out at night and transfer the wooden shingles into our basement. He stopped paying the electric bill that month, and when the electric company turned off the power, we spent two months cooking and heating our water over a fire pit in the backyard, where we burned a few hundred pounds of cedar shingles.

When we ran out of shingles, Dad paid the bill and got the electricity turned back on. He figured he saved us fifty or sixty dollars with that trick.

I was surprised how little I missed TV, as long as I could stare at a fire for a few hours every night.

35

That year at school I wrote yet another check with my mouth that my ass couldn't cash. I had a running beef with a kid in my grade named Chad Hicks. I couldn't even remember how it started, and normally Chad wouldn't have deigned to engage with a kid as far below him on the social totem pole as I was; he was smarter, better at sports, and had a lot more friends than I did. But he was also one of the only black kids in school, so after he'd established that he completely outclassed me in every conceivable way, I resorted to calling him a nigger.

If I'd done it once, I might have gotten away with it. Standards for that kind of thing were a lot looser in 1983. But I could tell as soon as it came out of my mouth that I'd finally found something that really pushed Chad's buttons, so I did it about twenty times over the next couple of months. I knew it was a bad idea. Leaving aside the fact that it was just an awful thing to say, I could plainly see that I was alienating everyone in the school. But I'd developed a weird itch that year, and sometimes it felt like the only way I could scratch it was by pissing off as many people as possible.

The problem that eventually caught up with me was that,

besides being better than me at pretty much everything, Chad was also, hands down, the toughest kid in school. It probably had something to do with being one of the only black kids in Ballard. He also had a lot of dangerous friends who all hated my guts. By Thanksgiving Chad had given me three of the worst beatings I'd ever gotten off another kid, and I was taking recess and lunch off campus to avoid picking up a fourth. Chad wouldn't be denied his justice though, so he called in a middle school friend of his named Mikey to wait for me after school. Middle school ended an hour before elementary school, so there was no way for me to avoid Mikey. He was four or five inches taller than I was, broader, and a lot stronger. When he confronted me one day after school I ran until he cornered me.

Getting my ass kicked at school was one thing—the fights were necessarily brief, because the teachers were always around to break them up. Off campus, Mikey wouldn't have to stop beating on me until he got bored. So when he caught me in a driveway, I pulled out my pocket knife and waited for him.

"You gonna stab me, you little faggot?"

"If you make me," I said. I tried to sound cool and collected, but I was already crying from fear.

"Pussy," Mikey said. "Faggot chickenshit. Can't fight fair. Need a knife to protect yourself?"

"You're two years older than I am!" I said. "This is bullshit!"

"I can wait here all day," he said, blocking me into the driveway.

"Then I'll cut you!"

"All right," he said, stepping back. "But you and me are gonna dance again. See if we don't."

I waited until he was out of sight before I went back out to the sidewalk, made sure he was gone, and went home. I didn't tell my dad about it. There was no point.

* * *

The next day I got called in to see Principal Adams. He asked me if I had a pocket knife.

"Sure," I said.

"Let me see it," he said.

I took it out and handed it to him. It was a four-dollar Barlow knife from Fred Meyer, with a two-inch blade that didn't lock. I used it to open boxes, sharpen sticks into make-believe swords and spears, and to clean my fingernails. And, that one time, to threaten Mikey. Mr. Adams set it down on his desk and opened one of his drawers. He took out what looked like a paperback book.

"These are the rules and regulations for the Seattle School District," he said. Then he opened the book to a page he had marked and read a passage that said that carrying a weapon on school grounds was a criminal offense.

"What I'm supposed to do now," he said, "is call the police and let them deal with you."

I started crying. It happened almost before I knew it was coming, but my face got hot and my nose clogged and I started sobbing.

My experience with cops was uniformly bad. They'd arrested my dad and let Carmella harass us with impunity. I'd had a few run-ins with them on my own. They'd never arrested me, but they never believed anything I said. When I was nine, one of them had threatened to beat my head in with his nightstick if I didn't rat out my friends for throwing rocks at a girl—who, incidentally, had been throwing rocks back. It didn't even matter that the only reason I'd gotten caught was that I stayed with her after she was hurt. Cops were pretty much the worst thing that could happen in any situation. Always.

"You can't call the cops!" I said. "Every kid in school has a pocket knife like that!"

"Every kid in school didn't threaten to stab someone with their pocket knife yesterday."

"Who told you that?" I asked.

"I got a call this morning, from a parent."

"He's an eighth grader who was going to beat me up after school. It wasn't even on school grounds. Why are you doing this?"

"I have the complaint, and I have this knife," he said.

I just sat there and cried. He leaned back in his chair and looked at me.

"I suppose," he said, "we can forgo the call to the police. But you'll get four swats, instead."

"Huh?" I said.

"Four swats," he repeated.

I stopped crying. Now I was confused. The deal he was offering was almost too good to be true. Corporal punishment was still used in my school, and I'd been on the receiving end of plenty of it. I'd been swatted in fourth and fifth grade, and once so far in sixth grade. The procedure was always the same: go out in the hall, stand with my legs apart, hands on the wall, and let some old guy hit me in the ass with a wooden paddle. It hurt, sure: the paddle was two and a half feet long, with holes drilled in it, and a tape-covered handle on one end. But really, it was nothing compared to what I got at home.

"Four swats?" I asked.

"Four," he said.

"And no cops?"

"No police," he agreed.

"Are you going to call my dad?"

"No," he said. "We'll handle it all here and now."

I didn't want to seem too eager, but I couldn't help it.

"Okay," I said.

"Okay," he said.

He got up and closed his office door.

"Are we . . . am I getting swats?" I asked.

"Yes," he said, returning to his desk.

He opened his desk drawer and took out his paddle. I'd never seen anything quite like it. It wasn't so much a paddle as a length of two-by-four with a big crack down the middle of it. It was held together at the handle with cloth tape and a length of twine. I couldn't really believe he was going to hit me with it, but things were happening too fast for me to think them through. I got up and went to the wall of his office to assume the position.

"Not like that," he said, turning his chair out. "Come over here, pull down your pants, and lie across my lap."

I turned around and looked at him. I was over five feet tall, and I weighed 115 pounds.

"I won't . . . fit," I said. There were more things going through my mind, but I didn't say them.

He sighed, opened his drawer, and put the paddle away.

"We can still call the police," he said.

I knew then what was happening, but I couldn't find an angle on it. He hadn't really done anything yet, one way or the other, so I didn't have anything I could hold over him. And even if I did, nobody would believe me. Nobody liked me. Nobody liked my dad—or at least nobody in this neighborhood liked him. I walked around Mr. Adams's desk and stood there staring at him. He raised his eyebrows and took the paddle out of his desk.

I slowly unbuckled my jeans and pulled them down. I was lucky, on this score at least. I'd only started wearing underwear a few weeks earlier. Dad didn't buy them for me. He said they were a waste of money for little kids. But I'd gotten big enough to start stealing Dad's, so I had one pair I wore all the time. They were dirty. I was embarrassed about that. And I was suddenly aware of how naked I was, standing there in my T-shirt, with my pants around my knees, and this man sitting in front of me holding a split piece of lumber.

"Over my lap," he said, positioning his chair.

I started to lean down and put my hands on his legs to position myself.

"No," he said. "Hands at your sides. Just get on your knees and slide across."

I stood back up and looked at him. He was such a mild-looking man. White hair. White mustache. White skin. Pale blue eyes, like everyone else in Ballard. Three-piece gray suit. Light gray. Like him.

I got down on my knees, laid my chest on his thighs, and pushed myself across until I was draped awkwardly over his lap. The fabric of his trousers was soft and thin. I could feel a bulge in his pants, up against my side, through my T-shirt. He picked up the paddle, put his free hand on my back, and hit me, once, hard.

It was different from the paddles the other teachers used. Less sting, but more force. Less like being slapped; more like being kicked. I felt the jolt travel from my ass up into my stomach. He took a few deep breaths and hit me again. I clenched my teeth and hissed, and tried not to cry. I didn't know why it mattered. I'd cried every other time I'd been paddled. But I didn't want to cry this time. Then I did anyway, when he hit me the third time. When he hit me the fourth time, I barely noticed.

He sat there for a few seconds, with his hand on my back. Then he put the paddle in his desk drawer and said, "Okay."

I slid off him, back onto my knees, and stood up, pulling my pants up as I stood.

"We done?" I asked.

"No," he said.

"Can I sit down?"

"Yes," he said.

I went back around the desk and sat down. I was numb. Defeated. I kept trying to think of a way where what I'd just let him do to me was okay, and not coming up with anything. It made me want to die.

"Why was he after you?" Adams asked. "The boy. The eighth grader."

"He's a friend of Chad's. Chad hates me."

"Why does Chad hate you?"

"Because I called him names," I said.

"Just called him names, hm?"

I nodded. I figured that was all it was, at the end of the day.

"All right. It sounds to me like we have an ongoing problem here. I want you to come back here, every Wednesday at lunch. For counseling."

"Okay," I said, standing up. "See you next Wednesday."

"I'll hang on to this," he said, dropping my pocket knife into his drawer.

"Fine," I said.

36

Trusting my instincts was hard for me where adults were concerned.

There had always been things about my home life that I wasn't supposed to talk about with regular people. When I was very little, most of them had to do with drugs and sex. Those were things that our people handled differently than the straights, and if the straights found out too much about us, they'd send police. Child Protective Services would come. I'd be taken away from my home, like I'd been taken away when I was three.

Then, around the time I started going to elementary school, Dad had added another item to the list of things I wasn't supposed to talk about to the straights: I was never supposed to talk about getting hit at home. And if I did, I should always use the word "spankings." It was also around this time—around the time I started going to Ida Patterson Elementary School, in Eugene—that Dad started telling me I was mistaken about how often I got hit. Or how hard I got hit. Or if I got hit at all. The conversations we had about whether he'd still be able to hit me when I was bigger, or what would happen then—those were conversations we had when he was threatening to hit me and the reality was present in the room with us. The rest of the time, he just denied he ever did it. If I brought it up, especially in front of other people—even our people—Dad would laugh and say, "I never hit you."

If I pressed him, he might admit that he spanked me. But he certainly never hit me. And anyway, I blew the whole thing out of proportion. I made it sound so much worse than it was. If I ever talked to someone about it, they'd get completely the wrong impression. But it wasn't nearly as bad as I made it out to be. Or it never happened. The point was, I shouldn't talk about it. Or I'd be taken away. I'd have to go live with someone else. Maybe my grandparents. Maybe a foster home. But I could never live with Dad again.

When I was little I accepted his explanation. It seemed plausible. There were lots of things I didn't understand; when I was three I got in trouble for pouring my milk down the sink, like I did with a half-drunk glass of water. I didn't understand that one came out of a faucet, and was basically free, and the other one was paid for at a grocery store. So maybe I didn't understand the difference between a spanking and a beating either. And once I made that leap, it was a tiny step to believing that it wasn't happening at all.

As I got older and started to understand the implications of what my dad was saying, my commitment to the idea that I was making the whole thing up only deepened. Because the alternative was that my dad was willing, however reluctantly, to make me question my own sanity; that he was trying to make me disbelieve a fact that was evidenced by my own senses and reason. Because I was wrong about getting hit, I lived my life with the understanding that I could be wrong about the color of the sky. I could be wrong about who was a friend and who was an enemy. I could be wrong about absolutely everything, because I was wrong about this really simple thing. But if I was right about getting hit—then maybe I was right about lots of other things.

That didn't make sense. That couldn't be true; he wouldn't do that to me. He loved me. So I must be wrong. About all of it. And if I could be wrong about that, who knew what else I could be wrong about? Only Dad knew what was safe and what wasn't; only Dad could tell me what was true, and who to trust.

And Dad said, trust no one.

37

It was around this time that Crazy Mike caught up with Olive in Seattle. It could have been worse. Calliope could have been home when it happened. But at thirteen she was an early bloomer. She was out of the country with her boyfriend when Mike showed up on their doorstep. The way Dad told me the story, Mike took his time with Olive. He beat her in every room of the house. Broke her jaw and some ribs, and knocked out all her teeth. He beat her until he got hungry, then he went into the kitchen to get something to eat. Olive was a tall skinny thing, maybe a hundred pounds soaking wet, but she had the constitution of a vending machine. When Mike left her in the living room, she got up and went after him.

She hit him with an antique iron. Back before electric irons were invented, people used an actual slug of iron to press their clothes; eight or nine pounds, shaped like a boat, with a long curved handle that was designed to stay cool when the main body of the iron had been heated up in a fireplace or over a stove. Olive had a couple of them around the house, as quaint preindustrial decorations and conversation pieces. While Mike was digging through her refrigerator, she picked one up off the bookshelf, walked up behind him, swung it from down low, over her head, and down as hard as she could—tip-first, right into the top of Mike's skull.

"It didn't even knock him down," Dad said. "He just turned around and looked at her and started kicking her ass all over again."

The iron didn't kill him, but it did give him a vicious cut on top of his head, and beating the shit out of Olive was hard work. Mike's heart really got going. As he dragged her around the house, kicking her and punching her, gouts of blood shot four feet out of the top of his head, spraying across the walls and the furniture. In some places, it was splashed on the ceiling. Between the two of them, they pretty much repainted the apartment.

By that time, Mike had been working Olive over for quite a while, and Will, the late-night crying masturbator, happened to come by for a social call. Will was half Mike's size, but he carried a straight razor in his boot. He went after Mike with the knife and splashed more blood around the apartment. Mike ran away. Will got Olive into a hospital and put the word out to all our people to be on the lookout for Mike.

"When's Calliope coming home?" I asked, when Dad was done telling me the story.

"Next week," Dad said.

"When's Olive getting out of the hospital?" I asked.

"Dunno," Dad said. "Be a lot longer than a week though."

* * *

I caught a bus over there a few days after Calliope came home. I found her in her room, cleaning blood off her comic book collection. She kept most of them in flat cellophane bags, so the damage wasn't as bad as it could have been, but there was more blood on everything else in the house—all over her bed, all over the kitchen. Rubbed into the carpet in the living room and the hallway. Splashed all over the bathroom. I could see the spatters Dad had talked about in Calliope's room. It looked exactly like someone had flicked a paintbrush soaked with rust-brown paint, spraying streamers of color across the smoke-stained walls and ceiling.

Calliope was wearing heavy yellow dish-washing gloves

while she wiped at her comics with a soapy sponge. She didn't look at me when I came into her room.

"You okay?" I asked.

She shrugged. "Not me that got my ass kicked."

"You wanna come over to our place?"

I hoped she would. I could weather all this shit easier with her there. I hoped she'd move in. I hoped she'd leave this fucking madhouse behind and come stay with me and keep me safe from all the bullshit going on in my life. We could protect each other. But she just shook her head.

"I'm gonna stay with friends for a while," she said. "But I've gotta clean all this up first."

I thought about offering to help, but I didn't know where to begin.

"How's Olive doing?" I asked.

"Fuck," she said. "Her jaw's wired shut. No teeth left. Half the bones in her fucking face are broken. Stupid. So fucking stupid."

"You gonna be okay?" I asked.

She finally looked up at me. She looked tired, but that was all. She frowned, like I'd just insulted her somehow.

"Why wouldn't I be okay?" she asked.

* * *

Olive was released from the hospital a few weeks later. She came by our place in Ballard once. The soft tissue and bones had mostly healed up, and she looked like she always had, except that her lips were kind of puckered because she was missing all her teeth now and she hadn't gotten dentures yet. She showed me the .22 caliber two-shot Derringer she'd picked up in case Mike came back.

"Shouldn't you have something . . . bigger?" I asked. "With more bullets?"

"No," she hissed through her wired jaw. "Anything I shot him with, he'd take it away from me and use it against me. This way, I shoot him twice, he's dying, he takes it away from me and it's empty. Best of all possible worlds."

Of course, everyone knew Mike's name. He had a lengthy arrest record. All Olive had to do was drop a dime on him and the cops would be all over him, but we just didn't do that. Ever. It was the only rule everybody stuck to. Everyone was breaking laws all the time. If someone called the cops, everyone could burn. So even for really heavy shit, if it happened between people who were in our network, it stayed in the network. Olive would tell the cops about who beat her up after she shot Mike, if it came to that. Otherwise, it stayed in the family.

It didn't leave Olive with a lot of options. So she was taking Calliope with her and moving to Hawaii.

"What's in Hawaii?" I asked. Everything I knew about Hawaii was derived from *Magnum, P.I.* reruns.

"Sun," Olive said. "And two thousand miles of ocean between me and Mike. He just drove up here, Jason. Just drove up from Oregon. Took him eight hours."

I saw Calliope twice more before they left, always on her way in or her way out. The last time I saw her before she left she was in her room at her house, packing up to go. She was hanging out with some girl I didn't know. I was wearing a bunch of army surplus clothes that I thought made me look cool, but really they just made me look fat. Or that's what my dad had been telling me. He was always on me about my weight lately.

When I came into her room, Calliope looked up from packing and smiled at me.

"What's up, doughboy?" she asked, using the World War I slang term for a soldier.

I didn't get the reference. I thought she was calling me fat, too.

I hung around awkwardly for a while. I didn't know what to say. Calliope's friend kept bad-vibing me, like I was messing up some intimate dynamic the two of them had going before I showed up. I tried to ignore it, but even I didn't know what I was doing there.

"All right," I said, after forty-five minutes or so. "I guess I should get home."

"Hey," she said, as I turned to leave. "Write me."

"I'll try," I said.

"You'd fucking better," she said.

38

I went to the principal's office every Wednesday for weeks. We talked. Sometimes he held my hand while we talked. He called me honey, sweetie, and dear a lot, but he never crossed any lines I could use against him. Not that I would have called the cops, or talked to a teacher about it. But if he'd done something bad enough, I could have told my dad. And for something like this, I figured Dad would probably call someone like Sean, our friend back in Eugene who'd shot all the windows out of his house.

But first, something would have to happen. I almost hoped it would. I wasn't sure how much longer I could handle having this smarmy fuck touching me and telling me how special he thought I was.

I was still having problems with other kids. Chad had friends in my class, and I was getting into arguments and shoving matches, even in front of my teacher, Mr. Burke. Mr. Adams was keeping Mr. Burke off my back, but he said we'd have to do something to settle the situation soon. He tried talking to me about "psycho-semantics," and how I carried myself like a victim. I thought that was funny, coming from him, but the insight didn't do much to keep me out of trouble in class. And there were no other classes I could go to. There were three sixth grade classes in the school. Chad was in one of them, and he had good friends in the other two.

"Have you ever had an IQ test?" Mr. Adams asked me one Wednesday, after I'd been coming to his office for about a month.

"No," I said. "Why would I want to do that?"

"Why wouldn't you?"

"I'm stupid," I said. "Why take a test that proves it?"

"Does your dad tell you you're stupid?"

"No," I said. "He's always telling me I'm too smart for school. But I can't spell. I'm bad at math. And every single other person here tells me I'm stupid all the time. You know they wanted to put me in special ed at Stevens."

He leaned back in his chair and looked at me.

"I'd like to call your dad," he said.

"What?"

"You're not in trouble," he said, gesturing for me to calm down. "I want to send you for testing. The school district does it. It shouldn't cost you any money. And it may mean we can get you into a class where you'll have fewer problems. A class where Chad doesn't have any friends."

I went home that afternoon with a sinking feeling. A few hours later the phone rang, and sure enough, it was Mr. Adams, wanting to talk to my dad.

"Jason," Dad said. "Why don't you go outside and play for a while."

I didn't have anything to do outside, so I went down in the

basement and used my BB gun to shoot targets I'd set up against one of the concrete walls, putting dings and dents in old toys I didn't play with anymore. I could hear Dad's voice through the ceiling above me.

A week later Dad took me to another school, in a part of town I didn't recognize. When we got there, I went into a classroom with some other kids and did a bunch of things that seemed like games to me, with shapes and matching symbols, and other tasks that didn't seem like a test at all. I was normally bad at taking tests. I had trouble with reading. Trying to write was even worse. I couldn't spell to save my life. But there was hardly any reading or writing in this test.

A week later Dad got a letter in the mail, from the school district. He opened it up and started laughing.

"What's it say?" I asked.

"It says you're in the ninety-ninth percentile," he said.

"Is that an A?" I asked, assuming there was a letter grade associated with the IQ test.

"Not exactly. They aren't scored that way."

"So how are they scored?" I asked. "What's a ninety-nine mean?"

"It means that if you take a hundred people at random and put them in a room, you're smarter than ninety-eight of them," Dad said.

I didn't believe that for a second. Nobody besides my dad and grownups who were basically family ever told me I was smart. Everyone—even Calliope—told me I was dumb pretty much all the time; teased me for not knowing things, or for misunderstanding things, or for not being able to read. This was just one more sick joke some bureaucrat at the school district was playing on me. Dad seemed confused by my reaction.

"You're going to be in the gifted program," he said. "They're moving you to a new class starting next week. One where you won't be so bored all the time."

The last time I'd gone to a class where I wouldn't be so bored all the time I'd ended up in counseling, but I had to acknowledge that Mr. Adams had put together a pretty good plan. The gifted class was, indeed, the only sixth grade class in the school where Chad didn't have any friends. I started there the following Monday, and it was everything I'd hoped it would be: a room full of kids where nobody tried to shove me into a wall when the teacher wasn't looking. I celebrated by unilaterally ending my Wednesday trips to Mr. Adams's office. He didn't make a fuss about it.

39

Dad started dating a new guy that year—Bruce. I was annoyed. I'd just started to like Charles, and now here was Bruce. But where Charles was all sharp angles and subtle, literate intelligence, Bruce was like a Disney version of an urban gay man: brightly colored, round, and resoundingly boring.

Bruce had worked as a display artist at one of the big department stores downtown for fifteen years. His favorite records were from the Pointer Sisters and Yma Sumac. He was the same height as my dad, but thicker in the hips and shoulders, with an oval face on an oval head—baggy eyes, too much jaw under too little mouth, and a straight nose that ended in a little ball. He was bald like my dad, and had a mustache like my dad, but none of it looked right on him. He smiled a lot but never seemed to get any of our jokes. He wore short-sleeved button-down shirts in colors like turquoise or magenta. His living room had a lot of potted palm trees and indirect lighting. After a few weeks of having him around the house, I happened to see him naked in the bathroom. He had the whitest, smoothest, most hairless ass I'd ever seen on a human being in my life. It looked like two pools of milk on a moonlit night. It didn't even look real. Dad and I made jokes about it when Bruce wasn't around, but whenever I expressed a desire to eject Bruce from our lives, Dad would bristle.

Because whatever I thought of Bruce, as far as Dad was concerned Bruce's most attractive feature seemed to be that he had been gainfully employed and extremely frugal since he was about twenty-two. He owned a one-bedroom condominium in South Capitol Hill and had about $10,000 in the bank. His job didn't pay especially well, and he didn't come from money. He was just careful, and lived within his means. Naturally Dad saw this as an opportunity.

"You owe me this," Dad would say to me.

"For what?" I'd ask.

"For everything."

We'd been fighting a lot since he got sick. He wanted me to work more, to carry my weight more. He wanted me to clean the house more often. Dad liked the house vacuumed twice a day. He liked me to do the dishes. Except for the compulsive vacuuming, it was all basic stuff—stuff any of my friends had to do at their houses. For some reason, when Dad told me to do it I dug in my heels. And lately he'd really started losing it when we fought. He'd always had a temper, but lately he'd started a new litany when we argued.

"You fat, lazy piece of shit!" he'd scream at me. "I can't believe I raised you! I can't believe I wasted my life on you!"

I didn't exactly blame him. I thought I even knew where his anger was coming from.

Every day we were hearing about more AIDS deaths. Newspapers were saying the infection could be much more widespread than people realized, because the disease stayed relatively dormant for the first couple of years after exposure. Billy was getting worse again. Bruce's last long-term boyfriend had died of AIDS the year before. He'd been one of the first in Seattle to die of it.

If Dad had previously assumed he'd have time to live his life after I grew up and got out of the house, he was reevaluating that assumption now. Even I could see it. If he died sooner rather than later, that would mean I was his life's work. And I wasn't good enough. It was that simple. What he saw when he looked at me didn't make him feel like his life had been worth it.

He liked everything about me less every day. He'd always told me how beautiful I was; how thick my hair was, what a good nose I had, how naturally graceful I was. Lately it was all about how fat I was. How I ate too much. How I didn't respect myself. How he was embarrassed to be seen in public with me. I used to be smart, but now I was lazy. I used to be full of love, but now I was just hateful and bitter. I used to be fun, but now I just took, and took, and took.

"Bruce can get us out of here," Dad said. "He wants to move with us, to Southern California. Someplace I can see the sun."

"I don't want to move to L.A.," I said. "I hated it down there."

"You'll move wherever I tell you to," Dad said. "But I don't want to move to L.A. either. San Diego. That's where we're going."

* * *

We moved in fits and starts as the weather got better. Dad and Bruce made a plan with Dad's friend Nikki, a submissive lesbian witch we knew from Capitol Hill. A month or so before the end of my sixth grade year, Dad announced we'd be moving into Bruce's one-bedroom condo to save money before the move to San Diego in October. I had mixed feelings about it, but there was nothing left for me in Ballard. I hardly ever saw Eddie, and after Gabe's mom married a rich lawyer and moved to a better neighborhood, the old D&D group didn't want to have much to do with me.

We put our stuff in storage that spring, in the garage of an old lady at the end of our block in Ballard. She'd once threatened me with her dead husband's .45 when she caught me stealing plums off the tree in her yard, but she didn't seem to recognize me when Dad gave her a check for $150.

Then we spent four months in Bruce's little one-bedroom condo while Dad and Bruce went on a landscaping and home repair spree, fixing up the building so the condo association would allow Bruce to rent his unit while we were in San Diego. Dad took some other steps to make sure we'd have a fallback plan in Seattle if San Diego didn't work out: he transferred our Section Eight housing to the apartment of his drug dealer, Scotty, on Capitol Hill. Scotty had a two-bedroom apartment in a converted house, and he agreed to risk losing the apartment to us, if we came back, in exchange for at least a year of reduced rent—plus our welfare checks and food stamps, which he'd also collect on our behalf. The arrangement carried a risk: at least three counts of fraud, and we'd never get on the rolls for any of those programs again if they caught us. But Dad didn't think we'd ever come back to Seattle, so he figured the insurance was cheap at the price.

Dad finally sold the Vega for scrap. He and Bruce split the cost of a '66 Volvo sedan to take to California with us.

I didn't bother registering for school in Seattle that fall. We'd be gone soon enough. Anyway, I needed to be home so I could take our dog, Thunder, for walks twice a day. In Ballard he'd been almost wild, with Dad letting him out all night, every night. Now he was cooped up in a tiny third-floor walkup, and I had to put him on a leash and walk him around the neighborhood while he did his business on the parking strips. However much I hated living in Bruce's apartment, Thunder hated it more. He exuded an almost existential angst. He also developed canine eczema on his lower back, which was pretty gross.

That October we packed everything from the garage in Ballard, and all Bruce and Nikki's stuff, into a U-Haul truck and a trailer, and began our five-day pilgrimage to sunny Southern California. Dad and I rode with Thunder in the truck. Bruce and Nikki took the Volvo.

It would have been a four-day trip, but we had to stop in San Francisco so Nikki could visit her dominatrix, Mistress Lisa. Mistress Lisa insisted we all come up and say hi. Her apartment was bright and homey. She had wainscoting in her kitchen and a lot of potholders with Midwestern ranch-themed prints on them hanging on hooks near the stove. I looked at a coffee table book about circus freaks while Lisa's slave brought us Red Zinger tea, and Dad and Lisa talked about gardening and interior design.

* * *

Nikki had a girlfriend in San Diego, in a neighborhood called Ocean Beach. When we got there, we spent a few hours moving Nikki and her girlfriend into their new apartment, but after that we were pretty much on our own with a truck full of stuff, no place to stay, and no income. It took Dad about two hours to rent a garage where we could store our things, on the ground floor of an apartment building next to the Ocean Beach Municipal Pier. We spent the rest of the day loading boxes and furniture into the garage before Dad and Bruce left me on the pier so they could return the truck to the nearest U-Haul place. Dad asked if I wanted Thunder to keep me company. I told him to take the dog with him in the car, and spent an hour walking around the beach by myself.

The fishing pier was enormous. It stood on concrete pillars twenty-five feet high and reached a good quarter mile out into the ocean. There was a building at the end of the pier, with the word CAFÉ painted on the side in huge black letters. The beach itself was dotted with public restrooms that had showers and working toilets; in Seattle most of the public bathrooms were closed nine months out of the year, and the toilets hardly ever worked. The Southern California air was warm. The smells were totally alien to me, some combination of sage and ocean. The sunlight made everything look white and blasted. It was unlike anyplace I'd ever been. I was willing to believe that was a good thing.

40

The first order of business was to spend as little money as possible while Dad and Bruce looked for work. Dad's solution was to get us all a room in a place called the Eagle Crest Hotel, between San Diego and Ocean Beach. The room cost ten dollars a night and had two twin beds and a small refrigerator. No TV, but that was fine—we just got one of ours from the garage storage unit. The bathroom was down the hall, and there were separate shower rooms. The men's shower room was a large open space with white subway tiles covering the walls and ceiling and small hexagonal tiles on the floor. All the tiles in the room seemed to be held in place by a dense black mold that was packed tightly into the crevices, like grout. A dozen shower nozzles poked out of the wall at regular intervals. When I went down the hall to check it out, there were three guys in there, and a cockroach running across the floor toward one of the open floor drains. We stayed in the Eagle Crest for two weeks. I didn't shower once.

Dad found a gig for himself and Bruce with a house-cleaning service that did one-time projects, like cleaning out trashed apartments so they could be re-rented. It paid more than enough to meet our needs. After that, he had no trouble finding us a place to live near the beach. Unfortunately, the town house wouldn't be ready until the end of the month, so Dad decided we should move into the storage garage to save money while we waited. We rearranged our things so there was a bed for Dad and Bruce in the back of the garage. I slept in the gap between two couches, where one was stacked on top of the other. We used the toilets and showers at the public bathrooms on the beach. We were careful not to be seen coming and going. Our rental agreement specifically forbade living in the garage.

I got to spend another two weeks lounging on the beach while Dad and Bruce cleaned the homes of dead shut-ins and junkies. I had to take the dog for walks, which I found annoying because I'd started to think of him as a spoiled sibling. But really, I'd had worse times.

41

We moved into the town house a month after we arrived in San Diego. Dad and Bruce took the upstairs, with the living room, the kitchen, and one of the bathrooms. I took the downstairs room that had its own bathroom and its own entrance. Once we were settled in, Dad registered me for the seventh grade at a nearby middle school. It was mid-November.

I didn't like the school. The layout was confusing to me; it was a bunch of separate one-story buildings connected by covered walkways, with no apparent rhyme or reason to how the rooms were numbered. A lot of my classmates only spoke Spanish in social settings. I was hot all the time. I didn't understand any of the classes because they were actual content classes instead of the general concept stuff I'd been learning in elementary school, and I was starting two months late. Computer science? Algebra? What? Oh, right, like those word problems I did in sixth grade where it says "n = ?" Now, what's this business with "x"?

After two weeks, I told my dad I didn't want to go back.

"Fine with me," he said. "Just don't sit around the living room watching TV all day."

I promised I wouldn't. I had cable in my room. I'd sit around down there watching TV all day.

* * *

At some point in early January, my middle school noticed that I'd been gone for kind of a long time and sent Dad a letter asking if I was coming back. When he called them to tell them he had no plans to reenroll me, they asked if I'd like to take part in their experimental learning program.

"What's that, exactly?" Dad asked.

The woman on the phone said that it was basically a home-schooling program. Every week a teacher would come to my house, drop off new assignments, and pick up my completed ones. The teacher would have up to an hour to spend with me if I was having any problems with the subject matter. Otherwise, there was a number that I could call during regular school hours if I was really stuck on a math problem or something. And I never had to set foot in a middle school again.

"What's the catch?" Dad wanted to know.

"He's got to take an IQ test to qualify," the woman said. "And some aptitude tests."

"Yeah," Dad said. "That shouldn't be a problem."

* * *

A week later I took another trip out to another remote administrative building and took another battery of tests. There were more questions this time, and more of them involved reading, but I did my best. As I finished each section, a tall bald guy in a suit and tie would collect my work. After about three hours, I joined Dad in a small waiting room while the school people finished their evaluation. The waiting room had windows that faced out into the hallway, and nice lighting. The furniture was a lot newer and nicer than what I was used to seeing in government offices. Everything had clean edges. Nobody had scratched their initials in anything. There were some Legos in a bucket near the door. I looked at them longingly, then started flipping through *National Geographic* magazines instead. I'd been avoiding Legos for two years, just to prove to myself that people like Carol couldn't hold anything over me.

After about forty-five minutes of us sitting in the waiting room, the tall skinny bald man in the suit came in. He sat down across from Dad, near me. I went and sat down next to Dad, so I'd be able to see the bald man's face.

"Thank you for waiting," said the man.

"Sure," Dad said. "Did he qualify? For the program?"

"Oh, I should say so. Has he had tests like this before?"

"In Seattle," Dad said.

"Ah," said the bald man. "Okay. So . . . based on these scores, what we'd like to do is, we'd certainly like him in the program this year. Of course. And, I don't know—I'm not sure there's much point in him starting eighth grade next year."

"Huh?" I said.

"Well," said the man. "We've got two choices, really, with these tests. He could start high school next year, and just skip the eighth grade. Or, instead of high school, we could also do an early admission program."

"Early admission to what?" Dad asked.

"College or junior college, if you want to go that way. I don't know what you can afford. If it's a city college we could cover part of the tuition. We've got a program for that. You'd have to go ahead and get a GED, but I don't think that would be a meaningful impediment."

"I don't understand," I said. "I don't even know algebra. How can I go to college?"

"Well, you don't know algebra," said the bald man. "Sure. But the thing is, we think you could learn, say, first year algebra, in a couple of weeks, if you had the right instructional environment. So whatever you know or don't know, teaching it to you isn't really going to be the hard part. Getting you into a situation that funnels information into you as quickly as you can learn it. That's going to be the real trick."

I just sat there blinking at him. Nothing he was saying made any sense.

"We'd like to start in the home study program," Dad said, after a minute. "And I think we can safely say we'd like to skip the rest of middle school. We'll have to talk about the college thing."

"All right," said the bald man. "Let me get some forms together for the home study program, and there's nothing to fill out about skipping the next grade—we'll just put that in his file."

"Thanks," Dad said, standing up and shaking the bald man's hand.

"Yeah," I said, from where I was sitting. "Uh. Thanks."

I followed Dad out to the car in a kind of daze. This was all totally ridiculous. Out of six and a half years of public school, I'd attended a grand total of about four. I'd never gotten better than a B average. Pretty much every kid my own age who'd ever offered an opinion on the matter had told me I was an idiot, and the teachers at Stevens had wanted to put me in special ed. I never really trusted the IQ test I'd taken in sixth grade. I figured I'd either gotten lucky or Mr. Adams had somehow falsified the score. And now here was this bald guy in a tie telling me I was such a mutant genius that I didn't even need to be in school if I didn't want to be. There was no question in my mind that I was worthless and stupid. Not being able to figure out why these bureaucrats kept lying to me about it was freaking me out.

"Well, that's pretty cool," Dad said, as we got into the car.

"Yeah," I said. "I guess."

42

Dad and Bruce didn't work for the cleaning service for very long. After about six weeks of cleaning up crime scenes and abandoned buildings, they got a call out to a mansion in El Cajon, a desert suburb of San Diego. The way Dad told the story, the job was just to get the house ready for the owner's in-laws, who were going to be visiting from Colombia. Bruce started cleaning as soon as they got there, but Dad looked around a bit and couldn't help noticing all the lightly armed men who just seemed to be standing around not doing anything, or the way there seemed to be a glass-topped coffee table in every room. The house itself was newly built, and the landscaping was only just beginning. Dad joined Bruce and finished the job for the day, but when it came time to get their time sheets signed, he asked to talk to the owner of the home.

"He's busy," said the man who'd been overseeing Dad and Bruce's work.

"We can wait a little while," Dad said.

Eventually the homeowner came to see what Dad wanted. The man's name was Karl.

"What can I do for you?" he asked, when he came into the room where Dad and Bruce were waiting.

"Well," Dad said. "I was actually hoping I could do something for you. I notice you're doing a lot of landscaping. I was a landscape architect in Seattle, and my partner and I work at a very reasonable rate."

"Not to be rude," Karl said, "but I can hire a landscape architect anywhere. What makes you special?"

"I'm a landscape architect. I can do the work that you need

done around the house. I can keep my mouth shut. I won't see or hear anything while I'm working."

According to Dad, Karl didn't need to think about it very long.

"You have references?" he asked.

"Felony possession with intent. In Eugene, Oregon. Nineteen seventy-five."

"I'll check it out and get back to you."

A week later, Karl called Dad and hired him and Bruce on as landscape architects at twelve dollars an hour, each. Cash. Plus expenses. Plus, every once in a while, he'd give Dad a goodie bag of drugs. The only condition was, Dad wasn't supposed to sell them. They were for personal use only; Dad the drug dealer was working for Karl the drug importer, and all he was doing was putting in garden irrigation systems, building decorative fountains, and taking care of the trees on the property. Karl didn't shit where he slept.

43

Under the home study program it usually took me about four hours to do all my homework for the week. After that, I spent most of my days down on the beach, which started at the end of our block. I had a $20 Styrofoam boogie board Dad had picked up for me at Target, but I mostly used it as a flotation device. On a low tide I'd go a half mile or so out to sea, then just let the waves carry me back in; then I'd swim back out and let the waves carry me back in. I could spend five or six hours doing that, three or four days a week. I kept the board with me as a kind of security blanket, in case I caught a rip or something. And to keep me from having to go down into the cold water, four or five feet under the surface. The feeling of those cold-water currents touching my feet was enough to send me into a panic. I imagined the water down there was black. I knew better, but that was what it felt like.

My dad got me a new bike for Christmas that year. I outgrew it almost as soon as he bought it for me. I was about five feet ten inches tall when I was twelve. But I rode it anyway. Mostly I rode it around the neighborhood, but every once in a while I'd cross over into Mission Beach to the north, or south toward Sunset Cliffs and Point Loma.

When I got home I'd shower in my room. Go upstairs and get some food, then take it to my room to eat it. I ate on my bed while I watched TV. My room always smelled like rotting orange peels. I hated the smell, but my best efforts at cleaning were thoroughly inadequate.

I watched shows about families. Kids with brothers and sisters and friends. Sometimes, for reasons I didn't understand, I'd start crying while I was watching TV. It used to happen a lot during a Coke commercial that showed around Christmas: snow, people holding hands, lighting candles, and singing about how they'd like to buy the world a Coke. When I watched it, a strange sort of panic would grab me. A crushing fear that everyone else was off somewhere, together, and I was alone in my basement room. That I'd always be alone in my basement room.

If it wasn't too late, on nights like that I'd get dressed and go down to the beach. There were big concrete fire rings down there. College kids would burn scrap lumber in them, then stand around them and drink on into the night. Sometimes they surfed by moonlight. I'd stand near the fires, looking at people's faces, just soaking up the presence of other human beings. Listening to their conversations and their jokes. It was never enough, but it was better than nothing.

* * *

Once every other month or so a big windstorm would blow in from the ocean. I'd put on my swimming goggles, wrap a scarf around my face, and go outside to watch. Because we lived so close to the beach, the windstorms sent tons of sand blowing down our street. Sometimes whole cars would be buried.

If it happened at night, I'd bring my flashlight and watch the sand stream down the street, like giant white snakes. If it happened during the day, I'd go to the beach and sit down with my back to the wind. Then I'd close my eyes and wait for the sand to bury me.

* * *

Dad and I fought about my room. A lot. He said it was attracting bugs. I thought he was probably right, but I didn't care. Or I didn't seem to be able to care. Once he told me to clean it by the time he got home from work or else. I went upstairs to watch TV in the living room and fell asleep on the couch. When he got home, he came back into the house through the basement entrance, took a look in my room, and came upstairs. He didn't even bother to wake me up, just started hitting me while I was on the couch asleep.

But it was getting harder. Hitting me. We were the same height now, and I was heavier. He was still a lot stronger, but the time was coming when he wouldn't be. Once we got in a fight about cleaning while I was in my room. He was yelling at me and I was arguing with him and he snapped and threw a punch at my head. A big looping haymaker. I blocked it with my elbow. We were both pretty surprised. Then he swung with his other hand, and I blocked that one, too. He screamed in frustration, shoved me onto the floor, and ran out of the room.

* * *

I took karate for a little while. I wasn't very good at it, and I didn't get along with the other kids in the class. Or the teacher. Or his kids. Or any of the grownups at the school. So I quit after a couple of months.

I tried writing to my friends in Seattle. Mostly Gabe. I'd send him enormous sheaves of paper with ideas for D&D games, or new gaming systems based on movies I'd seen on late-night cable. Sometimes I'd call him long distance, just to have someone to talk to.

"My mom says we keep owing postage on the stuff you send," he said. "She says to put more stamps on the envelopes."

I tried to write Calliope, too, but I gave up pretty quickly. I didn't really have anything to say.

Dad and Bruce made a lot of friends. Sometimes, if they were having a party upstairs, I'd go up and hang out. Everyone was always nice about it, but then I'd say something inappropriate or weird, and Dad would kick me under the table or something to try to get me to shut up.

"Why are you kicking me under the table?" I'd ask.

Then everyone would laugh awkwardly.

My life was breaking off from my dad's in a way that was confusing to me. More and more, he and Bruce had their own lives upstairs. He lavished affection on the dog. He bought a bunch of birds—parrots and finches, budgies and cockatiels—and started referring to them as his babies. Meanwhile, he and Bruce started calling me "Prophet of Doom," supposedly because I was always such a massive buzz-kill. Whatever we were doing, I could be counted on to point out what could go wrong or why something wouldn't work. They had a valid point, but I was twelve. Mostly it all just made me feel like I was in the process of getting divorced from the only family I'd ever known.

I started having trouble sleeping. I could go a few days with hardly any sleep at all. When I did sleep, it was usually from about three in the morning until noon. Then later and later, until I'd flip the clock and get back on a normal schedule for a few days.

I gained a bunch of weight. At five foot ten I was around 160 pounds, but it was soft weight, all baby fat. Whenever I did see Dad, he made a point of telling me how heavy I was getting. I tried sticking my finger down my throat, to make myself throw up after I ate. I'd heard about that on TV. Unfortunately I seemed to have virtually no gag reflex. I tried using some ipecac syrup that I got for free from the fire station a few blocks away, but the vomiting was so painful and it gave me such bad gas I never tried it again.

I had a horrible racking cough that lasted for three months. Dad said it was psychosomatic. Before it went away, my throat was so raw that I was spitting up blood. But then it did just mysteriously disappear, so maybe he was right.

Two or three times a month Dad would take me out to his boss's house in El Cajon, and I'd get paid $2.50 an hour to dig ditches or clear rocks out of the horses' paddocks. I used the money to order Domino's pizzas. There were no good toy stores in Ocean Beach, I didn't have anyone to play with, and I suspected I was getting too old for toys anyway.

* * *

Dad and Bruce liked to go on trips. Sometimes we'd go down to Tijuana, just the other side of the Mexican border, for shopping expeditions. I'd buy cheap souvenir bullwhips and throwing stars for a couple of dollars apiece. Dad would buy Mexican horse blankets, or semiprecious stones: opals, amethysts, and quartz crystals with veins of gold in them. Other times we'd go out to the desert, or we'd take a day trip to Torrey Pines Park.

We went out to Palm Springs a dozen or so times. Somewhere in the desert between San Diego and Palm Springs there was a truck stop that sold soft-serve ice cream. The place was always full of crusty old truck drivers, and the parking lot was always full of semis. The walls inside were covered with dried rattlesnake skins, from snakes that had been found dead on the highway. I loved it in there. And no matter where we were in the desert—even if we weren't actually going to Palm Springs—I could always find the truck stop. Dad was fascinated.

"Is it the lay of the land, or the direction of the sun or what?" he'd ask.

"I don't know," I'd say. "I can just . . . feel it. The ice cream calls out to me."

I liked the Palm Springs trips for other reasons besides soft-serve. Dad and Bruce and I would get a room in a cheap hotel we liked and take day trips up into the mountains around the town. Looking at the desert floor from so high up, I could see the shadows of clouds moving across it, and I saw mountain springs, and streambeds shining with quartz crystals, agates, and fool's gold. Palm trees hanging with dates. I saw caves, and bats, and coyotes. And mile after mile of pristine desert mountain streams, roaring through deep crevices in the exposed bedrock of the desert floor and tumbling hundreds of feet down the sides of mountains.

Then one night, after a long hike, I was sitting in the hot tub at our cheap hotel with my dad and Bruce and a few other guests, and this old lady kept staring at me and muttering under her breath. Eventually Dad and Bruce noticed her doing it, and Dad finally asked her what her problem was.

"It's just not right," said the old lady, glaring at me.

"What's not right?" Dad asked.

"Letting a girl that age run around without her shirt on."

I was twelve. Almost six feet tall. Overweight. I had shaggy, shoulder-length hair. And my voice hadn't changed yet.

Dad stared at the old lady, then sighed and closed his eyes. Did a thing where he massaged the bridge of his nose like it hurt. Scrunched up his face. Then opened his eyes and looked up at the woman.

"That's a boy," he said. "That's my son."

"Oh," said the woman. "Oh! I—"

"All right," I said, getting out of the hot tub. "That's great. Thanks."

"Nice work, you nosy cunt," I heard Dad say as I walked back to our room.

When we got back to San Diego, I did my usual thing of going to the beach. Only now I wore both my shorts and a T-shirt to swim in. I never took my shirt off in front of anyone again, if I could help it.

* * *

Late that spring, as I was nearing the end of my school year—such as it was—and thinking about going to Point Loma High School, Dad came down and knocked on my door.

"Yeah?" I said. I was sprawled in bed watching TV. As usual.

"Hey, Jason," Dad said, poking his head into my room. "I just got off the phone with Charles."

"How's he doing?" I asked.

"Billy died."

I looked at Dad. He looked like he was worrying more about me than thinking about what this might mean for him.

I couldn't decide if it would be better to get upset or seem like I was okay.

"That's too bad," I said. "Did it . . . how did it happen?"

"He just died. Pneumonia."

"The AIDS kind?" I didn't seem to be able to stop myself from asking.

"Yeah," Dad said. "That kind."

I looked at the wall above my TV and thought about Billy, tied to a stump, naked, and shot full of arrows.

"Okay," I said. "Thanks."

Dad lingered at the door for a second, then closed it and went back upstairs.

44

Near the end of our first summer in San Diego, Dad's boss got busted for tax evasion. Dad called a kind of family meeting to tell me about it.

"That still works?" I asked incredulously. Having been educated mostly by television, I couldn't find Kansas on a map, but I knew the Untouchables had put Al Capone away for tax evasion in 1931. I would have expected any competent criminal to know how to avoid such a thing.

"Well," Dad said. "It was sort of the lesser of two evils. He's been having some trouble with his in-laws. They've never really trusted him because he married into the family business, and I guess there's been some talk of maybe, you know, sending someone up here to blow his brains out over some perceived accounting irregularities. Or something. He was kind of vague on the details. So he may have engineered this tax thing so he could take a little break in Club Fed. Give everyone a chance to calm down."

"How long a little break?" I asked.

"Twelve to eighteen months. Give or take."

"Okay. So—" I realized why he was telling me this. "You don't have a job anymore."

"Right," Dad said.

"So what's that mean?"

"Well," Dad said. "We said we'd give this a year. We have our contingency plan back in Seattle, and that runs out in October. I can probably set something up again here. Something like what we had with Karl, or something better. But if we're going to leave, now's—"

"Let's go," I said.

"Well, I was—"

"What did Bruce say?" I asked.

"He wants to go back, too."

I wasn't surprised to hear that. Bruce hadn't been having an easy time of it in San Diego either. He wasn't as bored and lonely as I was, but he seemed to have a hard time matching the Southern California temperament. Which he and I agreed was uniformly rude and standoffish. It was pretty much the only thing we agreed on, besides our mutual love of Elvira, Mistress of the Dark, the campy hostess of a late-night TV show.

Bruce had mostly been keeping his unhappiness under wraps for Dad's sake, but he'd taken to pouring half a cup of pharmacy-grade grain alcohol into his coffee every morning to take the edge off. That was his traditional purchase on our Mexican shopping trips: I'd buy novelty weapons, Dad would buy rocks and textiles, and Bruce would buy Everclear.

"So," I said. "Are we doing it? Are we going home?"

Dad didn't want to say it, but he did.

"Yeah. I guess we are."

45

My return to Washington State wasn't especially triumphant. We had to spend a month living with Bruce's sister in Marysville while Scotty, the drug dealer who'd promised us his apartment if we returned, looked for a new place to live. I felt kind of bad about Scotty. He'd been in the same place on Capitol Hill since before the Indians came across the land bridge from Siberia, but a deal was a deal and Scotty had gotten a year of Section Eight housing, welfare checks, and food stamps for his trouble.

We were supposed to stay in Marysville until Scotty moved out, but after that first month, Dad said he couldn't handle Bruce's family anymore. He figured Scotty would be more motivated to find a place if we were in the apartment with him. He wasn't wrong.

* * *

Scotty's apartment, the one we were taking over, was in a converted house on the west slope of Capitol Hill. At some point in the distant past, it had been an enormous single-family home with a good-size backyard. Then it had been divided up into a bunch of sub-units. Each of the two main floors was converted into a spacious two-bedroom apartment. The attic and basement were turned into somewhat less spacious apartments. The backyard was paved over, for parking.

Whoever had converted the house into apartments had done kind of a half-assed job of it. There was one water heater for the entire building, and one fuse box. The fuse box was in the basement apartment, and each unit ran on one circuit. So if we turned on a space heater and a toaster at the same time, the whole apartment would go dark. Then someone would have to go downstairs and hope the neighbor was home to flip the breaker.

Otherwise, it was a nice apartment. There were two small bedrooms on the west side, with great views of the Space Needle and the mountains. The bathroom was next to the bedrooms, and there was a large kitchen with room for a table, and a dining room and living room on the east side of the house. The main entrance was a door on the west side that could be reached by going up an exterior staircase that was built onto the back of the building. There was also an old staircase left over from the original design of the house that went from the living room of our place, down to a lobby area on the first floor, and out to the front porch of the house. There was an awkward trapezoidal landing on our floor, outside the living room. The front yard was too small to use for anything, and it was mostly covered with some ugly, thorny shrubbery, just in case someone got any ideas about having any fun out there.

The refrigerator in our unit was self-defrosting, the cooking range was gas, and there was plenty of counter space.

When we moved in, Scotty had to retreat to one of the bedrooms on the west side of the house while he kept trying to find somewhere else to go. Dad and Bruce turned the living room into their bedroom, and the dining room was turned into a living room. Dad put all his birds on the landing, in the stairway outside their shared bedroom. I took the other back bedroom, across the hall from Scotty.

* * *

Scotty had always bothered me. When I was younger, it was because he didn't like kids and he was pretty open about that.

So I disliked him right back. As I got older, it got more complicated. Most of the gay men I'd met through my dad were just dudes who happened to have sex with other dudes. Plenty of them were palpably gay, but Scotty was the only full-on silk kimonos and eyeliner homo I knew personally. He lisped. He flounced. He actually had limp wrists, which I'd always thought was just some kind of weird story straight people made up to frighten their children. He shot smack, and when he was nodding he got even looser. I was thirteen years old, and I was trying to reconcile my dad's ever-shifting opinions on masculinity against what I was seeing on TV. Scotty just stressed me out.

One day Scotty found me in the bathroom, messing around with his hair products. He had various gels and mousses on the counter near the sink. I didn't know why he needed any of it. He had advanced male pattern baldness, and what hair he did have never seemed to be styled in any particular way. But my hair was always sticking out in ways that bugged me. I was trying to use some of Scotty's mysterious compounds to pin it down when I noticed him standing in the doorway, watching me and smoking a cigarette.

"Sorry," I said, stepping away from the counter. "I was just . . . I don't know what I was doing."

"It's fine," Scotty said, putting his cigarette in an ashtray next to the door. There were always ashtrays in the bathrooms of places where our people lived. He walked over and stood next to me, looking at me in the mirror. He was wearing a bright red embroidered kimono over a sleeveless undershirt and a pair of pajama pants. He was junkie-skinny, with big features and long fingers, like a cartoon. Small eyes. His light brown hair seemed to jump away from his head, like he'd been electrocuted.

"What are you trying to accomplish?" he asked.

"Just trying to get it to lie down," I said.

"Mm," he said. "I'm not sure that's the best look for you."

"What do you mean?" I asked.

He ran his fingers through my hair, pushing it into various shapes as he spoke.

"You have extremely thick hair," he said. "You can brush it down like that, but you're always going to be fighting with it. Why not brush it back, away from your face? That way it frames your features, and it's not always in your eyes."

"I don't like where my hairline is," I said. "It makes my forehead look too big."

He snorted. His forehead had probably been prominent even before he'd gone bald. My cheeks got hot, but I tried to keep my face blank.

"It's just not—" I stopped and tried to figure out what I was saying. "Most kids just have a part, then they let their hair fall down straight. Like the Hardy Boys."

It was 1985, but I still considered Sean Cassidy the height of fashion cool.

"So you want to look like everyone else?" Scotty asked.

"I guess," I said. "It's easier."

He shrugged. "Fuck those people, Jason. You can drive yourself crazy, trying to get them to accept you. It's a waste of your precious life, believe me."

He picked up his cigarette and started to leave the bathroom.

"Scotty?" I said. "Your friends—why don't they ever come over? Nobody's come over since we've been here."

I didn't know where the question came from, but I'd always had the impression, before we moved to San Diego, that Scotty had tons of friends—that his social calendar was always full. That he knew everyone, and that everyone knew him. But in the time since we'd been back I hadn't seen him leave the house, let alone have anyone over.

He smiled. "I'm a drug dealer, dear. We don't have friends, we have customers. And all my customers are dying."

Then he went back into his room, where I heard him turn the radio on to a jazz station. I'd surmised it was what he liked to listen to when he was shooting up.

I stood in front of the mirror for a while longer, pushing my hair down and brushing it straight with my fingers until I couldn't stand it anymore. I needed it cut, I decided. That was all. I just needed to cut it all off.

* * *

Scotty moved out at the end of that month, to an apartment a few blocks away. Dad took Scotty's room as his own. He still slept with Bruce in the living room, but he liked having his own room as a retreat.

"Is it true?" I asked Dad a few weeks later. "That Scotty doesn't have any friends?"

"Evidently," Dad said. "He always had friends as long as he was dealing. People wanted to talk to him so he'd get them high for free, over a cup of tea or something. Now? People are afraid to get too close. They don't want to have to take care of him."

"Take care of him?" I asked.

"He's got the lesions," Dad said. "Kaposi's. On his back, a couple of months ago."

46

Dad and I spent a few weeks arguing about whether I should go to high school or not. It was the same argument over and over again, once every other day or so. He thought I should get my GED and find a job.

"I'm thirteen," I said. "They don't let thirteen-year-olds work in Washington State."

"Then go to college," Dad said. "That way you can get a better job when you're finally old enough."

"Dad," I said. "I think maybe I need to spend some time around people my own age. I think there's sort of something wrong with me. From skipping so much school?"

"What are you talking about?" he asked.

"I'm not normal."

"What's so great about being normal?" he asked. "Normal people are monsters."

"I cry during Coke commercials."

"What?"

"And *Family Ties* reruns," I said.

"Are you making a joke?"

"Yes," I said. "I'm making a joke. But not about needing to be with some kids my own age. That part I'm totally serious about."

"Fine," he said. "Don't come crying to me when you can't stand it. Again."

"I won't," I promised.

* * *

I was intimidated by our new apartment. It was the first place I'd lived that was properly urban. I'd visited cities and slept over in apartment buildings, but I'd never really lived in one. Not since the place Dad had caught on fire, after we moved out of the Hayes Street house.

West Capitol Hill was a neighborhood full of apartments, condominiums, and town houses. Every block was a mixture of three- and four-story brick buildings from the twenties, converted houses, and various kinds of mid-century architectural monstrosities, about half of which had been built as hotels for the World's Fair in 1962. When the fair was over, the former hotels were converted into hideous, badly made, low-rent housing that festered around the neighborhood for decades. It seemed like I couldn't walk past one without witnessing some kind of ugly domestic violence drama in the parking lot, or seeing a couple of junkies screaming at each other on the balconies.

The people living in purpose-built homes weren't much better off. The news stories were always about how the whole country was in the middle of a massive crime wave. Poor people were still mostly concentrated in the cities, so the neighborhood had something of a bunker mentality. All over that side of Capitol Hill, windows were broken, boarded, painted over, or blocked up with stacks of garbage that had been shoved against them by pensioners or drug addicts, people who had been locked away from the sunlight for decades. Not one building in ten had been repainted since Nixon was in office, and driveways and garages were full of broken-down cars covered in layers of moss and rust, some of them packed to the gills with junk, like wheeled storage units with dirty windshields.

There was an abandoned house at the end of my block with a chestnut tree growing up through the shattered roof. Homeless people squatted there, and junkies used it as a shooting gallery. Ten years later the house would burn down and the land alone would be worth a quarter million dollars, but in 1985 it was just this black hole, kitty-corner to the convenience store and the laundromat.

There were almost no yards or parks in the neighborhood, which I assumed meant there were no kids. Or if there were kids, I wouldn't get to meet them, because they'd never have any reason to go outside.

When I took Thunder for walks, I went over to a vacant seven-story apartment tower half a block to the south. The building had a small grassy area behind it that was perfect for a doggy bathroom. Dad said the project had been started four years earlier, then run out of money before it was completed. I thought that must have been frustrating for the developers. The heavy work had already been done. The concrete walls, floors, and balconies were all poured and ready. The underground parking garage was completed. It was just missing its moving parts: doors, windows, and elevators. And, of course, people.

My dad had showed me pictures once of a place he'd visited with his mom when he was a kid, called Mesa Verde—an abandoned Indian city built in a cave on the side of a giant cliff. The empty tower reminded me of that. Not just forsaken, but hopeless.

* * *

Between the move back from San Diego, the stopover in Marysville, and the delay in getting unpacked while Scotty found a new place, I carried on my grand tradition of registering for school late. I signed up for ninth grade two weeks after classes started, in September of 1985. I ended up going to Garfield, one of several mostly black south end high schools in comparatively white Seattle. Dad had tried to get me into one of the north end schools, because that was what most white parents tried to do in the eighties, but Seattle had a mandatory busing program designed to desegregate the public education system. Apparently someone at the district office thought that busing me out of my neighborhood so I could go to school in a whiter part of town would undermine that mission.

Registering for school meant me and my dad going to the main office at Garfield and filling out paperwork. Bringing Dad to any place where there were a lot of straights was always kind of a nervous business, but I couldn't see any way around it. He made the appointment and drove me over there in the Volvo. He brought my records from San Diego with him in a beat-up manila envelope, which was his preferred tool for organizing papers.

The school was big; two blocks long, one block wide, and three stories tall over most of its length, with a redbrick and terra-cotta exterior. I didn't get much of a sense of how it was put together. Dad parked in the small lot near the main entrance of the building and we went up three flights of concrete steps to the front doors. There were trophy cases in the lobby, and we passed a psychedelic mural that included images of Jimi Hendrix, Bruce Lee, and some guy I didn't recognize who was playing a trumpet. Someone told me later he was Quincy Jones, and that the school auditorium was named for him.

When we got up to the office on the second floor, I found it was like most school offices I'd been in, only bigger: lots of wood trim and cabinets that had been varnished half to death over sixty years. Fluorescent lights, secretaries with big hair, and the smell of mimeograph solvent. Dad checked in with one of the secretaries and we sat down across from another family in a little waiting area; a very straight-looking older black couple and a girl about my age. The dad was actually wearing a tie.

We sat there for a few minutes before I caught the girl's eye. She had short hair and a tight-fitting yellow sweater over acid-washed jeans. Sneakers that looked almost like ballet shoes and socks with little ruffles around the ankles. I thought her outfit looked kind of 1950s.

"You signing up for ninth grade?" I asked.

"Yes," she said.

"Where'd you move here from?" I asked.

"Rainier Beach," she said. "You?"

"San Diego," I said.

"Is that where you're from?" she asked.

"No," I said. "Mostly I'm from here, I guess. Oregon before that. And sort of L.A. for a little while. We lived in Ballard before we moved to San Diego."

"Oh," she said.

"I'm Jason," I said.

"Sharon."

We all sat quietly for a while longer. Finally, one of the guidance counselors called the girl and her family into another office to fill out their paperwork.

"Maybe I'll see you in class," I said, as she got up to leave.

"Maybe," she said.

She was smiling when she left. I felt good. Proud of myself for overcoming my shyness and talking to someone right off the bat. A girl, even.

"You shouldn't be so chatty," Dad said.

"What do you mean?" I asked.

"You couldn't see how uncomfortable you were making her?"

I hadn't seen anything of the sort, but this was something Dad had been on me about recently—that I missed social cues. The nature of the thing meant that I had to take his word for it, or not. There was no way for me to judge whether what he was telling me was true.

"Why was I making her uncomfortable?" I asked. "Did I say something wrong?"

"Guys like you just don't talk to girls like that," Dad said.

I didn't know what he meant. I tried to picture it from his perspective, to figure out what he was seeing. I was big for my age, but my face still looked very young; I had a weak chin and I carried a lot of baby fat in my cheeks. I wore a brown polyester ski jacket—a thrift store purchase I wore more or less year-round, even in San Diego. It was getting to be too small for me. I'd solved the problem of my wild hair the week before by buying a camouflage-patterned cap at a surplus store downtown. It was the kind the Marines wore. Instead of brushing my hair in the morning I just shoved the hat over it before I left the house. My jeans were dirty, because I only owned two pairs, and my shoes were beat-up Chuck Taylor high tops. When I pictured that guy talking to a pretty, well-dressed girl like Sharon, I started to get an idea what my dad might be trying to tell me.

Eventually we got called into a guidance counselor's office. I didn't have much choice of classes because everything was already full, and I had a lot of mandatory courses I had to take. I wanted to learn Spanish, but I ended up in German. The counselor gave Dad a folder that included my schedule, a map of the school, and a sign-off sheet for my teachers to fill out. Otherwise I didn't follow a lot of what my dad and the counselor were talking about. I was having trouble letting go of the conversations I'd had in the waiting room.

47

Dad and I had registered me for school on a Friday, so I had the weekend home before I had to start yet another foray into public education. We spent part of it running laundry back and forth from the laundromat a block away. The distance was small but the load was big, so Dad had brought our clothes home in the car. I was taking a load up to our apartment when I saw a guy about my age stalking along the walkway of an apartment building two lots down, carrying a squirt bottle.

He looked like he was engaged in a TV shootout, except for the part where he was a teenager with a squirt bottle. I went back down and got another load of laundry from the car, and as I got up to my porch I saw another kid creeping through the backyard of the house next door—also carrying a squirt bottle. I dropped the laundry inside, then went and stood at the railing, watching to see what would happen next. When the kid in the yard next door noticed me he held up his squirt bottle, raised his eyebrows, and said, "You wanna play?"

"Uh, sure," I said. "I'll be right there."

I turned and took two casual steps back from the railing, then ran into the house and started digging frantically through the stuff under the kitchen sink, looking for our old green squirt bottle that we'd had since Eugene.

"Dad!" I shouted. "Where's the squirt bottle?"

"Hall closet!" he called from the front bedroom.

I found it on a shelf, then ran into the kitchen and rinsed it, in case it was full of bleach water or something. Then I was back out the door and pounding down the stairs.

The kid who was waiting for me down there was

strange-looking. Or rather, he was sort of classically handsome except for being kind of short and fat. He had a chiseled jaw, cleft chin, straight nose, high forehead, and thick blond hair that seemed to fall naturally into a perfect side part. It was the perfection of his face relative to his pronounced frumpiness that made him weird-looking. He was wearing baggy cargo pants and a sweatshirt; the preferred style of male teens with a weight problem, in my observation. It was similar to what I wore myself.

"I'm Ethan," he said.

"Jason," I said. "Nice to meet you."

"Come on," he said.

He led me between buildings, to the sidewalk out in front of my place. Then he waved down the block to one of his friends, who waved to someone else and came jogging our way.

A few minutes later there were three other kids on the sidewalk with us. One was a tall skinny guy with broad shoulders, enormous hands, a jutting lantern jaw, and tiny, close-set eyes that were magnified to almost-normal proportions by a pair of Coke-bottle glasses in thick plastic frames. He had a tuft of stiff dark blond hair jutting out of the top of his head, like a Muppet. Next to him was another tall skinny guy, with a wild mop of dark brown hair, terrible skin, and large yellow teeth, which were noticeable because he smiled almost constantly. Both the taller kids wore jeans, T-shirts, and button-down shirts in neutral colors. The guy with the glasses had a stencil of a bird's skull printed on his T-shirt.

Finally, there was another short, heavyset kid with light brown hair in a classic bowl cut. He looked like an understudy from the cast of *The Goonies*, with a child actor's round features, large eyes, and freckles. Like Ethan, he had everything going for him except his build, his height, and his sense of style: he was wearing a tight black T-shirt over a pair of navy parachute pants and some blue Nike tennis shoes with a bright yellow wave on the side. Even a fashion disaster like me could see that it was a bad look.

"Everyone," Ethan said. "This is Jason. Jason, this is Brunner." The giant with the weird face nodded at me.

"Kyle," Ethan said, gesturing at the kid with the teeth, who smiled and unleashed a string of gibberish.

"He pretends to be Australian when he's nervous," Ethan supplied.

"Oh," I said. "Yeah, I can see that."

"And this is my brother," Ethan said, pointing at the bowl cut kid. "Brandon."

"Hey," I said.

"Nice to meet you," Brandon said.

* * *

Brandon and Ethan lived in the house next door to mine. We spent most of the day taking each other's measure, trying to figure out if it was a good thing or a bad thing that we were neighbors. When they asked me questions about myself, I tried to sound more interesting than I was. My version of that involved talking about my love of martial arts and my exciting life as a surfer in San Diego. I giggled compulsively when I lied.

After a few hours of chasing each other around with squirt bottles, Ethan and his brother invited me to their place with the other guys, to get some food and cool down. Their house was roughly the same size as my building, but it had never been converted to apartments; it was still a single-family home. Normally that would mean money, but I wasn't sure what to expect here. The backyard was full of weeds, piles of broken masonry, and garbage. The front yard was paved over in red brick, with two cars parked there: a Honda Civic that had seen better days and an old red Volkswagen Beetle. The house itself was in poor repair from the outside, with peeling white paint, a few damaged and broken windows, and no real porch; just a set of wooden stairs nailed onto the front of the house, leading up to the door.

The inside, it turned out, was even worse off.

"We're renovating," Ethan said, when I paused in the doorway and looked around.

"Okay," I said.

The main floor was one large open space. The ceiling was made of clean, new drywall with recessed lighting fixtures. There was a bay window in the living room, with new venetian blinds on it. But everything else was gutted. The walls were either bare drywall with the mud and tape still showing, or they were exposed studs. The floors were chipboard, except where they were covered with carpet remnants or the battered remains of old Persian rugs. There was a kitchen in the back of the house, separated from the rest of the main floor by a long counter. The front of the room was home to a few chairs and couches and an old color TV. The open space between the kitchen and the sitting area was occupied by a grand piano.

Kyle, Brunner, and the others made themselves at home. I stared at the piano.

Ethan caught my look.

"It's Brandon's," he said.

"It's . . . a piano," I said.

The instrument was all polished wood and majesty. As I circled it I saw the name Steinway & Sons above the keyboard cover. I had a vague recollection that it was a good brand, in sort of the same way that I knew Dom Pérignon was good champagne, some half-remembered quote from a movie or something.

"Our parents got it for him when we were little," Ethan said. "I got a violin. It's downstairs. Smaller, but worth about as much money."

253

"How much is that?" I couldn't stop myself from asking.

"Now? Fifteen thousand. About."

"So that's worth $7,500?" I asked, pointing at the piano and thinking about the fact that my dad and I got something like $4,000 a year in welfare.

"No," Ethan said, looking annoyed. "Fifteen thousand each."

"I love this thing," Kyle said, sitting down and opening the fallboard that covered the keys. He started to play a few Joplin tunes that I recognized from elementary school music classes, blending one effortlessly into the next. I suddenly felt very much out of my depth. I'd never met anyone my own age who could play an instrument, let alone just sit down and start improvising.

"How . . . does one come to . . . buy a piano?" I asked Ethan.

"You mean how did we find it?" Ethan asked.

"No," I said, trying to figure out how to phrase the question. "I just mean—I don't think I've ever seen one in someone's house before."

Kyle glanced up from where he was playing and gave me a very different kind of smile from the goofy, affable one he'd been showing me all day. It gave me the idea that I'd just stepped in something.

Ethan cocked his head like a confused cocker spaniel, but Brandon, who was assembling sandwiches in the kitchen, answered the question I was trying to ask.

"Our dad's business partner ripped him off," he said. "We used to live up north, by Montlake. Big house. Big yard. Tennis courts. Fountain out front. Dad had to sell all that off to cover the losses from the business partner thing, but Mom insisted we keep the piano and the violin. When all the dust cleared, Dad had just enough money left for one investment. So he bought this place to fix it up and resell it. The plan is that he'll use the profits to buy two places, fix those up and resell them. And so on."

"What was your dad's business?" I asked. "Before?"

"Investment banker," Ethan offered.

I'd never heard that answer to that question before. I wasn't even sure what it meant. I decided to change the subject.

"How long have you been working on the house?" I asked.

"Two years," Brandon said.

"You should have seen it when we bought it," Ethan said. "The family that lived here had been here pretty much since it was built, but they went broke twenty years ago. Then they just sat in here and went crazy. They had so many cats in the basement that the cat pee leaked into the foundation and disintegrated the concrete. The whole house was listing. We had to jack it up and repour the foundation. That was twenty grand right there. For cat pee."

Brandon nodded. "Rotten books and magazines in all the rooms, rats everywhere in spite of the cats. Old clothes, rotten food. It was disgusting."

I looked around at the bare, unfinished floors and the exposed wiring.

"So it's better now," I said.

Brandon made a "so-so" gesture with his hand.

48

I caught my school bus on the corner of Broadway and Republican Street at seven o'clock in the morning. Broadway was the Seattle equivalent of San Francisco's Castro, or New York's Fire Island; it was the center of the city's gay community. But at seven on a weekday morning it was mostly just cold, wet, and empty. I stood on the corner for five or ten awkward minutes, next to the Fred Meyer where I used to buy my action figures. A few more teens came from down the hill: A tall older guy with big features and light brown, wavy hair. Denim jacket, jeans and sneakers, all well broken in. A compact, dark-haired kid about my age, with weirdly pale skin and new clothes—new jeans, new shoes, new jacket. Looked like a vampire, for some reason. Then Brandon and Ethan. I was glad to see some familiar faces, but they didn't go out of their way to be friendly and I didn't push it.

When the big yellow school bus finally came along and stopped for us, I got on and sat near the front. Brandon and Ethan sat farther back. The smell of the green vinyl seats was strong enough to make my head spin. I tried to breathe through my mouth and not to make eye contact with anyone.

Getting off the bus and walking into the school was completely disorienting. A lot of the "kids" looked like adults to me, and the halls were packed solid with them. It was impossible to move without bumping into someone. I'd looked at a mimeographed map of the school the night before to figure out where my classes were, but the reality was just overwhelming.

I found my way to my first period World History class and stepped gratefully out of the crush of people moving through the hall. The layout of the classroom was similar to the classes in my school in Ballard, with desks for about thirty students, all facing a teacher's desk and the blackboard behind it at the front of the room. The students' desks were different than they had been in elementary school. In Ballard, the desks had flip tops, so we could store our supplies and books in them. Here, the desks were simple plastic chairs with wood writing surfaces attached and a small wire rack underneath the seat. The rack was ostensibly for storing books, but it was too small to put things on and it divided the space under the seat so I wouldn't be able to fit my backpack down there—which would mean I'd have to put my gear in the aisle.

That would be no small thing. I'd been told when I registered that all the lockers were taken, so I was going to have to carry all my textbooks in the blue nylon backpack my dad had used for community college back in Eugene.

The room itself was comfortingly old—light-colored hardwood floors, plaster-and-lath walls under thick layers of dark purple paint, wood trim, built-in wooden supply cabinets with leaded glass windows, and the blackboard set in an age-darkened wooden frame. The school colors were purple and white, so every wall in the place was painted various mismatched shades of purple.

The desk at the front of the room was made of battle-scarred oak, with an oak swivel chair parked behind it. The room had fifteen-foot ceilings, with banks of fluorescent lights dangling down on steel cables.

There was no teacher at the desk, so I picked out the first white kid I saw who wasn't involved in a conversation. Some Ballard-style headbanger in a denim jacket, with a mullet.

"Is there assigned seating?" I asked.

"What?" He frowned at me.

"Is there assigned seating?" I asked again. "I'm new. Can I just sit anywhere, or is there assigned seating?"

"I don't know, man."

Yeah, okay, I thought. It's going to be that kind of day.

I picked an empty seat at random and sat down in it. Sure enough, a few minutes later, a girl in a tight pink sweater walked in, scowled at me, and said, "You're in my seat."

"Sorry," I said. "Is there an empty seat?"

"I don't know," she said. "But that's my seat."

"Screw it," I muttered. I felt too conspicuous standing at the front of the class, so I sat in the teacher's chair and watched the room fill up.

A minute after the bell rang a harried-looking woman in her mid-thirties came in, clutching a giant stack of books and folders. She had black plastic glasses with enormous frames, and short-cropped curly dark brown hair. She was wearing a sweater vest over a blouse, and wool slacks.

"Ms. Gibson?" I asked. "I'm Jason. I'm new. I'm supposed to get your signature on my registration form and ask you for a textbook."

She looked at me and blinked owlishly.

"You're in my seat," she said.

* * *

The rest of the day went pretty much like the first part of it had. I had swimming for second period, which I'd chosen because it seemed less awful than regular physical education. After first period I asked someone at random where the swimming pool was. It wasn't on the map I'd been looking at the night before.

"It's on the fourth floor," the kid said.

"The . . . ? I didn't think there was a fourth floor."

"You've gotta take the elevator," he said.

"Where's that?"

"End of that hall," he said, pointing.

I went where he'd directed me, but when I found the elevator it had a key lock.

"Hey," I said to a guy who was standing by the corner watching other kids go by. "How do I work this?"

"You don't," he said. "It's only for crippled kids."

"Then how'm I supposed to get to the fourth floor?"

"There is no fourth floor," he said.

"That's what I thought," I said. "But where's the pool?"

"Oh," he said. "The fourth floor pool gag. Sorry, man, someone was fucking with you. The pool's outside the building, down the hill. Big concrete thing. Looks like a bomb shelter."

"Which way?" I asked.

"That way," he said, pointing toward the north end of the school. "Out the doors, down the stairs. You can't miss it."

I didn't entirely believe him, but I asked a few other people and got the same story. The pool was half a block north of the main building, in an underground building that looked like a giant concrete bunker. When I found my way inside, I located the teacher, Mr. Ryerson, a hugely overweight white guy in his early sixties with a well-oiled pompadour, a broad, jowly face, and a bulbous nose. He was wearing nylon trunks under a bulky sweatshirt, but he didn't look like he'd been in the water since he destroyed the *Pequod* and dragged Ahab screaming into the depths. I gave him my registration form to sign and asked him where I was supposed to get shorts.

"You don't have any swimming trunks with you?" he growled.

"Uh," I said, "I thought I'd get them here. Like a textbook or something?"

His expression said he thought I must be joking. In a bad way.

"Christ, Schmidt," he said, pointing to the bleachers that overlooked the pool. "You can sit it out today. Tomorrow, bring some goddamn shorts."

* * *

Finding the cafeteria for lunch, at least, was no problem. It was a large room located on the first floor. We ate in two shifts, and it looked to me like a pretty significant number of kids ate off campus. Anyone was allowed to leave school grounds for lunch, but I didn't have money for restaurant food. A full lunch in the cafeteria was a buck ten, and milk was a quarter. I qualified for the free lunch program automatically, because my dad and I were still on welfare, but I'd learned in elementary school that using a free lunch card was more trouble than it was worth. Students on the regular meal program got a blue card. Free lunch kids got a pink card; anyone saw that pink card, it was nonstop bullshit for the rest of the year.

As I walked down the stairs to the cafeteria I passed some guys sitting at the base of the stairs. They were laughing and telling jokes, and one of them was doing . . . I didn't know what the hell he was doing. I'd never seen anything like it. He had his hand cupped over his mouth, and he seemed to be spitting into it. And hissing. And then making some kind of other weird noise. As I got closer I realized he was making a pretty consistent rhythm, like a cheap synthesizer. Suddenly we made eye contact and he stopped and pointed at me and started laughing.

"Man," he said. "Check that dude out!"

He looked at his friends and opened his eyes wide, then mimed staring at something that was going past, like some slack-jawed rube seeing his first horseless carriage. My face got hot and I stormed past him while he and his friends laughed at me.

* * *

When the day finally ended I went out the south doors of the school and found bus #320 parked with a dozen or so others. I sat down in the front-most seat, across the aisle from the driver, and felt the tension oozing out of my body. I'd survived. And more than that, I'd been vindicated. After the isolation of San Diego, the feeling of being packed into that enormous building with so many other students was like staggering onto land after a shipwreck. Making friends was almost secondary. All day, I had to talk to people, negotiate with people, listen to them, and be listened to by them. All different kinds of people. If four years in that place didn't pound me into some semblance of normalcy, nothing would.

49

I had one sheet of paper where I kept all my phone numbers. They were written in a dozen different kinds of pen, the sheet folded and unfolded so many times there were holes where the creases intersected. Eventually I sat down with the telephone in my room and put my sheet of paper in front of me.

I'd always had an extremely active imagination. In San Diego a lot of my imagining had been about my friends in Seattle. I played out scenarios in my head where I'd visit or move back, and they'd be really glad to see me. There'd be some kind of party. Hearty handshakes and welcome homes. And we'd do things. Better things than we'd done before. Water parks and movies. All-night Dungeons & Dragons marathons. Acrobatics. In my mind, getting to play with other kids again would feel like doing backflips. Like breaking free of gravity.

My problem—or one of my problems—was that even I couldn't delude myself into thinking anyone besides Eddie would be glad to see me again. Sitting in my bedroom, looking at my phone list, I knew I had to internalize the idea that calling the guys I'd known in Ballard wasn't going to be a good experience. There was no question of not doing it. In spite of having met and hung out with Ethan and Brandon, precedent suggested that

I shouldn't assume I was going to make even a single friend in my new neighborhood or my new school. So it was this or nothing. But the trick I'd only recently learned was that expecting things to suck—really convincing myself ahead of time that everything was going to suck big dirty ass—significantly reduced the sting when the reality lived up to my worst expectations. So there'd be no party. There'd be no water park. Most of them probably wouldn't be happy to hear from me.

I swallowed the idea as many times as I had to in order to make it stay down, then I picked up the phone and dialed Gabe's number.

He was the first friend I'd made at my elementary school in Ballard, and he was geographically closest to me. The lawyer his mom had married owned a big house in Montlake, an upper-class neighborhood on the north end of Capitol Hill, where a lot of University of Washington faculty lived.

I called the last number I had for him, with a Capitol Hill prefix.

"Hello?"

I recognized his voice immediately.

"Gabe," I said. "It's Jason. I'm back in town."

"Who?"

"Jason Schmidt."

"Oh . . . okay?"

"I'm back in town," I said.

"Right. You said that."

"Yeah. I was thinking—you wanna do something sometime?"

"I'm kind of busy," he said.

"I . . . okay. Uh, like maybe next weekend then?"

"Nope," he said. "Got plans."

"Sure, okay . . ." I said.

"Hey, I gotta go," he said.

"I'll try you some other time."

"Uh. Sure. Okay. Bye."

I hung up the phone. Then I went to the kitchen and got a piece of bread. I wadded it up and tucked it into the corner of my mouth as I went back to my bedroom, lay down on my bed, and stared at the ceiling for a while. I waited for my face to stop feeling hot; I waited to stop wanting to punch things. I sucked on the wad of whole wheat bread like a piece of candy; it was a trick I'd learned for staving off hunger without eating very much actual food. Besides curing my munchies, it was also strangely relaxing.

When I thought I was back under control I got up and called Ryan, in Ballard. That call went better. No water parks or parties, but I went over to his house later that afternoon and we sat around in his living room watching football on TV. I didn't know anything about football, in spite of having watched hundreds of hours of it at my grandparents' house. I didn't understand the rules or the scoring. I didn't care. We talked about kids from Mr. Fields's class during commercial breaks. He told me about a new gaming system he was into.

For the first time in months I felt like I existed.

50

About two weeks after school started, Eddie and I decided to go fishing down at Shilshole Bay, as sort of a reunion tour. I got a bus to Ballard early in the morning, and we made it out to the bay in time to lay down a dozen or so drop lines. Then we went to all our old haunts: the dinghy we used to hide under during rainy days, where we'd eat lunch and Eddie would get high; the rope swing above the railroad tracks, where a child molester had once approached us and tried to lure us into the bushes so we could watch him jerk off. We brought our slingshots and spent a few hours breaking beer bottles the hoboes left in the drainage ditches next to the tracks. Then, as it started to get dark, we went back to the bay and checked our lines. We hadn't caught anything. So we walked to the Ballard Locks and caught a bus up to his house.

We got off on 3rd and Market, where we'd always gotten off. As we were leaving the bus, we ran into David Milcher, a kid who'd been in Mr. Fields's class with us.

"Hey, Dave," I said, as we went past him.

"Hey, Jason!" he said, getting on the bus.

I turned around in time to see Eddie cutting around the front of the bus. Normally that wasn't a good idea, but this particular bus stop was at an intersection with a terrific light. I assumed the light was red because the bus wasn't moving, but the way it was blocking the crosswalk, I couldn't see the pedestrian signal on the other side. I assumed Eddie had checked it though, so I followed him into the street. That was as much as I remembered, afterward.

* * *

When I woke up, my head hurt. It took me a second to figure out that I was in the back of an ambulance. There was a man in blue coveralls sitting on a bench on the other side of the ambulance, just at the edge of my vision. Eddie was sitting next to him. The ambulance was moving. And my head hurt because it was taped down. I'd been taped to a gurney, and the tape on my forehead was so tight that it was pulling the skin. Just like when I'd fallen off the high dive.

I opened my mouth to talk, but my face was just one big wound. My mouth sent stabs of pain shooting down my jaw and into my spine. I felt around with my tongue and realized I was missing one of my top front teeth. My lips were hamburger. When I explored my bottom lip I could feel a place about halfway down where something was cold. It took me a second to realize that the cold feeling was air. There was a hole in my bottom lip, about a half inch down from my mouth. I'd gotten braces while we were in San Diego. It was one of the things Dad had done during our short burst of prosperity while working for Karl the drug trafficker. They were gone now—just scraped off my teeth, leaving pieces of dental cement behind. Apparently at least part of them had been scraped off right through my face.

"Eddie," I whispered. He looked down at me. He looked mad. In a scared and worried kind of way. "What happened?"

"You got hit by a car, dude," he said.

"Where's my front tooth?" I asked. "Did you find it?"

"No," he said. "I fucking looked, while they were loading you up. It could have come out anywhere."

"Did you look on the ground?"

"Dude," he said. "You bounced for about fifty fucking feet. You flew all the way across the fucking street and partway down the next fucking block. I fucking—I checked in all the places I saw you skid, but—fuck, dude. I don't know what to tell you."

"Can you move your toes?" the medic asked.

"Yeah," I said, wiggling them.

"Fingers?" he asked.

"Sure. I'm really worried about the tooth though."

"Don't be," he said.

"Eddie," I said. I was starting to panic, thinking about my tooth. And my braces. My dad was going to kill me. I started crying.

"Jason," Eddie said. "You need to be quiet. Your mouth—I'm worried you're gonna tear it."

I closed my eyes and tried to think about what else might be wrong. I could feel all my parts. I could breathe. Everything seemed to be where it was supposed to be.

"How's my brain?" I asked the medic.

"It's fine," he said. "Or it seems fine. You mostly landed on your face."

I almost laughed. Then I stopped.

"Someone called my dad?" I asked.

"Yeah," Eddie said. "Someone called him. He'll meet us at the hospital. Now seriously, dude. Shut the fuck up."

* * *

When we got to the hospital, a doctor came and looked at me. He flashed a light in my eyes and checked my reflexes. He told me I seemed to be in surprisingly good shape, all things considered. My spine seemed fine, but they needed to do some tests before they let me move. Then he took off and left me taped to the gurney in the hallway. Eddie was leaning against the wall a few feet away, looking exhausted. I was about to say something to him when I heard my dad's voice, calling my name. Eddie glanced up, and his face went scared again. Dad was coming from the direction my feet were pointing so I couldn't look at him, but he was saying my name over and over again, and then his face came into view. It was his purple-bulging-vein face, more than his oh-son-how-are-you face.

"Jason!" he hissed at me as he got closer. "What. The. Fuck?"

"Dad, I'm sorry. I—"

"Let me see your—oh shit! Goddamn it!" He fingered my mouth to move my lips around, looking at the condition of my teeth. "What the hell? Your braces. Your tooth. Oh my fucking— after all the money I spent on these? Are you kidding me?"

266

"Dad—" I said, when he took his hand away from my mouth.

"And you!" he shouted, turning on Eddie. "You mother-fucker, I knew something like this would happen if he just kept hanging out with you long enough! I fucking knew it! I told him a million times you were a bad influence—and now look at him!"

"Dad!" I said.

"You shut your goddamn mouth!" he yelled at me. "And you," he said, turning back to Eddie. "Don't ever let me see you darken my door again. I mean it, you piece of shit. I ever hear about Jason so much as walking down your block, I'll be calling Child Protective Services on your junkie mom faster than you can say what the fuck happened!"

"Dad!" I shouted again.

Eddie looked from me to my dad. His face was red and clenched, and I could see that Dad had just said what Eddie had been thinking the whole ride in the ambulance. He didn't even say anything back. He just turned around and left. I was sobbing by that point.

"Dad!" I said.

"Mr. Schmidt?" I couldn't look up, but I knew the doctor was back.

"Mr. Schmidt," the doctor said again, as he walked up next to me. "I'm going to have to ask you to wait outside. You're upsetting him."

"I'm upsetting him?" Dad sneered.

The doctor surprised me by grabbing Dad's arm. Hard.

"Yes," the doctor said. "You're upsetting him. Whatever you think happened here, I assure you, he's been through enough. Can I talk to you outside, please?"

The doctor physically dragged my dad down the hallway, toward the same door Eddie had just gone out of. I expected the doctor to come back, but he didn't. I was alone in the hall-way for so long that I was starting to fall asleep when I heard footsteps nearby. I opened my eyes and there was a cop standing over me. Cop uniform, cop face. Dark brown hair. Dark brown mustache. Glasses with thick plastic frames.

"Jason Schmidt?" he asked.

"Yeah," I said. My throat seemed to have gotten dry while I was lying there.

He held up a pad and tore a piece of paper loose, then put it on my chest.

"What is that?" I asked.

"Jaywalking ticket," he said. Then he turned around and left.

* * *

The doctors wanted to keep me overnight for observation, but they couldn't stop talking about how incredible it was that I was even alive, let alone so relatively unharmed. I didn't feel unharmed. I felt like I'd been dragged over a mile-long cheese grater. I had a scab that went from my forehead to my chin. My lips were puffed up to three times their normal size, and my face was full of tiny pieces of gravel. The insides of my lips had been ground into raw meat by my braces. My nose was completely crushed. My hands, knees, and elbows were all shredded. I had a cut on the side of my left knee that went past the skin, down to some kind of white material that was either fat or cartilage. Everything hurt. On the other hand, except for my nose and my tooth, I hadn't broken a single bone, and I'd nearly totaled the car that hit me. So maybe it was another miracle tale of survival after all.

On the morning after my overnight observation, the hospital brought in a dentist to look at my face. She was Swedish.

"Ya," she said, peering into my mouth with her little penlight. "We're going to need to do some major work in here. Get this old cement off. Put in new braces. But there is no point replacing that tooth right away. I am not even sure you will keep the ones around the missing one. They are all completely shattered. Like a teacup? The kind with all the cracks, that holds together anyway? That's your front teeth. The only thing holding them together is what's under the enamel."

"So I have to just . . . have no tooth?" I asked, when she was done.

"For a while," she said.

"How long is a while?" I asked.

She shrugged. "A year or two."

Dad picked me up that afternoon. He'd called my school and told them I'd be out for two weeks, and asked them if they could send my homework to me. Brandon and Ethan came by after school the next day to drop off my assignments.

"Wow," Brandon said, staring at my face.

"Dude," Ethan said. "Did the car hit you, just, like, right in your face?"

"Is that my homework?" I asked, nodding at the paper Brandon was holding in his hand.

"Uh," he said, glancing down. "Yeah. Are you okay?"

"Great," I said, plucking it out of his hand. "Thanks."

I did my homework for the week in a few hours. Then I went to bed for three days. The accident had happened on a Saturday. I went back to school the following Thursday, as soon as the swelling in my lips went down. My teachers were all surprised to see me. I said I was fine. It looked worse than it was. And, unlike at home, at least nobody at school was yelling at me about my fucking braces.

269

51

Some kids at school started right in on me about the missing tooth. A guy in my history class started calling me Gappy, which, fortunately, didn't stick. But the accident seemed to earn me some cred with Ethan and Brandon, who, having seen me in the immediate aftermath, were loudly amazed by how little I bruised and how quickly I healed up. They were especially impressed when I squeezed the odd piece of black gravel out of a healed cut, which I was able to do pretty regularly for a few weeks.

"You're like that Wolverine guy, in the comics," Brandon said.

If we'd been on a date, that line would have gotten him to at least third base.

I eased into my friendship with the brothers, playing it as cool as I could given how desperate I was to make friends. We started out in the backyard, messing around with a throwing knife their dad had brought back from Indonesia a decade before. We could spend hours taking turns hurling it at a piece of plywood that we'd leaned up against their back porch. Then I had the idea to bring down some of the cheap bullwhips I'd bought in Tijuana, and that was another skill set we built together. We practiced on milkweed and thistles at first. When Halloween rolled around we tied pieces of braided copper wire to our whip tassels and used them to slice pumpkins to shreds.

In between all the wanton destruction, we watched movies on their fancy top-loading VCR. Summit Foods, the corner store down the street, had a selection of VHS tapes they displayed on an old wire rack designed for paperback books. They only carried a dozen or so movies we ever wanted to watch. *Star Wars, Time Bandits,* and *Escape from New York* featured prominently in our rotation, plus a few things Ethan and Brandon had recorded off HBO at their cousin's house, like *The Terminator* and *War Games,* both of which we regarded as deeply philosophical.

Like a lot of people, we were mostly just caught up in the novelty of being able to watch whole movies, on demand, at home. Until about two years earlier, if we'd wanted to rewatch one of our favorite sci-fi adventures, we'd have had to wait for it to come around at the Neptune, a repertory movie theater in the University District that showed double features, grouped by theme, Sunday through Thursday—and *The Rocky Horror Picture Show* at midnight every Friday and Saturday. Calliope had taken me to *Rocky* once when I was ten. The police searched us at the door to make sure we weren't bringing any glass bottles into the theater. I was a fan of the repertory theater model, but *Indiana Jones and the Raiders of the Lost Ark* came through there about once a year, so getting to watch it three times in a day at home, where we could pause it for bathroom and snack breaks, felt like a bizarre futuristic luxury to us.

I didn't have a clear picture of which of the brothers I was actually friends with at first. Brandon was in my grade, and he was only a year older, while Ethan was three years older and an eleventh grader. But Ethan and I had more in common: he was the one who liked weapons and Dungeons & Dragons and was more of a committed sci-fi geek. Unlike Brandon, he also liked to wrestle. I still suffered from my inexplicable desire to jump up and down on people, so Ethan's willingness to scrap with me was a major plus—until it wasn't. Ethan liked to spar, but he also liked to physically intimidate people during arguments. And because I was always looking for something to push up against, I didn't back down. It only took about a month for us to end up rolling around on his kitchen floor, trying to hurt each other without being obvious about it. Ethan, who was older, with an adult's muscle density, was the clear winner.

The next day at the bus stop, Ethan studiously ignored me, but Brandon stood next to me on the corner.

"I was thinking we should take the whips down to Discovery Park this weekend," he said. "Kill some plants. Maybe jump down those cliffs by the sewage treatment plant."

"That'd be great," I said. "It's not going to . . . cause a problem for you?"

"Dude," he prison-whispered to me, "Ethan's been pushing me around since I was five. You see this scar here?"

He pointed to a horizontal line between his bottom lip and his chin, very similar to the one I had left over from the car accident.

"Ethan did that when we were kids. Tied a giant Tinkertoy on a string, swung it around, hit me in the face with it. My bottom teeth went right through my lip. The only thing you could have done the other day that would have made me happier was if you'd kicked his fat ass from one end of the house to the other."

"I . . . will work on that," I said. "Next time."

"Cool. Meanwhile—Discovery Park? Saturday?"

"Sure," I said.

52

I waited a few months to try to reach Eddie again. Partly it was to give my dad time to cool down, and partly it was to give Eddie some breathing room. Things Eddie had said to me back when I lived in Ballard, things I'd seen him do, I knew he'd always worried in the back of his mind that he was a bad influence on me. He knew I was no normie, but he also knew I was clean by choice, and he worried that me hanging out with him was going to work against all the other good decisions he thought I was making in my life. So Dad had really gone right for the nuclear option head-fuck with the stuff he'd been screaming at Eddie in the hospital. I figured giving him some time to walk it off would make it easier to get past it.

Not such a good plan, it turned out.

I started calling him in mid-November, but it always went through to the answering machine. I left messages, but never got a call back. Finally I gave in and just went over there to see him on my way home from a weekend sleepover at Ryan's place.

Eddie's mom's boyfriend, Dan, was in the driveway next to the house, working on his van. I'd met him a bunch of times— even gone trailer camping with Dan, Eddie, and Eddie's mom once, on some land Dan owned out on the Olympic Peninsula. But he didn't seem to recognize me until I asked him if Eddie was around.

"Oh," he said. "Jason, right? Eddie's friend."

"Yeah," I said.

"Eddie doesn't live here anymore, man."

"I . . . what?"

"Shirley just got too goddamn strung out," he said, fiddling nervously with a socket wrench. "Coke, man. Bad news. She still calls me asking for money. That's why I never answer my phone anymore."

"You know where they went?" I asked.

"No," he said. "Up north, I think. Shirley was hooking Eddie up, too. That was part of why I told Shirley to leave. It happened fast, man. One day it was just a line or two every once in a while, the next day Eddie was breaking into places and stealing shit to sell, to buy coke for him and his mom. Didn't figure it was safe to have them around anymore. Fucked up, but I had to do it."

I looked at his van and his house. The van had the full A-Team muscle kit: a GMC V8 with red detailing and a spoiler on the roof. The house was a mansion, by Ballard standards. Maybe by anyone's standards. He made good money as a contractor, and Eddie had been living in his basement for three years. What did it take to make someone a parent? It didn't matter. He and Eddie had never really gotten along.

"Okay," I said. "Thanks."

I walked to the nearest bus stop. It was the same stop where I'd gotten hit by the car.

I never saw Eddie again.

53

I came home from school one day in December, and Dad said he needed to talk to me in the kitchen. He was dressed like he'd just come in from outside; he had on a black wool coat, a brown scarf, jeans, and his broad-brimmed brown Stetson hat.

It was dark out. That time of year, between the overcast skies and the early sunset, it was nearly full dark by four o'clock. The kitchen was lit by a bank of fluorescent lights set into the ceiling behind a warped cover of beaded plastic. The plastic was impregnated with decades of grease and smoke. It gave the blue-green fluorescents a comforting yellow cast, like a bright incandescent bulb.

I sat down at the kitchen table, and Dad sat across from me, with his back to the living room.

"I went to the doctor today," he said.

I said, "Oh yeah?"

I knew what the rest of the conversation was going to be. I had no idea what to do about it, but I knew where it was going.

"You know I've been sick," he said, like he was explaining something to a five-year-old. "Last month, the doctor drew some blood for a test. There's a test for AIDS now. It's—the virus that causes AIDS is called HIV, and people get antibodies if we're infected. They can't find the virus, but they can find the antibodies. So they test for those."

He looked at me like he wanted me to say something. I had no idea what to say, but I figured I should do something. I narrowed my eyes. I chewed my lips and crossed my arms. I was wearing too many layers. Crossing my arms pulled my jacket and shirts tight across my shoulders. It all felt too bulky. Too constricting. I couldn't move.

"I got the results today," he said. "When I went to the doctor, they told me. The test was positive."

"Positive?" I asked. "Positive good, or positive bad?"

"Bad," he said.

He was starting to lose it. His face was getting red. His eyes were welling up. It made me uncomfortable, so I looked at the table.

"Is there . . ." I said. "Do they ever get false positives?"

"Sometimes," he said. "But not this time. The—I guess the numbers were pretty high. The number of antibodies. Conclusive."

"What's that mean?" I asked. "Conclusive. What happens now?"

"Most people . . ." He stopped to catch his breath. He was having trouble getting it out. "Usually most people last about six months. That's what usually happens. About six months."

I looked up at him. His face was a wreck. When our eyes met he started gasping and crying.

"I don't know what to do," he said. "I don't want to die. I'm so sorry. I won't be here. I don't want to die."

I took a deep breath. I was starting to panic, because I wasn't having any kind of reaction. I didn't feel anything. I tried. But there was just nothing there. I couldn't tell him that. He was sobbing across the table from me, and I had to do something or he'd realize I wasn't going to cry. I moaned and put my elbows on the table and used my hands to cover my face so he wouldn't see that I wasn't crying. I tried to think of things that made me cry. I cried in movies all the time. I cried over that Coke commercial. None of it gave me so much as a stuffy nose while my dad was telling me he was dying. I couldn't feel anything. I bit the insides of my cheeks, but it just hurt. Finally, the combination of the pain and the fear of getting caught caused enough anxiety to elevate my breathing and my pulse. I'd have the right expression on my face. My cheeks would be flushed. I took my hands away. Dad and I looked at each other and stood up to hug. I was thirteen. I was two inches taller than he was. He sobbed against my shoulder. I stood there, holding him, and thinking about myself.

* * *

I got up for school the next day. I went to class. I came home after school. Dad wasn't home. Bruce wasn't home. I wanted to talk to someone, but there was nobody to talk to, so I went into my room and watched TV. At some point I turned off the TV and tried to do my homework, but I didn't seem to be able to give a shit. I turned the TV back on and thought about the Cambodian girl I'd met in Ballard—the one whose family had been trampled by elephants, while I and everyone else I knew went about the daily business of our normal lives, thousands of miles away. But not me. Not anymore. As of yesterday, I was living in a war zone.

54

Ryan and his mom still lived on the same block in Ballard that they'd lived on when I left for San Diego, though they were in a different apartment now. They'd moved out of their old apartment when their downstairs neighbor, a woman whose kids Ryan used to babysit for, was smothered with a pillow while her two toddlers were asleep in the next room. They knew the neighbor's death didn't imply anything about the safety of the apartments, or the neighborhood; the murder was an outlier. But they moved anyway, to another apartment across the street and half a block to the east.

I didn't like Ryan's new place much. It was a 1960s duplex, with a basement unit and an upstairs unit, torchdown roof, low ceilings; the entire front of the building was a bank of garages, with a wide concrete driveway where a front yard should have been. The backyard was a sunken concrete patio and a raised "garden" full of beauty bark and juniper bushes. The place had all the charm of a TV dinner, but Ryan liked the abundance of concrete surfaces. He liked to start fires, and he was glad to have a place to do it without having to worry about burning down the entire block.

The bus ride from my place on Capitol Hill took more than an hour, so it wasn't worth the trip on a weeknight. Even on weekends, it was only worth it if I stayed the night. The first couple of times I did it, there was a nod to the whole idea that I was a guest. Ryan's mom would make dinner, and I'd share breakfast. But they really didn't have the money to feed another kid two days a week, so after a few weeks I started bringing money to buy my own food. I'd sleep on Ryan's floor on Friday night, get up with him at six o'clock on Saturday morning to help him put rubber bands on newspapers for his paper route, and split the route with him, working one side of the street while he worked the other. Then we'd goof around all day Saturday. Every other weekend or so, I'd sleep over on Saturday night, too. Get up with him Sunday, do his route with him again, goof around a while longer, then head home.

Ryan didn't have a VCR—most people didn't—so when we were on our own, we spent a lot of time recounting the plots of horror or science fiction movies one of us had seen that the other hadn't, or talking about our favorite parts of a movie we'd both seen. Sometimes we went fishing down by the locks with Ryan's neighbor Brian. If we could get enough other kids together we'd have rubber band wars or squirt gun wars.

Every so often some toy company would make a toy gun that fired plastic or rubber projectiles hard enough to cause physical pain at close range. We spent a lot of time stalking around the neighborhood with other kids, shooting spring-loaded guns at each other with no eye protection of any kind, and leaving the projectiles scattered around each other's houses for younger siblings to find and choke on. Eventually the guns would break, and we wouldn't be able to buy new ones because the toy company had been sued and had stopped making that particular model. Then a new kind would come out and we'd buy a bunch of those and start up our endless war all over gain.

We also played Dungeons & Dragons, and other role-playing games with names like Gamma World, Teenage Mutant Ninja Turtles & Other Strangeness, and Car Wars. We painted lead figures. We went to movies at the Bay Theatre in downtown Ballard—usually war movies or science fiction flicks. Sometimes Ryan could put together enough guys for a softball game or touch football. No matter how many times we played, I never did understand the rules for football.

Ryan and his friends smoked a little pot together from time to time. I never smoked with them, which gave me a reputation as kind of a Goody Two-shoes. For some reason, the irony was totally wasted on me.

* * *

Ryan was friends with most of the kids in his neighborhood, including two guys at the end of the block named Dale and Daryl Johnson. Daryl had been in Mr. Fields's class with me and Ryan, but Dale was a couple of years older. Their home situation was unusual. Their parents were still together, which was almost unheard of in our school. They had a stay-at-home mom and their dad made them call him sir. He worked in lumber or farming or textiles. Also their house was full of guns. Once when we were all still in elementary school, we'd been playing hide-and-seek and I'd crawled under their kitchen table and found a loaded .357 revolver in a metal bracket, bolted to the underside of the table and pointed at the front door. There were other pieces stashed around the house in various easily accessible places, in case drug-crazed hippies kicked down the door while the family was watching TV, or while Mr. Johnson was sitting on the toilet. And there was a stockpile of assault rifles, handguns, and shotguns in a large gun safe in the basement. By the standards of the time, this sort of behavior was considered eccentric but not worth calling CPS over.

Dale and Daryl's dad didn't just own guns; he liked to shoot them. A lot. When he wasn't shooting them, he was pretending to shoot and reload them, while his wife timed him with a stopwatch. He traveled all over the state, and sometimes around the country, participating in shooting competitions. He spent hours at the range every week. He fired so many bullets through his many, many guns that eventually he figured out that he could save money if he just made his own bullets. Which meant that not only was his house full of guns—it was also full of gunpowder. He kept really close track of what happened with the guns. For some reason, he was a lot less careful about the gunpowder.

This was how Dale, Daryl, Ryan, and I came to be standing in front of Ryan's house late one night arguing over how best to detonate a large pile of gunpowder that we'd dumped on the sidewalk. The other three had carried out various experiments in making things go boom, such as packing tennis balls full of gunpowder, sticking a waterproof fuse in them, wrapping them tightly in duct tape, lighting them, and throwing them in lakes. Evidently this created a large splash and, on a good day, a few dead fish. To hear Ryan and the Johnson brothers talk about it, you'd think they'd been on Normandy Beach at D-Day but, of course, rather than making me annoyed, their endless repetition of the stories just made me jealous. Now, standing on the sidewalk next to the boom-y stuff, I wasn't sure jealousy had been the appropriate response.

"This is retarded," Dale was saying. "It's not gonna explode!"

"Come on!" Ryan said. "Let's just try it!"

The pile of gunpowder was a loose heap, about six inches high and as many inches across. A thin trail of primer powder extended about three feet from the large pile, like a fuse. Later on, after everything went horribly wrong, we could never remember exactly who had suggested this arrangement. But we all agreed we'd gotten the idea from Wile E. Coyote.

What we thought was going to happen was that we'd light the very end of the trail of gunpowder and it would hiss toward the big pile, like it did in the cartoons. When the spark got to the main pile, there'd be a modest explosion. We didn't actually know if this would work; part of the experiment was to find out if the cartoons bore any relationship to reality. That four children were using live explosives to test a hypothesis based on a cartoon didn't raise a warning flag for any of us.

"It's not going to explode," Dale kept saying. "It needs to be tamped down. It needs to be under pressure. It's just gonna fizzle like this."

"I just want to see what will happen," Daryl said. "Let's try it and see what happens."

"It's a waste of gunpowder," Dale said.

"Would you guys hurry up?" Ryan said.

He was looking around anxiously. Ballard was usually pretty dead by midnight, even on a Saturday, but he was worried about the neighbors seeing us.

"Come on," I said. "Let's see it already."

"Fine," Dale said.

Me, Ryan, and Daryl stepped back, while Dale lit a wooden match, crouched down low, and reached out for the tail end of the fuse from as far away as he could get.

All of us were watching the match except Ryan—who was watching his house. Just as Dale was about to light the fuse, Ryan thought he saw his upstairs neighbor's curtain move, and he panicked.

"No!" he yelled, leaping forward—over the pile of gunpowder—to kick the match out of Dale's hand. He didn't quite make it. To those of us who were standing there watching, it looked like Ryan yelled, "No," jumped forward, and exploded in a cloud of smoky black fire. When the smoke cleared, Ryan was gone. There was just a giant blackened circle on the sidewalk where he'd been. Then we heard him screaming.

All three of us looked up, expecting to see him shooting toward the horizon like one of the cartoon characters we'd based our experiment on. But then we heard him scream again and spotted him, sprinting down the sidewalk about half a block away.

We took off after him. We had no idea why he was running, and no idea why he'd jumped into the gunpowder. As keyed up as we were, taking off after him was pure herd instinct. We chased him for about a block before he ducked into a sunken driveway and leaned against the wall, panting. We charged in after him and took cover against the same wall.

"What the fuck?" Dale hissed. "Did you see a cop or something?"

"What?" Ryan said. "No, no cop. The old lady. Upstairs. Looking out the window. Tried to stop you."

"Then why'd you run?" Daryl asked.

"Run?" Ryan said. Evidently he hadn't noticed he'd been running. "Shit! Am I on fire?"

He started swatting frantically at his clothes. We all circled him and looked him over, but he was fine. The explosion had been too brief to ignite him. His bangs were singed, and all the hair had been burned off his legs, but that was it. No tissue damage. No shrapnel.

It was all funny when it was over, and we told and retold the story at every opportunity; the match, the curtain, Ryan jumping over the gunpowder at the exact instant it caught fire. It was the kind of story that never got old, because it was exciting and nobody had died.

* * *

Sometimes Ryan and I would go up to Northgate Mall with a bunch of guys from his Ballard crew. We'd goof around and prank each other, go to toy stores and sporting goods stores and look at all the cool stuff we couldn't afford. We'd all pretend I was one of them.

Ryan had a gag he liked to run when we were up there. If one of us bought a soda, he'd wait until we were walking down the main concourse of the mall, then ask if he could have a sip. He'd take it. He'd drink out of it. Then he'd look at whoever had given him the soda with wide, terrified eyes, and shout, "What?! You've got AIDS?"

Ryan and his friends always thought that was hilarious.

55

Once, in San Diego, I'd met a kid my age at the beach. It was on Christmas Eve. The local chamber of commerce had a giant Christmas tree lighting ceremony that drew thousands of people down to the parking lot next to Ocean Beach's main lifeguard station. The mood was festive. Lots of people partying, lots of bonfires. I climbed up onto a lifeguard tower to get a better view and there was another kid up there already. We spent the whole night goofing around together. He seemed cool. Denim jacket. Medium-length mop of dark brown hair. Pierced

ears. He mentioned at some point that his parents were dealers. I told him mine were, too. He asked if I lived with my mom
or my dad and I told him I lived with my dad and his boyfriend.
Maybe I was caught up in the excitement of the night, or maybe
I just didn't think it should matter, but his reaction was everything I could have hoped for.

"Your dad gay?" he asked.

"Yeah," I said.

"A lot of people think I'm gay," he said. "Because both my
ears are pierced. That, or they think I'm a girl. I don't give a
shit."

When we parted ways early on Christmas morning, he told
me where he lived, in an apartment next to the freeway overpass.
He said we should hang out again sometime. When I mentioned
him to my dad the next day, I said I'd just come right out and
told the kid about Dad and Bruce. It was really liberating, not
to worry about it for once.

Dad got really quiet.

"Listen," he said after a while. "I should meet people before
you tell them that."

"He seemed fine," I said.

"Yeah," he said. "But I should meet them."

"What's the big deal?" I asked. "If he'd been a dick about it,
I just would have blown him off. That'd be that."

Dad sighed. "If the wrong people find out about us, the cops
might try to take you away. But that would be one of the least
bad things that could happen, really. People could come to our
house, burn it down with us in it, and nobody would try to
stop them or punish them for it. No law protects gay men."

"That's ridiculous," I said.

"Jason . . . a couple of years ago some Jesus freak walks into
San Francisco City Hall and shoots the mayor of San Francisco
in cold blood, because the mayor supported a gay city council

member. Then he goes and shoots the queer city council guy. Gets arrested. Goes to trial. Gets five years. He got out of jail last year. This guy shot the mayor, Jason. You understand what that means?"

The kid I'd met down by the beach really had seemed okay. But I never did go to visit him in his apartment by the overpass.

* * *

Our apartment on Capitol Hill wasn't a place for me. It certainly wasn't meant as somewhere I could bring friends back to. It was an apartment where two gay men lived. I happened to live there, too.

My bedroom was next to the back door. I had two windows; one facing north and one west. The window to the west gave me a view of the mountains and the Space Needle and Puget Sound. It overlooked the stairs that were built onto the back of the house. When people came or went through our back door, they walked past my bedroom window. The window swung into the room on a pair of top-mounted hinges. It was surprisingly heavy. I used a piece of a broom handle to prop it open. I was always afraid it would come loose, slam closed, and shatter. The north-facing window was a sash window that looked down on the street below. Both windows had gray venetian blinds that had come with the apartment.

My closet was on the east wall, in the north corner, adjacent to the sash window. There was no door on the closet. I had a pair of heavy red velvet curtains covering the closet doorway. They hung from a curtain rod that I'd improvised out of a piece of bamboo. The curtains were made from a set of much larger curtains that Dad had stolen out of a condemned mansion in L.A. in the late sixties. We had a few more sets of curtains and three or four chairs that were upholstered in the same fabric: deep bloodred velvet, with swirls of paler fabric worked in, like ocean waves.

I had an old deer skull nailed to the closet door frame, above the red curtains.

The light in the room came from a frosted glass light fixture on the ceiling, a sort of inverted umbrella of glass with flowers etched into it. I didn't like it. It collected bugs.

The walls and ceiling were painted white, but they were smoke-stained and dirty from previous tenants. The floor was real linoleum rather than vinyl, patterned in large gray and brown squares. It was so scratched, and there was so much dirt ingrained in its surface, that no amount of mopping or sweeping could make it look truly clean.

My bed was against the north wall, in the northwest corner, with the foot pointing toward the closet. It was an old latex foam twin mattress on a box spring. I had always tossed and turned so much at night that I couldn't keep sheets on it: I woke up every morning tangled in them. So when we moved into the Capitol Hill place, I just stopped using sheets altogether. The mattress got dirty pretty fast after that, but I didn't really care. I slept fully clothed, in jeans and a T-shirt. Sometimes I even wore my shoes to bed.

I had a bookshelf nailed to the wall above my bed. When I moved in, there were just some knickknacks on it. Later, I filled it with cheap sci-fi and fantasy paperbacks.

Clean clothes went in the dresser up against the south wall, next to the bedroom door. Dirty clothes went in a pile in front of the closet. The closet itself didn't have any clothes in it at all. It was just packed full of junk.

The nearest laundromat was a block away, next to Summit Foods. I rarely changed or washed my clothes. I didn't own very many that fit me. I wore my pants for weeks without changing them. I stuffed candy wrappers and bus transfers in the pockets until they were bulging with garbage. I put all my useful stuff in my coat pockets: tools, weapons, toys. I always carried a spool of twine or cord, a screwdriver, and a Swiss army knife of some kind. I always had a flashlight. I carried a long, narrow chisel that I'd sharpened to a point. I always had a ball—usually a handball or a tennis ball—to bounce against a wall or the ground if I got stuck somewhere and didn't have anything better to do.

I never had enough socks or underwear. I wore them until they rotted. I didn't use deodorant until Ryan couldn't stand it anymore and begged me to buy some Right Guard or something. I hadn't even known I smelled. The idea that it could be that bad without me knowing it was disturbing.

I took a bath at least once a day, but I wore the same dirty clothes for days or weeks at a time. Dad never talked to me about any of it, or explained to me that I stank. He'd always been squeamish about bodily functions. Once, when I was seven, my ass had itched so bad that the doctors thought I had worms. Turned out I just wasn't wiping well enough, and never had; Dad had just never been willing to talk to me about it. It was the same way now. He told me my feet stank, but he didn't suggest that buying more socks might help with it. At some point he started sneaking into my room at night and dumping huge quantities of foot powder in my sneakers. It just crusted around my toes.

I didn't brush my teeth unless I was going to the dentist. The walls of my bedroom next to my bed were stained with grease from me rubbing up against them at night.

I slept only four or five hours a night. Sometimes I'd wake up on my box spring, with my mattress on the floor next to the bed. I had a tendency, when I was asleep, to try to crawl under the mattress, and I'd end up shoving it off the bed entirely. Almost like I was trying to hide.

I didn't like for my straight friends to see my house, or for anyone to see my room. It was just this embarrassing physical manifestation of my dysfunction, the same way our apartment reflected my alienation from my dad, and I didn't like people to see those things spelled out so clearly. Of course, my attempts to handle my problems by keeping them secret gave something away, too, but my introspection stopped short of recognizing what that might be. That may have been part of the reason it took me almost a year to notice that Brandon's room, in the house next door, looked a lot like mine.

In some ways, his was worse.

* * *

Garfield had 1,700 students, which meant Brandon and I had a lot of room to avoid each other at school. After school, we started spending most of our time together. He showed me pieces of himself a bit at a time. I saw his room, and the basement where he lived with his brother. They shared a bathroom that had no walls, just sheets thumbtacked to the studs where walls would be someday. They lived in bedrooms with doors that slid back and forth on metal rails, instead of having hinges. The doors didn't meet up with the walls or the floor—there were several inches of clearance on all sides—so they didn't offer a lot of privacy. Brandon and Ethan's beds were mattresses set in wooden boxes hinged to the wall and supported by lengths of nylon rope. The sort of thing you'd expect to find in a prison or a barracks. Ethan kept his room comparatively neat, if only so he could manage his extensive pornography collection. Brandon just kept his room dark. The concrete floor was always covered in clothes and loose bits of junk—electronics, and art projects Brandon worked on for fun.

We spent most of our time together avoiding being home. Freshman year we got into skateboarding. Neither of us could do any tricks, but we liked riding quickly down the street, or in parking garages. We knew all the covered garages in our neighborhood, and which ones tended to be empty at midday. We'd take our skateboards there on school holidays and spend hours skating in circles, shooting soundlessly along on the smooth-finished cement, kicking every so often, but mostly just enjoying the wind in our hair, and the silence.

We also started going for walks at night. Brandon claimed to sleep better than I did, but when I went and knocked on his window at eleven o'clock or midnight, he was always ready to spend a few hours walking around the neighborhood, talking about girls or movies or whatever.

It took me a while to get used to Brandon's version of friendship. My D&D group back in Ballard had hopelessly skewed my perceptions when it came to the difference between friendly teasing and outright abuse. Even with Eddie, who I thought of as my one true friend, we tended to communicate by mocking each other, pushing, and shoving. Brandon had no patience for any of it. Our first few months hanging out I repeatedly pushed him too far only to have him stop whatever we were doing, tell me I was being an asshole, and go home. Up to that point in my life, I'd really never seen anything like it. But I was intrigued by what it implied.

At school, Brandon had his own friends and his own social life. But it almost never came home with him. The kids he hung out with at Garfield were just kids he bantered with, kids he took classes with. Freshman year, and most of sophomore year, those kids didn't even know his phone number. He had some friends from his old neighborhood who he introduced me to: rich kids in big houses who went to private schools. They were too far away to be regular hanging-out friends. Day-to-day, around the neighborhood, it was usually just him and me.

We spent a lot of time talking about school, and the social

dynamics there. We talked about clothes, and our body types, and how we could dress to look cooler. We talked about our haircuts. My missing tooth, and how it probably meant I'd never get a girlfriend—as if that was the only thing holding me back. We almost never talked about Brandon's dad and how he seemed to be in the process of going nuts, or Ethan and how he seemed to be following their father down the rabbit hole. Or my dad.

We pretty much never talked about my dad.

56

The summer I turned fourteen, Kris moved north to Seattle with her five-year-old daughter, Lizzie. Jimmy stayed in Arizona. Things hadn't gone well for them down there. Kris said it was because they got married: no better way to fuck up a perfectly good relationship than to get married, she said. Then the two of them had Lizzie together. That might have been stressful, too. But I thought it probably had more to do with Jimmy's drug habit. He worked as a miner, and like many people who work sixteen-hour shifts in jobs where a moment's inattention can result in the violent amputation of an arm or a leg, Jimmy mainlined a shitload of speed. Nobody really blamed him for it until one of his drug buddies molested Lizzie when she was three. After that he was persona non grata for a while. Kris divorced him and moved out on her own. When Dad told Kris that the apartment under ours was coming up for rent, she came to Seattle and moved in downstairs.

Having Lizzie around was weird. The only way I knew how to interact with little kids was to roughhouse with them, so after she and her mom moved to Seattle I spent a lot of time chasing her with a squirt bottle or smacking her around with a pillow. I usually didn't go after her—she'd come to me for this abuse, which I thought meant we were just playing around. I knew my compulsion to bounce her off a wall every ten minutes—and her compulsion to come looking for it—probably came from some more deep-seated issues, but I didn't have a lot of extra mental capacity for productive introspection. I managed to avoid injuring her, and she learned how to pick the lock on a pair of handcuffs.

* * *

Not long after Kris and Lizzie arrived in Seattle, I was talking to Kris and made some offhand comment about how my dad never hit me. Kris stared at me like I'd just grown another head.

"Are you serious?" she asked.

"About what?"

"That your dad never hit you."

"Well, of course he spanked me sometimes."

She didn't seem to be able to make up her mind how to respond. After a minute she said, "Jason, when you and Mark were in Arizona with us, Jimmy and I got in a huge fight about this. Your dad did more than spank you. We could hear it through the wall, and I was saying we should go in there and cool him down, and Jimmy was saying it was none of our business. It was the same thing in Eugene. You don't remember that?"

"I remember it," I said. "I just thought—I was making it out to be worse than it really was."

"How so?"

"Well, it's not like he beat me with a coat hanger."

This was something my dad used to say when I complained

about him hitting me. I didn't even know what it meant, but I repeated it without thinking about it.

"Okay . . ." Kris said. "I guess that's true, if that's the goalpost. He wasn't beating you with a coat hanger. But he was flipping out, totally losing control, and hitting you in a way that was pretty scary to witnesses. So I don't think you were probably making it out too much worse than it was."

"Huh," I said.

"He still do that?" she asked.

"What?"

"Hit you."

"No," I said. "I'm too big for it."

It was mostly true.

"Well," Kris said. "What doesn't kill you makes you stronger."

"I guess," I said.

During my many years of being home during the day and watching *Dialing for Dollars*, I'd seen a lot of old movies. One in particular that had always disturbed me was an Ingrid Bergman movie called *Gaslight*, about a woman whose husband tries to drive her crazy. He uses small tricks: He takes a picture down from the wall of their house and says she did it and just doesn't remember. When she hears noises from the attic, he tells her she's imagining it. The whole scheme turns on a simple device— take someone who's socially isolated and dependent and make them doubt the reality of their own senses. I'd even heard it used as a verb: gaslighting.

In the end of the movie, a detective comes into the house and tells the woman he hears the footsteps in the attic. That was all it took. One other person to confirm the truth.

"Hey, Jason," Kris said.

I looked up at her. I realized I hadn't spoken in a while.

"Don't make a big thing out of it," she said. "With him. I'm just not sure it's worth it at this point."

"Sure," I said. "I won't make a thing out of it."

57

Around the middle of my sophomore year I realized I was sort of falling in love with my high school. It started as a physical thing. The building was full of little pieces of other people's lives. The seats and soundproofing in our auditorium were all from the late fifties, but the stage was part of the original building, and the walls in the backstage were covered with graffiti. Not the wild styles that had been popular since hip-hop; mostly it was just the names and graduation dates of students, going back to the thirties. JB, class of 1940. Class of '52. Class of '63. Kids who had fought in Europe. Kids who had gone off to march on Washington with Martin Luther King Jr., and kids who had joined the Black Panthers. Japanese kids, who'd been shipped off to concentration camps in California and Idaho. Kids who had seen and done everything I'd learned about in history class, or seen in movies. Kids who had grandkids now. Kids who ran businesses or invented new medicine; who had changed the world. Kids whose bodies were buried in some field in France, or in a rice paddy in Southeast Asia.

The more I looked at the school, the more there was to see. Coal chutes and loading bays. The old greenhouse, where the botany classes did experiments with avocado plants. A giant clock in the office, full of gears and switches, that used to control the bell system for the entire school. We had a new gym down the block, next to the swimming pool, where all the regular physical education classes happened. It was a gigantic building with four full-size basketball courts and a weight room. But there was another gym in the middle of the main building that nobody used anymore—two rooms, each a quarter of the size of the new building, with thick maple floors, forty-foot ceilings, and peaked skylights. One of the rooms had a cork-floored jogging track on a mezzanine that could only be reached through a narrow spiral staircase.

The school had its problems. Building maintenance was massively underfunded, so finding a working bathroom could be a challenge. The textbooks were trashed; there were only one or two computers in the whole school. The landscaping and shrubbery were crawling with rats, and there were crack houses across the street on three sides. But none of that mattered to me. The classrooms were always warm, nobody ever told me to leave, and pretty much everyone ignored me. I could shower after swimming class. I got more sleep in school than I did at home. I'd never felt so safe in my life. I wanted to be a teacher when I grew up. I wanted to go back to Garfield after college. I wanted to spend the rest of my life there.

Even I recognized that the school had won my heart by just not caring enough about me to reject me. But, from my perspective, Garfield was also the first place I'd ever spent a significant amount of time where none of the adults called me stupid, hit me, or tried to cop a feel, and where none of the kids went out of their way to hurt me or make fun of me. I got into a couple of fights at Garfield, and had a couple of long-term hassles with people, but all those situations, without exception, were my fault. I could retrace every one of them to the exact moment when I broke the rules and started the problem for myself. And if I was willing to let the conflict go, it always disappeared in the rearview.

That was my definition of the Promised Land: the only bad things that happened to me at Garfield were bad things I caused. Hallelujah, and praise mandatory busing.

* * *

While I was developing a passionate relationship with my school, I was also learning to develop shallow relationships with my classmates. I regarded this as a significant improvement in my social skills. Up to that point in my life, I was so desperate for friends I tended to latch on to anyone who spoke to me, like a drowning person clinging to a piece of driftwood. At Garfield, I finally learned the art of forming satisfying nonfriendships with other kids in a bunch of my classes.

One of my long-term nonfriendships was with a girl in my German class named Marti. She had short brown and blond hair, a pixie's face, sapphire-blue eyes, and a mischievous smile. Her high, breathy voice reminded me of Marilyn Monroe. If she hadn't had kind of spotty skin and a slight mustache issue, she probably would have been a cheerleader—but her loss was my gain; if she'd been more popular she probably wouldn't have talked to me.

We chatted at the beginning and end of class. Sometimes we passed notes about something funny the teacher said, or another student. She said hi when I passed her in the hall. When I missed school she asked me where I'd been.

It was nice. I felt like I was a regular person for a change. I knew better, but I enjoyed the experience anyway.

* * *

Brandon's version of Garfield was better than mine in a lot of ways. He had more friends, got better grades, and just generally did better in school than I did. He hated it anyway. He hated the way all the girls he knew kept him in the friend zone; he hated the way the bigger kids bullied him and the cooler kids ignored him. It was hard not to take it personally—not just that he didn't seem to love the school the same way I did, but that he seemed to feel like his life, which was better than mine in every measurable way, was just a long string of unbearable indignities.

One day early in our sophomore year, he wasn't on the bus going home. He'd been there that morning, but he never showed up for the afternoon bus. When I went by his house to see where he'd disappeared to, his dad told me he'd come home early.

"Was he sick or something?" I asked.

"No," his dad said. "He got in a fight. Came straight home after. He's been downstairs in his room ever since."

"Can I check on him?"

"Sure."

I went downstairs, but it was quiet down there. I found Brandon sitting on his bed in the dark, wrapped up in a blanket.

"Hey," I said, stepping carefully into the sea of junk on his bedroom floor. "Your dad said you got in a fight. You okay?"

"Go away," he said.

"What happened?" I asked. "Was it someone we know, or . . . ?"

"I didn't get in a fight. I got mugged."

"You got . . . ?" I tried to figure out what the difference might be. "Like, someone robbed you?"

"In the hall," he said. "I was going to the bathroom during class, when the halls were empty. Some kid told me to give him my money. When I said I wouldn't he hit me with a bottle."

"Jesus! Are you all right?"

"He hit me in the arm. Then he ran off. It hurts, but I'm fine."

"Can I take a look?"

"No. Go away."

"Brandon . . ."

"Go away!" he shouted.

I backed out of the room and went home. I tried calling a

296

few times that night, but Brandon's dad said Brandon didn't want to talk. When he came to the school bus stop the next morning, I asked him if he was all right.

"Don't ever bring that up again," he said.

"Why not?" I asked.

"Just don't," he said.

I tried to accommodate him, but I also wondered what he thought made him so goddamn special. The idea that he just thought all of us were entitled to more, and that he might be right, never crossed my mind.

58

Dad did the five stages of grief on a weekly rotation, at random. Denial, anger, bargaining, depression, acceptance, whatever. Once he woke me up at three in the morning to help him move all the furniture in his bedroom. He read magazine articles about AIDS: treatment options, politics, and conspiracy theories.

"Doesn't it seem convenient?" he asked. "That there's this disease that mostly kills gay men, junkies, and Africans? That it spreads fastest in places that have overpopulation? I'm not saying it was engineered by the government. I'm not saying that. But if Ronald Reagan were going to design a virus, this is the virus he'd design."

I had to admit it: he wasn't wrong.

He read books about religion and spirituality at the meta-level: Carlos Castenada, Alan Watts, and their contemporaries. There was a long-standing family rumor that Grandpa's mother had been Jewish, so that was the religion Dad settled on. Not in the sense that he studied Hebrew or learned anything about the religion, the history, or the culture. But he started wearing his gold Star of David necklace all the time, and sometimes for a goof he'd wear a yarmulke.

Some days he yelled at me for not doing the dishes or for leaving my shoes in the bathroom, but most days he barely seemed to notice I was around. One night I came home at two in the morning and he was waiting up for me in the living room, with the phone on the couch next to him.

"Where the fuck have you been all night?" he screamed at me. "I've been worried sick!"

"What are you talking about?" I said. "I've been doing this four nights a week for months!"

It was true, but it wasn't like I was out partying and having fun. Usually I was just walking with Brandon, or by myself, and actively not being home.

Dad tried to hang out with other people who had AIDS, so he could learn how to be an AIDS patient, the same way he'd learned how to be gay. But it was hard to form a community with other AIDS patients. Everyone was going through their own long dark night of the soul, so they weren't at their most social. Plus, of course, people kept dying.

"I met this couple today," Dad would say. "Al and Pat. It's the saddest story. They've been married for twenty years. Al had one gay affair, because he was sort of questioning his sexuality. He got infected, then infected Pat before they had the antibody test. He didn't even know he was sick."

Then a few weeks later, "Pat's been really sick."

Then a few weeks after that, "Pat died. Al's devastated."

Then, "Al's been in and out of the hospital all month."

I never even met most of them. They were like TV shows. He'd find one he liked, get into it, and start telling me how good it was. Then it would get canceled before I had a chance to watch it.

Bruce, meanwhile, seemed to be in perpetual syndication. Somehow, in spite of having two boyfriends with AIDS, he was still HIV negative. Not that anything else was going particularly well for him. Everyone he knew was dying, and he and Dad were on the rocks.

Dad had never been easy to live with, but I suspected the underlying problem between him and Bruce was emotional exhaustion. When we got back to Seattle, Bruce had gotten a job at one of the downtown department stores—a different one than he'd worked for before we left for San Diego—but then he'd been laid off. He hadn't taken it well. Like me, he seemed to have been operating under an assumption that everything would be okay if we could just get the hell out of San Diego; that we'd be made whole, and get back everything we gave up before we moved down there. Instead, Dad was sick, Bruce was unemployed, and his life savings were long gone. His three years with Dad had been, probably, about the worst thing that ever happened to him. Not that I forgave him for spending three months hanging around the house, drinking and sponging off our welfare, but I at least had to admit that it was karma.

Finally, Bruce got another job at another department store and things started looking up for him—though not so much for his relationship with Dad. Bruce moved back to his condo at the beginning of my tenth grade year. He and Dad were theoretically still a couple; once Bruce had a little money in the bank they planned a big trip to Mexico together, to the Yucatán Peninsula. But even I could tell it was a last hurrah.

* * *

I didn't mind that Dad was going to the Yucatán Peninsula to look at Aztec pyramids without me. I didn't even mind that he was planning to be gone for the better part of a month. What I did mind was that he wanted me to take care of his birds while he was gone.

Dad still had most of his birds. I hated them. Bruce hated them. Our neighbors really hated them. Dad had taken to moving all the cages onto our back porch on sunny days, and the noise had kicked off yet another feud with the guy who lived in the house to the west of us. I'd told Dad from the minute he started talking about going to Mexico that he'd need to arrange for someone else to take care of the birds while he was gone, because I just wasn't doing it.

We fought about it for a couple of days. My solution was that he should get rid of the birds, but he wasn't having it. At one point he tried the old "You live under my roof and I pay your rent!" thing, but I'd recently had a realization about that, and I took this opportunity to trot it out.

"You don't pay my rent!" I said. "I pay yours! If I didn't live here, you wouldn't get welfare or food stamps. So go ahead and kick me out. Try getting by on just SSI, I fucking dare you. You might be able to pay rent, but that drug budget's gonna take a big hit."

At that point in the conversation he said, "You motherfucker," grabbed a bottle off the knickknack shelf in the hall between our rooms, and tried to brain me with it. I snatched it out of his hand and pushed him away.

This was how our conflicts had been going lately. He still got to smack me around sometimes, if he caught me sleeping or something, but in a waking confrontation we'd switched roles: I was three inches taller, faster, and much stronger than he was. Anymore, I got the feeling he only tried to hurt me as a form of protest, just to let me know how pissed off he was.

Except that he'd taken to trying to use things that were lying around the house as equalizers. Before the bottle he'd come after me with a wooden spoon, a shoe, and once with a kitchen knife. It always went the same way. I just snatched the weapon out of his hand and told him to back off. Once, in the kitchen, I sat on him until he calmed down. Bruce, who'd sat calmly by while Dad had beaten the crap out of me back in San Diego, was horrified.

After I took his bottle away, Dad screamed obscenities at me for a minute longer before he stormed off into his room.

Then, a few weeks before he was supposed to leave, the situation seemed to take care of itself. Bruce had met a woman named Cathy at one of his earlier department store jobs, and Cathy needed a place to stay for a month while she was between apartments. Her need happened to line up with the time that Dad and Bruce were going to be in Mexico. They made arrangements for her to put her stuff in the living room of our apartment and sleep in Dad's room. I'd never met Cathy, but I said it was fine with me as long as I didn't have to deal with Dad's birds.

It was all set to happen on the night before Dad and Bruce were leaving. Cathy would come over with her stuff. Dad would show her the birds. Then Dad would go to Bruce's for the night and Cathy would move in. Unfortunately, at the appointed time on the appointed evening, Cathy didn't show up. She didn't show up at six o'clock, when she was supposed to. She didn't show up at seven. And there was no way to call her or figure out what was going on. By eight o'clock Dad was in a rage. By nine, he was apoplectic. I tried to pretend I didn't notice what was happening or guess where it was leading, but around ten he came and stood in my bedroom doorway, fuming for a few minutes.

"This is ridiculous," he said after he'd worked up a head of steam. "If she can't even bother to get here when she's supposed to, she can't stay here. Fuck her. Tell her she missed her chance. You'll have to take care of the animals."

"Nope," I said as I sat in bed reading a book. "She'll be here tomorrow. She can take care of them."

"I said she can't stay here."

"What do you care? You'll be in Mexico."

"This is my fucking house, and I said she can't stay here! And you'll do as you're told or so help me God—"

I looked up at him with the same expression I'd had on my face when I took his bottle away from him.

"You'll what?" I asked. "Call me names? Look, she'll be here tomorrow. And it's really none of your business whether she stays here or not. I'll have to deal with her. You'll be gone. And I'm sorry but there's just no way I'm taking care of those goddamn birds while you're partying in Mexico on Bruce's dime. Just deal with it."

"You'll do what I say while you're living under my roof!"

"Not this time," I said, and went back to my book.

He stared at me for a while. I read. I could feel him looking at me, but I wasn't going to engage.

"You know," he said. "I can have you committed."

It was so out of the blue that it took me a minute to understand what he'd said.

"What?" I asked.

He smiled. "I looked into it. You've got a history. Your mom's crazy. I can have you committed if you don't do what I tell you. I'll turn you over to the state."

I narrowed my eyes at him.

"And if you lay a finger on me," he said smugly, "I'll have you arrested for parent abuse."

I expected to get mad. I thought the sheer audacity of it would make me mad. Instead, I could feel myself starting to panic. There were a lot of things converging in my head, but one of them was that I'd thought I was finally safe from him—I was bigger, stronger. I didn't think he could keep hurting me. And now this. Having that feeling of safety taken away was worse than never having had it.

"I'll run away," I said.

"That just makes it easier," he said, still grinning like a vindictive child.

"What would you tell them?" I asked.

"That you're a danger to yourself. That you're a danger to me. You are. I'd tell them about the cat. I'd tell them about the time you whipped the dog. All of it."

The panic jumped and slammed into me like a wave.

"None of that's true," I said.

"You hurt that cat. You hurt Tom."

"That was an accident."

"What about Kit-Kat?"

"I had nothing to do with that!" I shouted. "She got hit by a car!"

"Really, Jason? Really? Or is that just what you tell yourself?"

"What are you talking about?"

"Did Kit-Kat really get hit by a car? Or are you just blocking out what really happened?"

"You can't do this," I said. "You can't. You're the one who hits me. You're the one who used to kick the dog until he couldn't walk straight. You. Not me."

"How do you know? How do you really know?"

"I know."

"It doesn't matter," he said. "They'll take my word over yours."

I noticed my hands were shaking. My face was hot. I realized I was finally crying.

"I fucking hate you," I said.

His face went purple, and he stepped into the room and jabbed his finger at me.

"You know what?" he hissed. "Someday I'll be gone, and you're going to look back on all this and you're going to be sorry. I fought with my mom when she was sick. And when she was gone, all I wanted was to have her back. You'll see."

"No I won't," I said. "I'll be glad when you're dead. So glad. I hate you. I fucking hate you."

"You need to watch what you say to me," he said calmly. He'd won. He could afford to be calm now.

Then he left. I stared at the place where he'd been for a second, in disbelief. Bruce was waiting in the living room and had probably heard the whole thing. But he'd never gotten between me and Dad. I could hear them in there a minute later, talking in quiet tones.

I sat on my bed for a while, hyperventilating. Then I got up and closed my door, went back to my bed, grabbed my phone off the floor, and set it in front of me. I had no idea who to call. My phone list, my piece of paper with all my personal phone numbers on it, was next to my bed. I picked it up and stared at it for a while, then dialed a number in Hawaii.

The phone rang a few times and someone picked up.

"Hello?" said a woman's voice. She was chewing on something.

"Calliope?" I asked.

"Yeah. Who's this?"

"Jason."

"Jason who?"

"Your brother," I said. "In Seattle."

We'd started referring to each other as siblings right before she left for Hawaii. It explained to us, and to everyone else, why two people who got along so badly were also so important to each other.

"Jason?" she asked. "What's—oh, fuck. Did Mark fucking die? Shit, Jason, I'm sorry—"

"No," I said. "He's not dead. I wish."

"You guys had a fight or something? You know it costs, like, twenty-five cents a minute to call from the mainland, right?"

"Cal, he said he was going to lock me up."

"What?"

"He said he's going to lock me up. He's gonna have me committed. Like, to a mental institution."

"Oh!" she said, getting it. Then, "Oh . . . really? He said that?"

"Yeah."

"Wow. Boy. Pot, kettle, huh?"

"What am I gonna do, Cal? I can't—if he does that, I don't know. I don't know what I'll do. I can't go into a place like that. I can't!"

"Calm down," she said. "He's not going to commit you to a mental institution."

"He said he was! Just now!"

"Look, your dad can't scratch his ass without making a big production out of it. If he actually gets around to doing it, he'll tell you exactly what he's going to do before he makes the first phone call. You'll have plenty of warning."

"So?"

"So just leave. If it comes to that. Just leave. Go someplace else. Go to New York. Screw it, go to Canada. Come here. I don't know. Just leave. Living on the streets is fucked, but if the alternative is letting your dad give you the Frances Farmer treatment, to hell with it. Eventually you turn eighteen, and after that he can never mess with you again. This isn't the rest of your life. It's three years, at most. Assuming he lives that long, which he probably won't. You just have to gut it out."

"That's good," I said after a pause. "That's a good point."

"Sure it is," she said.

"What about you?" I asked.

"What about me what?"

"How are you and Olive getting along?"

"Great, right now. She's on the big island for a few months, in a shack in the jungle, guarding a pot farm."

I laughed.

"Our parents suck," I said.

"Yeah."

"Cal . . . what if he's right? What if there's something wrong with me?"

"There's no 'if,' dude. There's something wrong with you."

"I'm serious," I said.

"So am I. Look, the shit we've been through, there's something wrong with both of us, and there probably always will be. We're never gonna be happy people. We're never gonna be like everyone else."

"Is that a good thing? Sometimes I think I see life more clearly than they do."

"I think we probably do see life more clearly than they do, but I'm not sure it's a good thing. It's like having a magic power. You can hear things nobody else can hear. But the special frequency that you're tuned into is the screaming and suffering that everyone else ignores. What's so great about that? You get a free cable channel nobody else gets, but all they show is snuff films."

"You're totally cheering me up," I said.

"Hey, you called me."

"Yeah," I said. I'd stopped crying. My heart had stopped racing.

"You think he's right? About me being messed up? Hurting animals and whatever? Thunder. The cat in Ballard."

"No," she said. "I was there for the thing with Thunder,

remember? You were being eight. That's all. You never shot birds with your BB gun, or any of that shit. You never went off and hurt animals in private. You told your dad about the cat, for God's sake. Still a complete mystery to me, that. You couldn't even punch a bully at school. You don't have that in you. It doesn't mean he can't use it to fuck you up, but as far as it being true—don't even think it."

We were quiet on the phone for a while.

"I'll be so glad when he's dead," I said.

"Yeah," she said. "I know."

I rubbed my free hand across my face.

"Thanks," I said. "I feel better now. But, like you said. Twenty-five cents a minute."

"All right," she said, turning on a dime. "Later."

"Later."

I hung up.

Cathy showed up about twenty minutes later, apologizing profusely. It had taken her longer than she thought it would to get her stuff packed up. Dad let her in and showed her the birds. I peeked out into the hallway and saw a pretty blond woman in her mid-twenties. She was wearing a white button-down shirt and a pair of jeans.

"Jason, this is Cathy," Dad said. She turned to look at me. She had a nice, open face. Glasses. Friendly eyes. She reached out to shake hands, and her palms were cool and soft.

"Hi, Jason," she said.

"Hi," I said, staring at her chest just long enough to be embarrassed about it later.

Dad left without saying goodbye. I didn't come out of my room again. When I went to sleep that night I could hear Cathy and someone else moving boxes into the living room.

* * *

Dad and Bruce went to Mexico the next morning. I lived with Cathy for three weeks. She wasn't home much, but when she was we read through her collection of vintage *Time* magazines, and talked about how women used to dress in advertisements, and what messages the advertisers were trying to send about their products. She told me why she loved theater. She told me about how she'd lived in Paris once. She asked me what my high school was like, and if gangs were really a thing in Seattle. She tactfully ignored the crush I obviously had on her, and she was kind and funny and fun to talk to. For three weeks, I went home after school, and I slept well at night.

59

Dad and Bruce broke up when they got back from Mexico, pretty much just like I knew they would. I'd never gotten along with Bruce, and in the alternate universe where my dad wasn't dying, I would have been happy to be rid of the annoying boyfriend so Dad and I could get our groove back. Unfortunately, in the universe I actually lived in, losing Bruce meant taking care of Dad myself, and I wasn't up for it. I wasn't up for it because I was still a kid, and I could barely take care of myself. And I wasn't up for it because the idea of my dad dying bothered me less every day.

* * *

Dad kept wanting to have little talks with me when he was high. It took me a while to figure out that was what was happening. I'd spent so much of my life around people who were living in one kind of altered state or another that even the most deeply aberrant behavior barely registered with me, or if I did notice it I thought it was just an exceptionally heavy mood swing. Dad had spent about half my life up to that point stoned on pot, or in withdrawals from pot, or high on MDA or mushrooms or the chemical of the week, so it was especially difficult for me to pick out when he was on drugs because I didn't have a baseline of normalcy to compare it to. Since he'd gotten sick he'd been taking handfuls of painkillers like Valium, Demerol, codeine, and Seconal. Anyone else would have been unconscious or dead, but Dad just got weirdly flat. And then sometimes he'd say things like "Hey, Jason, come in here and talk to me for a sec. We don't talk enough anymore."

So I'd stop, on my way in or out of my room, and cross the hall and sit awkwardly on the end of his bed. He'd lie there under his Pendleton blanket, joint in one hand, smiling at me, and looking at me through lidded eyes.

"How's school?" he'd ask.

"Fine," I'd say.

"You meeting any girls?" he'd ask.

And I'd shrug. I was still missing one of my front teeth, my clothes were all trashed, and I didn't have any friends. So really, what was the point?

And then the conversation would go somewhere else.

Once it started with him saying, "I tried with your mother, you know."

"Sure," I said.

"She's just—you know how she is. She just makes you nuts. She could push Gandhi into punching her in the mouth. I'd come home from work, you'd be sitting on the floor screaming, with a diaper full of shit, there'd be a sink full of dirty dishes, she'd be pulling her hair out and crying. We just fought all the time."

"Sure," I said again. Most of my life, my dad had been telling me that he and my mom had broken up because he couldn't stand what a slob she was. So this lined up with the story I'd always heard.

"We used to fight," he said. "We'd fight all the time."

I remembered them in the Hayes Street house, before Mom moved to San Francisco; the two of them, standing at either end of the dining room table, screaming at each other. I remembered them screaming at each other on the phone. In the park. Once at a doctor's office.

"Like one time," Dad said, "we were just going at it. Seemed like for hours. The fight went out in the hall. We were living in this apartment building. Nice older place in downtown Eugene. We'd been fighting for hours, and I decided to leave. She followed me out into the hall and I totally lost it. There was this big wide stairway down to the lobby of the building. I just grabbed her and threw her down the stairs."

I looked up. I'd never heard this part of the story before.

"You threw her down the stairs?" I asked. "Like, actually—threw her? Down the stairs?"

"Well, yeah," Dad said, pausing to take a hit off his joint. "I was trying to kill her. I threw her down this long flight of wide stairs, and she just screamed and cursed all the way down. Didn't shut up. So I went down, grabbed her by the hair, dragged her back to the top of the stairs and threw her down again."

I blinked.

"Didn't kill her that time either," he said regretfully. "Never could shut that bitch up. Hit her. Threatened her. Tried to strangle her once. Never could shut her up."

He gave me a pleasant, stoned smile.

"Hey," he said. "How's school? You meeting any girls? I

didn't date much in high school. I took a girl to prom. Japanese girl. Mom flipped out. But she was just a friend. The Japanese girl. After a while people started saying I was queer, so my buddies set me up with this girl. Laurie Gannett. She'd had a crush on me for years. Got me high and we had sex. She said later I got her pregnant. I was leaving town anyway by then. I gave her two hundred dollars and told her to take care of it. I think she probably did. I never heard anything about her having a baby. But I guess you never know. You should check that out later. Maybe you've got a brother or a sister or something."

Sometimes I used these retrospectives to ask any pressing questions I'd had floating around in the back of my mind.

"Hey, Dad, how did you actually get out of jail? I was never clear on that."

"Marianne and some other people got money together for bail," he said.

Again, this was what I'd always been told: Dad's friends bailed him out. That was how he got out of jail. It was only when I was older, into high school, that I realized bail was a pretrial thing. It didn't explain how he'd gotten probation instead of doing hard time. Oregon was notoriously hard on drug offenders in the seventies. Dad stared out the window, thinking.

"Then," he said, "while I was out on bail, I was staying in this hotel, and I . . . sort of tried to kill myself. I got in the bath and I cut my wrists. But I chickened out. I called an ambulance. There was a psychological evaluation. The shrink told the judge I was . . . something. Maybe paranoid schizophrenic? Anyway, the doctor said there was no way I could do the time. I'd crack up in jail. So the judge gave me probation. Barely left a scar."

He held up his arm for me to look at his left wrist. And, sure enough, he had two hair-thin lines of scar tissue across the base of his wrist. I couldn't believe I'd never noticed them before. Then I realized he usually wore a watch on that wrist.

"That reminds me of this time," he said. "Before I was with your mom. I was living in Venice Beach, with these two guys. Boyd and Aaron. We were dealing out of our apartment and the cops were onto us, but we only dealt with people we knew, so they couldn't get probable cause for a warrant. To get around it they sent two narcs—not cops, but confidential informants—around to pick a fight with us. They just knocked on the door, shoved their way in, started beating the shit out of us. One of them almost bit my ear off. The other one was beating on Boyd. Aaron came out of the kitchen and stabbed the one that was beating on Boyd with a kitchen knife. It went all the way through him. Through his back, came out of his chest. The other guy ran off. I hid the drugs in a vacant lot next door. The cops were furious. They took me to a hospital to get my ear fixed and the doctor let me sneak out the back door."

"Okay," I said. "I've got to go. I need some fresh air."

"Hey, Jason. Come here and talk to me for a sec. We never talk anymore."

"I can't, Dad. I have to be somewhere else."

* * *

I finally got rid of Dad's birds. Some of them went to friends, and some of them went to pet stores, but all of them went and I didn't bury any of them in the garden. Thunder had been spending more and more time down in Kris's apartment. I didn't mind. I'd never liked him much, and the fewer things I had to take care of besides myself, the happier I was.

60

Sometime during my tenth grade year, I told Brandon my dad was gay. I got Dad's permission first, but I had to argue my case. Dad didn't think it was anyone else's business. I basically agreed, but the traditional lie—telling people Bruce was my uncle—wasn't going to fly anymore.

"Dad, Brandon lives in the same neighborhood we do. He sees gay guys all day every day. If he had a problem with it, I'd expect to have heard him say something by now. And one way or the other, he's going to figure it out. Better I tell him, don't you think?"

"Fine," Dad said. "But don't come crying to me if it blows up in your face."

One of Dad's great fears in life was me coming crying to him for any reason.

I didn't know how to approach Brandon, so I just invited him up to my place, sat him down on my bed, and told him.

He stared off into space for a minute, then said, "So . . . how were you born?"

"I—" I paused. That wasn't the response I'd been expecting. "Dad was married for a while. To a woman. I was born. It's not like every guy can just be who he is. Most guys take a while to come out, and sometimes, before they get there, they have kids. And some guys are gayer than others; some of them are into men and women both. That happens, too."

"Okay," he said. "That all?"

I took a deep breath.

"Not exactly," I said. "Remember how I told you last December that my dad had been diagnosed with tuberculosis?"

313

"Yeah," he said. "Not tuberculosis?"

"No," I said.

"Okay. I knew. You know that, right?"

"I guessed. I just wanted to get it out there."

"Sure," he said.

"Any questions?"

"Nope," he said.

And that was pretty much the last time we ever talked about it.

* * *

While Brandon could be exceptionally cool about some things, he pushed hard against the glass ceiling that relegated him to hapless dork status, and he wasn't picky about whose back he stood on while he did it. Midway through our sophomore year he started hanging out with a crew of girls at school who occupied kind of a weird social niche.

I didn't know them, but I'd noticed them around school. They generally hung out with guys who were on the chess team or in Latin Club. Some of them had some nerd chops of their own—they were in advanced math courses and physical sciences classes. Most of them were in marching band. Their clothes, body types, and hairstyles varied widely. Their most notable feature, from where I stood, was that they didn't seem to be able to keep their hands to themselves. It seemed like whenever I saw them, they were laughing and tickling some poor band geek, or wrestling him to the ground, or ganging up on him and putting makeup on him or something.

Brandon and Ethan were well networked with the pocket-protector-and-slide-rule set, but Brandon had shunned them for most of his first year of high school. Then, at some point, he leveraged those connections to start spending a lot of time with these geek divas. None of it meant much to me, except that sometimes when I saw the band geek girls mauling a guy, it turned out to be Brandon. And sometimes he'd drop off the radar for a few days.

"What do you do with them?" I'd ask, when he came up for air.

"You know," he said. "We just goof around."

"Like how?"

"A little making out. Whatever."

"Which one?" I asked.

"It varies," he said.

Then after a few months he started spending most of his time with a girl named Sadie. Sadie didn't look like someone Brandon would be into. One of the things he and I talked about when we went for walks was what we liked in girls, and Sadie didn't have a single item on Brandon's list, except maybe her vagina.

She was tall and broad-shouldered, with a flat face, a heavy forehead, and a nose like a veteran prizefighter's. She had terrible skin, and braces, and she generally dressed in oversize flannel shirts and jeans. I liked to imagine she'd undergo some kind of developmental transformation and turn out to be a future Miss America, because God knew she had something like that coming, karma-wise, but in the meantime she was not remotely Brandon's type. And yet, when he disappeared lately, he disappeared with Sadie.

Then, suddenly, he had all this free time again and I didn't see him with the geek girls anymore. I didn't think much of it. We went back to hanging out on weekdays—watching movies and going for walks around the neighborhood at night. And one day we were sitting on his front steps talking when Ethan poked his head out the front door.

"Brandon," he said. "Phone for you."

"Who is it?" Brandon asked.

"Sadie," Ethan said.

"Tell her I'm not home," Brandon said.

"Okay." Ethan disappeared back inside the house.

I looked at the space where Ethan had been, then back at Brandon.

"Were you and Sadie going out?" I asked.

"Not really," he said.

"But enough to break up?"

"I guess."

"Why'd you break up with her, man?"

"She got too attached."

"Hold up," I said. "You just said she got too attached?"

"Yeah."

"You know, that's funny. If someone else said that, I'd think it was because she put out, and he kicked her to the curb after he got what he wanted."

He looked at me, but he didn't say anything. We stared at each other for a while, then I looked away.

"That's cold," I said.

"She a friend of yours?" he asked.

"Nope. Don't even know the girl."

"Then what do you care?"

Maybe he had a point. What would Han Solo do? Mind his own goddamn business, probably. But I couldn't shake the feeling that I was letting someone down. Maybe it was Brandon.

61

The summer after my tenth grade year, the dentists at the free clinic where I got my teeth worked on finally replaced the tooth I'd lost in the car accident. That also happened to be the summer I started working out—and the summer my wardrobe improved, courtesy of the AIDS epidemic.

A lot of the gay men on Capitol Hill had been effectively disowned by their straight families when they came out of the closet so when they died, there was no grieving mother to sort through their stuff and dispose of it. The straight family didn't even come to the funeral a lot of the time. For the first couple of years, dead gay men's property typically went to their closest friends. But then those friends started to die or their apartments filled up, and suddenly there was this ominous surplus of secondhand rattan furniture, glass-topped coffee tables, posters for Broadway musicals—and clothes. Lots and lots of young men's clothes in a wide variety of styles. And, after about the time I turned fifteen, that was how I dressed myself.

Some of my new clothes came from people I'd known. I got a collection of really nice St. John's Bay button-down shirts that used to belong to Billy. The sleeves were a little short for me, because I was taller than Billy had been, but I kept them rolled up, and otherwise the shirts fit fine. I had some jeans and T-shirts I got from a guy named Mac, who was a friend of my dad's. The T-shirts were different than the ones I got on the cheap at JCPenney—they were tight, single-color shirts made out of some kind of stretchy cotton-synthetic blend. And I had a lot of other clothes I just picked up in alleys, when some landlord would have to throw an entire apartment full of stuff in the Dumpster—pants, shirts, and belts. I still didn't have enough underwear or socks, but I was all set for outerwear. My new look was topped off when Bruce gave me a leather bomber jacket for my birthday that year. He and my dad were still broken up, and he and I still didn't get along, but he was part of our network and he wanted to do me a favor. He used his employee discount to get it for me at the big downtown department store where he worked. Even with the discount, it was the most expensive thing I'd ever owned.

I undertook this makeover with no particular expectation that it would pay off for me, and it didn't seem to amount to much at school. On Broadway, however, the effect was immediate and in no way subtle. Or maybe there was a subtle component that was just drowned out by the guys who hooted at me from passing cars, came out of bars to yell things like "Gimme some of that!" and followed me home, got my name off my mailbox, looked my number up in the phone book, and called me to ask me out on dates.

I didn't think any of the guys who were cruising me realized that I was jailbait. I'd always looked older than I was, and I was already shaving. But I was still a little unnerved by the intensity of their interest.

The new attention was confusing in other ways, too. I couldn't talk to my dad about it. Even if he hadn't been stoned on pain medication night and day, he had too much of an agenda when it came to stuff like this. I could sort of talk to Brandon or my friends at school about it, as long as I kept it philosophical—as long as I talked about how over-the-top the men were being, and how inappropriate it would be for a straight guy to hit on a woman like that. But as soon as I started to take the conversation toward the thing I actually wanted to talk about, the reactions I got were so negative that I'd stop immediately, change course, back up, and cover. Because the thing I actually wanted to talk about was the fact that I liked it.

I liked the attention and I liked the affirmation. It made me feel good to be wanted, and it didn't matter much who I was wanted by, or what they wanted me for. The wilder the pass, the better it made me feel about myself. When a muscular blond guy with a chiseled jaw and a California tan drove his convertible over the parking strip and cut me off on the sidewalk across the street from Volunteer Park to ask me if I wanted to take him for a ride, I told him I wasn't interested. It was half true. I didn't want to have sex with him. But I'd absolutely been walking near Volunteer Park in the hope that someone like him would give me that little boost. I felt better about myself for the rest of the week.

Which was extremely confusing. I didn't have a single role model in books, TV shows, or movies to tell me what it meant to be a fifteen-year-old tease in one of the gayest neighborhoods in the country. Even the idea of a teenage boy basing his self-esteem on his looks or having people hit on him was uncharted territory for me. My dad and his friends had said some things that referred to it, but I'd never seen it anywhere in my own world—in my world of comic books and war movies, after-school specials and syndicated sitcoms.

I was pretty sure Han Solo wouldn't approve. Though, really, who knew? He had a certain swagger. Meanwhile, I just had to find my own way with it, and I had no intention of forgoing all that attention just because I liked girls.

* * *

Living in a gay neighborhood, dressing in the clothes of dead gay men—and trying to get live ones to hit on me—did yield other kinds of attention. During my afternoon walks around the Hill, guys with mullets and trucker caps would sometimes slow their cars down on the street next to me, roll down their windows, and yell "Faggot!" at me. Or "Faggots!" to everyone on the street, depending on where I was. At first I just thought it was funny; the fact that these redneck assholes drove out of their way to cruise through my neighborhood and shout insults from passing cars, like a bunch of cowards. But then one day a pickup truck with two guys in the back stopped about twenty yards ahead of me and one of the guys yelled, "Hey, faggot!"

And I yelled, "Come over here and say that shit to my face!"

I was pretty sure he'd be too chickenshit to actually do it.

But then he said, "All right," and jumped out of the back of the truck, followed by his friend. The driver got out and watched over the cab of the truck.

In spite of my wardrobe upgrade, I still carried a lot of odds and ends in my pockets, so when they got out of the truck I took my sharpened chisel out of one pocket and an expandable club out of the other pocket. The expandable club was a cheap version of the kind police carried: it was made of three steel tubes, one inside the other, that could be extended and locked into position to form a club about eighteen inches long. I'd bought mine at a martial arts store in the International District, Seattle's Chinatown, for twenty dollars. It was a piece of junk, but when I snapped it to full extension the two guys coming toward me slowed down.

I wanted to say something tough, but I was so scared I was afraid my voice would crack and give me away. I had six inches on either one of them, and I had my little weapons, but two on one was bad odds no matter what. Three on one would be a massacre, if the driver got into it. Even assuming he wasn't just staying near his truck because that was where he kept his gun or his baseball bat or whatever.

"The fuck?" one of the guys said, eyeing my club.

"Come on," said the first one.

"Naw," said the second one slowly. "He ain't worth it. He's probably got the AIDS or something."

"Ronnie!" said the driver. "Let's get going, man!"

"All right," said the one who'd started it. "Let's go. Leave the faggot alone."

They went back to their truck and drove away.

My hands were shaking so badly it took me five or six tries to get the telescoping club closed up and put away.

A few months later I was out on one of my late-night walks with Brandon when a car came out of nowhere and jumped the curb to block us in. Someone shone a spotlight in our faces. When we put our hands up to shield our eyes from the glare, a voice called out over a loudspeaker.

"Awww, what's the matter? Does the light hurt your eyes? Too much time in the closet?"

"What?" I asked.

"No faggots on the streets after midnight!" barked the voice. "You've been warned!"

Then the spotlight went off, and the car slammed into reverse and disappeared around the corner, while Brandon and I were still blinking the spots out of our eyes.

"Was that a cop car?" I asked after a minute.

"Yep," Brandon said. "Sure was."

* * *

Ironically, the self-esteem boost I got from being cruised by hot guys on Broadway led pretty quickly to dating in high school. I still didn't have any real friends in school; just my few acquaintances, Ryan, my weekends-in-Ballard buddy, and Brandon as my invisible at-home-only friend in my own neighborhood. But I started getting looks from girls—looks I probably wouldn't have understood if I hadn't seen a similar expression on the faces of a few dozen guys over the preceding year. I had a girlfriend by the end of the year, which made me a late bloomer compared to everyone else I knew, but I felt like the king of the world. Dad being in a drug coma so much of the time meant I could even bring my girlfriend, Alexis, back to my apartment for extended make-out sessions. My room still wasn't very clean, but Alexis had lived on the streets of the University District for a few months, so she had a pretty wide filter when it came to housecleaning and personal hygiene.

One night we were making out in my room with the lights off and someone started screaming on the street outside my house. I barely registered it. People were always screaming in the streets around my neighborhood. Alex stopped for a second and whispered, "Is that okay?"

"Don't worry about it," I said. "It happens all the time."

After a while I was vaguely aware that the screaming stopped. I heard what sounded like a CB radio, and my brain filed it away, but I didn't think anything about it in the moment.

The next day, Kris told me that Scotty had died the night before. I was taken a little off guard by it; I'd seen him just a few weeks earlier. He'd loaned me his tent so I could take it on a school camping trip. I'd been surprised that someone like Scotty owned a tent, but he'd been really nice about it. He'd seemed fine. Now he was dead.

"What did he die of?" I asked.

"Yellow fever," she said. "It happened really fast."

"Jesus. Who dies of yellow fever?"

"People in the tropics. And AIDS patients, evidently."

"Who found him?" I asked.

"Nobody. He died in the hospital. He was actually here last night. He crawled from his apartment. Three blocks on his hands and knees. But he couldn't get up the stairs, so he just lay there in the street screaming for Mark. I found him when I came home from work and called an ambulance."

I stared at her, replaying what I'd been hearing the night before. Had it been "Help me, Mark"? Was that what I'd been hearing? I played the sound over and over in my head, until I could pick out the words. My breathing got fast. I started to sweat.

"Are you okay?" Kris asked.

I shook it off. Or tried to.

"Yeah," I said. "I mean—no. Jesus. That's awful."

"Yeah," she said. "He was off his head with fever. It was terrible."

I nodded and changed the subject.

A week later, my dad came home and gave me three pairs of jeans and a dozen pairs of wool hiking socks.

"Where'd these come from?" I asked.

"Scotty's apartment," Dad said. "His landlord was throwing everything away, but these looked like they'd fit you."

62

Alexis was my first girlfriend. I'd met her in Marine Science class in the winter of my eleventh grade year. We got partnered up to work on clay models of animals that live on the wooden pilings of piers. She was a big girl—five foot seven or so, broad-shouldered, and a little on the heavy side. She had curly brown hair, full features, and large blue eyes. She always looked startled. Her jeans were tight. Her shirts had gathers and ruffles around the shoulders and neck. She wore too much perfume, and tacky jewelry. I didn't know her personally before we were partnered together for class, but I watched people at school and I'd seen her date two geeks from the marching band—best friends, that she dated one after the other; guys I never thought would have girlfriends. After she dated them both, they repaired their friendship and became reasonably popular, having solved the mystery of girls. I watched all of this from a distance. None of them knew me. But when Alexis started giving me the look in Marine Science class, I had an idea where things might be headed.

After school that day, while I was sitting on my school bus, Marti, the girl from my German class, got on the bus and sat down next to me.

"Hi," she said.

"Hi," I said. "Don't you have a car? I thought you had a car."

"I do," she said. "I—"

"And also, you live in a completely different neighborhood."

"Yes," she said patiently. "I'm here to give you this."

She handed me a folded piece of paper.

"What's this?" I asked.

"It's a phone number. My friend Alex wanted me to give it to you. She'd like you to call her."

"Alex . . . Alexis? From Marine Science class?"

"Yes. She's my best friend. She found out I knew you, asked me to give you this."

"Okay," I said.

"Don't freak out," said Marti.

"I'll do my best," I said.

She got up and left the bus.

I had to admit, I was a little freaked out.

* * *

Brandon wasn't on the bus that day. Screwing Sadie seemed to have worked some kind of magic on his self-confidence, and his social life at Garfield had blossomed accordingly. He'd gotten on the staff of the school paper, and he was on the debate team, which he insisted was a great place to pick up girls. He even had a couple of friends who hung out with him outside of school. Some of these new guys had cars, so he ended up catching rides home more than half the time lately. I was sort of happy for him, in the conflicted tradition of the uncool guy whose partner in uncoolness suddenly becomes cool, but I wished he was on the bus to give me some advice about this Alexis thing.

When I got home I spent twenty minutes or so dithering, then called Alexis. She answered the phone at her house.

"Hello?" she said.

"Hi. This is Jason. Marti's friend. I mean—from Marine Science."

"Oh, hi!"

"Hi."

Long, awkward pause. The lines buzzed quietly.

"So, how's this work?" I asked. I realized it was something I'd heard in a TV show, where some rich guy was talking to a kidnapper about how to ransom his son.

"You wanna hang out tonight?" she asked.

"Sure," I said. "I mean, yes."

"Great! I'll come by and get you. Where are you?"

I gave her my address and she said she'd be there in about forty-five minutes. After I hung up I felt vaguely nauseated. I got up and changed clothes. Then I changed them again. One more time for good measure.

She showed up right on schedule. I was sitting on the porch waiting for her when she arrived. When she came up the stairs she was wearing a pair of tight cutoff jeans, rolled up and hemmed, and a loose rugby shirt and a pair of Reeboks. Her curly, light brown hair was tied up in a kind of topknot.

"You ready?" she asked. Her smile was huge. Her eyes were huge. Her teeth were huge. Oh, Grandma . . .

"Sure," I said.

She drove an old Saab in one of those modern noncolors; silver-white with an undertone of blue or something. When we got downstairs and climbed in, she put on a pair of fingerless leather driving gloves.

"Are we going fast?" I asked.

"Only way I like to drive," she said, putting the car in gear and launching us up the hill toward Broadway in a smooth, constant acceleration.

"Where are we going?" I asked.

"Marti's house," she said.

I knew Marti lived somewhere up north, but I was fuzzy on the details. Alexis took the long way, so she could hit more straightaways. She kept looking at me out of the corner of her eye to see how I was reacting, but I kept cool. There were plenty of things I was afraid of in life, but dying in a car accident wasn't one of them. She seemed to regard my lack of reaction as a challenge and kept pushing the little car harder, pounding out of stoplights in first and standing on the gas for fifty or sixty yards before she shifted up and let the engine take a breath. She blew through Montlake, took us across the ship canal, and was making her way into a north Seattle neighborhood called Wedgwood when the car suddenly stalled.

"Shit," she muttered, throwing it into neutral and restarting before we'd come to a complete stop on the road. We got another few blocks before the car died again. She did the same restart trick, but she looked worried now. We pulled in at an ice cream place next to a trestle bridge for the old Burke-Gilman railroad, and Alexis used a pay phone to call Marti, who suggested running the car up to a garage just north of her house if we could make it that far.

Alexis coaxed the engine back into life and managed to get us sixty blocks north to the garage.

"You know anything about cars?" she asked me.

"Not really," I said.

"All right." I couldn't read her affect. She seemed sort of mad and businesslike, while at the same time she was trying to maintain some kind of mood. Like an actress whose script reading has been interrupted.

We got out of the car and a tall skinny guy in his early twenties came out of the garage to see what we needed. Only now that we were here, it didn't look like much of a garage. More of a gas station, with an advertisement saying they could do brakes and lube.

"You all need some help?" the skinny guy said. He was wearing blue coveralls and had a greasy rag in his back pocket.

"My car died," Alexis said.

"Well," said the gas station attendant. "Let's take a look at that."

He popped open the hood and proceeded to engage in a weird pissing contest with me, asking me what I thought was wrong with the car, then talking about his own theories when I said I didn't know. I realized after a minute that he was trying to show off for Alexis, and that my role was to be all jealous and weird about it. I had just enough experience with girls to know that I was perfectly capable of being jealous and weird. But the fact was, I didn't know Alexis well enough to have that much invested in the situation. So, for once in my life, I got to play it cool. And, just like in the car with Alexis driving, my reserved behavior seemed to push the guy to want to do something stupid.

"Well," he said finally. "I think what happened here is you

just overheated her. We put some water in there, she should be good as new."

I perked up a little at this, remembering something Sean, our mechanic/dealer friend in Eugene, had said about cars and engines and how they had different systems that operated in different ways.

"Isn't the cooling system pressurized right now?" I asked.

"There is no cooling system," he said. "Just the water in the radiator."

"Uh. Okay. But, I mean, if you . . . the water's hot now, right? And it runs through the engine, to cool it off? Engine's hot, water's hot. So, if I understand how this works, when the car overheats, it's because the engine kind of swells up and stops working. The parts stop fitting together right. Water swells up, too. Lots of pressure. If you open the radiator, won't . . . something bad happen?"

Alexis and the attendant stared at me.

"Good point," the attendant said, taking out his grease rag and wrapping it around his hand. "I'll use this, in case some comes out of there when I open it."

"You think that'll do it?" I asked doubtfully.

"Sure," he said.

The attendant reached in carefully and started to unscrew the radiator cap. He did it from as far away as he could, arm fully extended, rag-encased hand working quickly. He got it through about six turns before it exploded, violently. Alexis screamed. The radiator cap shot twenty feet into the air, blasted out by a geyser of steam and boiling water. The attendant ran out of the blast area before the hot water came back down, then stood in the middle of the parking lot jumping in circles, cursing and waving his scalded hand around.

"Well, shit," the attendant said, when he'd finally calmed down. I could see from a distance that his right hand was bright red, and there were white blisters forming on his thumb and forefinger. "Guess we may as well at least get our money's worth out of that little show."

He went to the gas pump island and reeled out the water hose toward the car. Another fun fact about engines and heat was percolating around in the back of my head, but I didn't manage to recall it before the attendant started running water into the radiator. When he had it topped off he told Alexis to try starting the car again.

I pursed my lips, but I was too embarrassed to say anything. For some reason, being right about the radiator pressure seemed like a bad thing in this context. I had a feeling that the only thing worse than being right about something else would be saying it and having it turn out to be wrong. So I stood there, trying to figure out what I should do, while Alexis got behind the wheel and tried to start the car.

It made a sad little whirring sound and then just stopped. After that, it wouldn't even turn over. I leaned awkwardly down to look under the car without actually getting on my hands and knees, and saw a mixture of water and antifreeze leaking out of the bottom in a slow, ponderous drip.

"Maybe the oil," said the gas station attendant.

"Maybe not," said Alexis. "Can I leave this here until I can have it towed?"

"Sure," said the attendant.

Alexis walked over to the bank of pay phones next to the parking lot and called Marti to come pick us up.

"Marti!" she said. "My car just exploded!"

She paused to take in Marti's reply.

"I know! I love that car! I hope it doesn't cost too much to fix."

I just listened. I was pretty sure the gas station moron had just cracked the engine block, but it didn't seem worth saying so at this stage.

* * *

Marti came to pick us up in her little yellow Volkswagen Beetle and drove us back to her place, fifteen blocks to the south. I was quietly appalled that people from this far north were being shipped all the way down to Garfield, at the same time I was being quietly appalled that there were people this far north at all. As Marti turned left onto a tar-and-gravel residential street with no sidewalks, I could see block after endless block of ugly mid-century suburban-style houses on oversize lots, reeling off in every direction.

"I've never been to this neighborhood before," I said, as I followed Marti and Alexis into the house.

"It's nice," Marti said. "Lots of room to move around."

The house reminded me a lot of the places my dad's family lived in, up in Stanwood and Camano Island: California-style architecture imported to the Pacific Northwest during the housing boom after World War II. The ground floor had a living room with wall-to-wall mustard yellow carpeting and a kitchen separated from the main room by a bright orange counter. The walls were covered in fake wood paneling. Big glass doors led out onto a deck that I couldn't see very well. An overweight white guy was sitting in an easy chair next to the front door, watching a baseball game. He wore a blue button-down shirt and a pair of well-used jeans; shoes off, holes in his socks; short, light brown hair with some gray in it; silly little mustache. Big soulful eyes.

"Jason," Marti said. "This is my dad."

"Nice to meet you, Mister . . ." I dived for Marti's last name and came up with "Brower."

"Hiya," Mr. Brower said. Then he did something unusual among easy-chair-sitting, baseball-watching white guys in my experience—he got partway out of his chair to shake my hand; firm grip, lots of calluses.

"And my mom," Marti continued. I realized there was a skinny, anxious-looking woman standing in the kitchen. The sun was going down outside, but there were hardly any lights on inside. Mrs. Brower had been nearly invisible in the shadows on the other side of the counter. She was medium height, with dark brown hair piled up in a loose arrangement of hairpins and clips. She wore cat-eye glasses, complete with the elaborate necklace-like retaining strap that was draped over her yellow polyester turtleneck. She was, at least, wearing blue jeans. It was her only concession to the fact that it was 1988. Looking back and forth from Mr. to Mrs. Brower, I could see how if you added them up and divided by two, you'd get Marti.

"And this is my rat," Marti said, pointing to a glass cage on a shelf next to the television, "Roosevelt."

"Hi, Roosevelt," I said.

"We're going upstairs," Marti announced.

"Okay," Marti's mom said.

I followed the girls to a doorway at the other end of the living room, which led to a steep flight of stairs that turned sharply up to an attic room. When I got up there I saw the usual teenager stuff: bookshelves, a small portable stereo, clothes scattered everywhere, and a twin bed next to a filthy bathroom. Then, on the other side of the room, I saw a mattress laid down on the floor with a stack of neatly folded clothes next to it.

"I'm staying here for a few days," Alexis said. "Just long enough for things to cool down. I'm having an issue. With my parents."

"Sure," I said, thinking I wished I had a mattress and some extra clothes at Ryan's house. I still went over there most weekends, and we still did mostly the same stuff we'd always done: sports I didn't understand the rules for, watching TV, role-playing games, blowing things up, trespassing, and petty larceny. He'd traded his paper route for a job at McDonald's, so instead of getting up with him and delivering newspapers, I got up with him and walked him to work, then hung around in a nearby park and read until he finished the breakfast shift. I'd been sleeping at his place six or seven nights a month for more than two years, but I still slept on the floor, under my coat, with my backpack as a pillow. Not that Ryan and his mom owed me anything, but boy—I would have loved a mattress.

"Alex is always having issues with her parents," Marti volunteered, when I didn't respond to Alexis's declaration.

"Who doesn't?" I said.

Marti giggled nervously. Alexis smiled. She seemed to approve.

Marti mostly left us alone after that, under the pretext of going downstairs to help her mom get dinner ready. Alexis played me Amy Grant songs on Marti's stereo, and told me how her and Marti's dads were both Masons, and how Alexis and Marti had both been members of a girls' auxiliary group called Job's Daughters.

"It was fun," she said. "In a way. We did car washes to raise money and stuff. But everyone was always in everyone else's business. That was why I kind of had to quit after I got pregnant. After I got rid of it."

"Okay," I said.

"I mean, I kind of actually got kicked out. But they would have let me stay if I'd been sorry, so I figure not apologizing was sort of the same thing as quitting."

I made a noncommittal noise, and thought about how interesting this day was working out to be. I'd gotten up that morning, gone to school, with no idea that anything out of the ordinary was going to happen. Now here I was, having this conversation, in this place, with this girl. And why was it all happening? What had it taken to launch my life into the Twilight Zone in one afternoon? A little exercise, a replacement for one of my front teeth, and a leather jacket.

Jesus.

I realized that the experience I was having right that minute actually explained a lot about why cool, attractive people acted so strange so much of the time. Their lives were always like this, only the girls were prettier, the houses bigger, and the cars nicer. They didn't even live on the same planet as I did.

I had no illusions about that point: I did not belong in this place, doing these things, with these people. Brandon might be able to handle social mobility, or evolution, but I was utterly incapable of adapting. It was only a matter of time before I screwed something up, tipped my hand, and got sent back to the Dungeons & Dragons table in the metaphorical cafeteria of life.

I realized Alexis and I had been staring into each other's eyes for kind of a while.

"So," she said. "Are you going to kiss me or what?"

We were sitting next to each other at the top of the stairs that led up to Marti's room. The best model I had for this kind of thing was Princess Leia and Han Solo at the end of *The Empire Strikes Back*. I did my best.

"That was pretty good," she said when I came up for air. "But you should use your tongue. Like this."

We kissed again, and her tongue peeked into my mouth. I was surprised by how intimate it was, given how gross the idea sounded. I tried to replicate what she was showing me and she pulled back.

"Little motions," she said. "You're not trying to lick my tonsils off."

"Okay," I said. I did better the next time.

Marti's mom must have picked up on what was happening, because Alexis and I only got about fifteen minutes of kissing before Marti came up and said she had to take me home. I made small talk on the way back, but all I could think, over and over again, was that everything was different now. Again. Everything was just going to keep being different—changing—from now on.

It was a terrifying realization.

* * *

Words were abstract to Alexis. The things she said always meant something else. When she asked me questions, she read things into my answers—things I didn't mean to say, didn't think I'd even implied. Then she explained to me why I meant the thing she'd heard, instead of what I'd said. I found it discomfiting and avoided the problem by not talking much when we were together. I was honestly surprised when she seemed to find my brooding silences intriguing.

The second time she came over to my house, she told me she'd run into Lizzie on the stairs and that Lizzie had asked who Alexis was.

"I said, 'I'm Jason's girlfriend!' " Alexis announced proudly.

"You did?" I asked. It was news to me, but I didn't see the harm in it. There wasn't a lot of competition for the position.

The only real instruction I'd received about how all this worked was from Brandon, who, in the wake of the Sadie thing, had adopted a decidedly mercenary approach to relationships. He'd told me the worst thing I could do in a new relationship was to push too hard. But, so far, that didn't seem to be a problem with Alexis.

"I love you," she said, the next time she came over to my house. I'd cleaned my room so we could make out there, since she was still staying at Marti's place. We were lying on my bed, fully clothed, making out. I had one hand on her hip. It was as close as I'd been willing to come to trying to feel her up.

"Uh," I said. "I love you, too?"

"Are you a virgin?" she asked.

I blinked in surprise. "Yes."

"Hm," she said. "We'll have to work on that."

"Okay."

"Would you like that?"

I wasn't sure what to do with that question.

"What do you like?" she asked when I didn't answer. "What are you into?"

"I just said—I haven't done anything yet."

"Fine, but what do you think about when you jerk off?"

"I don't."

"You don't think about anything?" she asked.

"No. I mean, I don't—the other thing you said."

"You don't jerk off?" she asked.

"No."

She narrowed her eyes at me.

"Are you telling me the truth?" she asked.

"Yes," I said.

"Never?"

"Never," I said.

"That's totally bizarre," she said.

She was right, of course. My attitudes about sex were weird. I'd only recently started to appreciate how weird they were, compared to most other people. Kris had been giving me shit about it when she thought I was being prudish. Which was pretty much every time the subject of sex came up in any context.

"How a kid who grew up around as much balling as you did could be so sex-negative is just beyond me," she'd say.

I thought she was probably just trying to convince herself that the human sexuality lesson she and Jimmy had given me when I was four was a good thing, but I didn't need any convincing on that score. When I thought about it—which I really hated doing—I figured that my attitudes about sex, and about male sexuality specifically, were mostly based on everything I'd seen and heard *after* watching Kris and Jimmy screw. Because sure, there was all the theory about humping and fucking and all that silly kid stuff we used to talk about when I was little. But in practice, in the real world, most of the stuff I heard about men was unspeakably bad.

Back in Eugene, Marcy's boyfriend Kenneth had supposedly molested Marcy's daughters, Faith and Crystal. Jimmy's drug buddy had molested Lizzie. Calliope had woken up in the middle of the night and found Will jerking off and crying next to her bed. One of Dad's teachers had molested him when he was young. I had my own experiences with Principal Adams, ambiguous as they were. Prison, which was a constant backdrop in the mythology of my people, was virtually synonymous with rape. And wherever I went when I was little, there were always the warnings: never get into a car with a strange man; never trust strange men; if a strange man tries to grab you, scream; if a man touches you in your bathing suit area, tell someone. It wasn't just a lot of talk. It happened to me and Eddie that time by the railroad tracks, when an actual strange man had asked if we wanted to go into the bushes with him and watch him beat off.

In spite of all this, I had, by some miracle, managed to avoid the trap of believing that I might secretly have one of these monsters lurking inside of me. I never worried about waking up one morning with an uncontrollable desire to use my penis to ruin someone else's life. But I hated those people—those *men*. I hated them with an elemental purity. After Principal Adams it was like a constant hum, like the feeling of standing under high-tension electrical wires. It made the hair on my arms stand up. And I'd get a little zap if I thought about touching myself at night. Or looking at dirty pictures. Or looking down a girl's shirt when she bent forward. Until finally, right around the time when I might have been motivated to try to get past all that negative reinforcement, there was the thing where my dad and Billy and Scotty, and every third guy I saw walking down the street, were all suddenly dying of a horrible wasting illness. That they got from having sex.

None of it meant that I'd given up on sex. I wanted romance. I wanted to date. It was just that, without knowing what the reward was, I hadn't had enough motivation to figure any of it out. And, really, I didn't think I'd need to figure it out on my own. I'd always had some idea that there'd be some natural process of discovery that I'd go through, that I'd meet a girl who was as inexperienced as I was and we'd learn this stuff together. Then I'd work my way up to kissing and copping a feel and heavy petting and so on. But that wasn't how it was working out.

With Alexis, sex felt like a cross between an aptitude test and a kids' game. I was supposed to let down all my defenses and let her touch me—like we were playing doctor or something— except I was being scored the whole time. And it was pretty obvious from Alexis's attitude that my test results this time around were not going to be in the 99th percentile. I tried to slow things down, but I couldn't articulate the why of it; I kept stumbling into platitudes about respecting her too much to rush things. The idea that I might want to take things slow for my own reasons was a nonstarter. It was an article of faith for Alexis and everyone else I knew that a healthy teenage boy would crawl a mile on his hands and knees over broken glass for the privilege of sticking his hands down some girl's pants.

Brandon's recent behavior certainly seemed to support that mythology.

Maybe there really was something wrong with me.

A week or so after we started dating, Alexis moved out of Marti's house and back in with her parents. She lived in the same part of North Seattle as Marti, but in a much nicer house, with nicer furniture and a nicer yard. She only took me up there a couple of times, usually when nobody else was around.

She introduced me to her mother once, in passing—literally. We were passing through the living room, on our way to get a textbook from her bedroom, and her mom was in there on the couch. Alexis said, "Mom, this is Jason," as we were walking by. I wouldn't have been able to pick her mom out of a lineup afterward. I never met Alexis's father. She was still mad at her parents. She'd been mad at them for a long time. It took me about a week to get the story out of her.

"They locked me up," she said one afternoon in my bedroom.

"Like, in a hospital?" I asked.

"Yeah."

"Why?"

"I tried to kill myself," she said.

"How?" I asked, thinking about my dad, and the scars on his wrist.

"That time?" she said.

"There was more than one time?" I asked.

"Yeah," she said. "That time it was with a bottle of aspirin. The time before that I cut up my stomach with a kitchen knife."

"You can't kill yourself with a bottle of aspirin," I said.

Or by cutting up your stomach with a kitchen knife, I thought.

"Well, sure," she said. "I know that now. It happened because I ran away. I mostly lived in the University District. In squats, or with friends. I told people my name was Lauren, so it would be harder for the cops to track me down. Eventually they caught me and sent me home. My parents went with me everywhere for a week, to keep me from running away again. So I swallowed a bottle of aspirin to get away from them. Afterward, they said they were taking me to family counseling. We went to this place up north that turned out to be another hospital. But I didn't know that. We all went in together, and I was in front, and I went through this doorway ahead of them and the door closed behind me. When I turned around and tried to open it, the doorknob just spun."

I frowned. I was thinking that someone who did something like that to me would be taking their life in their hands to sleep in the same house I did every night. But then, my dad had done plenty of awful shit to me—including threatening to have me committed—and I had never killed him in his sleep. So maybe it was all relative.

"I fought the nurses for a while," she said. "They tied me down. Four-points restraints, they called it. I was like that for days. Eventually I just gave up. They kept me for a few weeks. Counseling. Group sessions."

"Why'd they let you out?" I asked.

"The doctors said I was better. I think really our insurance just ran out."

She never asked me anything about my dad or my home life. She never asked me where Dad was all the time or why he never came out of his room when he was home. Never asked me where my mom was. I wondered who she thought she was talking to, what she thought I was thinking while she was telling me these things.

"Anyway," she said, "they're not my real parents."

I jolted back into the conversation.

"What?"

"I'm adopted," she said. "You can't tell?"

"How would I be able to tell?" I asked.

"They're white."

". . . and you're not?"

"I'm one-eighth black," she said. "That's why my hair's so curly."

"Oh," I said.

It was sort of possible. Her hair *was* curly. She had blue eyes, but that didn't mean much. Even at Garfield I knew a few blue-eyed black people. Still, I figured that about half of everything Alexis told me was pure bullshit. I could just never tell which half.

"How do you know?" I asked. "About being part black?"

"It's on my birth certificate," she said.

I sighed. That was no help. I decided it didn't matter. I'd let her have this one.

63

Brandon and I spent a lot less time together during junior year. Partly it was just that we were heading in different directions personally. But there was a social component as well. Since his initial foray into womanizing, Brandon had gone through a couple of evolutionary downgrades, each one harder to respect than the last.

Appearance-wise, he'd stepped up his game considerably. He trimmed his old bowl cut down to a standard side part, which he held in place with enough hair product to achieve what we used to call the wet look. He got rid of his parachute pants in favor of artificially distressed jeans, and he started wearing an old denim jacket of mine, with the sleeves rolled up, over designer T-shirts. He was still kind of chunky and his skin wasn't great, but he had kind of a nerdy River Phoenix thing going on that seemed to work for him.

Once his physical transformation was under way, he had apprenticed himself to a guy named Andre, who he'd met through one of his cousins, or who maybe was one of his cousins. Brandon's extended family relationships didn't make a lot of sense to me. Andre didn't go to our school. He wasn't even a kid—he'd graduated from high school three years earlier, in 1985. He had a day job of some kind and owned a nice car, and he was an unnerving amalgam of hotness: short, spiky black hair, pale skin, thick black eyebrows, dark eyes, and a hawklike nose over a wide, angular mouth and a sharp chin. He was medium height, rail-thin, and ridiculously muscular.

Andre and Brandon spent a lot of nights cruising the all-ages clubs in South Lake Union and the University District. The summer before our junior year, Brandon told me he'd had sex with thirteen girls in parking lots, alleys, and the bathrooms at Skoochies—arguably the most important downtown hangout for teenagers looking to score since the closing of the Monastery a few years earlier. I never went to either place, but I heard a lot of stories.

Apart from his formidable skills as a pickup artist, Andre also had a black belt in tae kwon do, which was something Brandon had been interested in since the mugging incident where the kid hit him in the arm with the bottle. They started training together, and Andre introduced Brandon to the Guardian Angels, a local chapter of a New York–based vigilante organization that got its start doing community safety patrols in the New York subways. The Seattle Angels were a mixed bag of prison guards, full-contact martial artists, cop wannabes, and local busybodies who were just looking for some shit to get into. Brandon started going on patrols with them, and pretty soon he'd mastered not only sex but violence as well. And, by extension, fear.

Once Brandon got over the rush of being able to have meaningless sex in parking lots whenever he felt like it, he settled down and got a regular girlfriend. Or, actually, two regular girlfriends in a row. The first one was named Jane, and the second one was Jane's best friend, Meadow.

Meadow and Jane were a couple of private school kids from the east side of Capitol Hill who, for administrative reasons I didn't pretend to understand, happened to be on Garfield's speech and debate team. Brandon started out with Jane around the middle of our junior year. I knew almost nothing about her or their relationship, except that she bit him. Hard. Every couple of days he'd show up for school looking like he'd been mauled; dark red tooth marks on his neck, his arms, his shoulders. Everywhere. They were together for a few months, and he professed to be very happy with her. Then, one day while we were sitting on his porch, he admitted to me that he'd made out with Meadow, at a debate tournament that Jane hadn't attended.

"Why would you do that?" I asked.

"I don't know," he said. "It seemed like a good idea at the time. Meadow's . . . very pretty."

Never having seen either girl, I had no basis for comparison.

"Well, what are you going to do?" I asked.

"Not much I can do," he said. "Meadow and Jane are best friends. There's no way Meadow will keep it a secret. She's already feeling guilty about it. The best I can hope for is to end up with Meadow. There's no version of this where I get to stay with Jane."

"Which is what you want to do?"

"Yeah," he said. "I think I'm kind of in love with her, actually."

"Well, then why the fuck did you mess around with Meadow?" I nearly screamed at him.

He put his head in his hands and sighed.

"I have no idea," he said.

64

Dad started taking AZT that year, the year I was fifteen. It was the latest thing in AIDS drugs. It was supposed to slow the replication of the virus. It didn't seem to do much for Dad's health, but it did mean he had to get something called a PICC line, which was basically a catheter that went from the inside of his left arm, through his brachial artery, to his heart. Drugs of all sorts could be injected into the catheter through a rubber gasket that hung out of Dad's arm near the bend of his elbow. A nurse came by a couple of times a week to administer the AZT by connecting the PICC line to a machine that would then spend a few hours slowly pushing this ridiculously toxic material into Dad's system. The PICC line was necessary because the AZT was so poisonous that it would burn his veins if it was injected directly into them. It had to be administered in such a way that it was able to mix with the large volumes of blood near his heart, to dilute its effects.

AZT was originally developed as a chemotherapy drug, and it hit Dad like chemotherapy hits cancer patients. Every time he got a treatment, he would spend the next twelve hours in the bathroom, throwing up and crying. Sometimes he'd talk while he was in there. He'd say things like "Oh, Jesus Christ, please make it stop! Help me! Fuck, someone, Jesus." It would come out between sobs and horrifying bouts of retching. And it didn't stop. It wasn't like a few minutes of that, then silence, then a few minutes. It was twelve solid hours of that kind of thing. It was like listening to someone being tortured to death. Or what I imagined it would be like, listening to someone being tortured to death.

I tried not to be around for it. If I was home, it was usually because I needed to sleep. Which didn't really work. I'd end up lying in bed, staring at my ceiling reminding myself that, as unpleasant as it was to listen to, at least I wasn't the guy in the bathroom hugging the toilet and praying to a God I didn't believe in for salvation that wasn't coming.

* * *

At some point during eleventh grade, I noticed that Dad wasn't really Dad anymore, and hadn't been for a while. He was never fully present. His hair was stringy and dirty and his eyes were clouded over. Even when he wasn't stoned, he was exhausted and sick all the time. It was easy to forget there was a person in there. That he was dangerous. He couldn't keep track of time. Sometimes he'd suddenly get mad at me about something I'd done two years ago and try to ambush me—hit me with a broomstick or a bottle, or try to punch me. But mostly he just staggered around. He didn't eat much. He couldn't cook. He was down around 120 pounds. When he held his arms out I could see both the bones in his forearms.

Amid all the general deterioration, it took me a while to notice that something more specific was happening. He was sleeping harder than he used to. He was falling over a lot. He'd spend two or three days in agony, then he'd spend two more days in a drug coma. I just figured it was the disease. He was having good days, and bad days. Or something.

Finally, one day in January of 1988, when I was fifteen, I came home from school and he was standing in the kitchen in his underwear with his back to me. Every bone in his body was visible through his skin. His briefs hung off him. He had the gas stove on, and he was doing something in front of the stove. A gesture I recognized—his left arm was extended, and his right arm was curled in front of him. Head forward, focused on what he was doing. I was only a few feet from him when he realized I was there and turned around to look at me with an expression of naked panic on his face.

"Shit!" he said. He dropped the syringe he'd been holding, ran into his bedroom, and slammed the door.

I stood there, looking the situation over. There was a spoon on the stove with a few empty gelatin tablets lying next to it. The spoon had a clear residue in it, from whatever he'd been cooking down. The bottom of the spoon was scorched. The syringe was lying next to the rest of his works.

So he was cooking down his pain pills and shooting them into his PICC line. Of course he was. Why wouldn't he be? And suddenly I understood the weird cycles I'd been seeing. He was stockpiling the meds. He'd spend a few days in agony, then a few days slamming the drugs, stoned to the gills. Agony, ecstasy. Back and forth, no in-between.

* * *

Dad's doctor was a well-known local AIDS doctor that everyone called Dr. Barton. Dad had been referred to him shortly after he was diagnosed, but I'd only recently started to have a lot of contact with him. He was hooked into the whole community, trusted and respected. Once I got to know him I started going to him for my medical needs as well—like the HIV tests I took once or twice a year, just in case Dad used my razor by accident, or if it turned out the virus was transmittable from cleaning up puke after all.

When I saw what Dad was up to I called Dr. Barton and told him what was happening. He gave me a choice. I could either have Dad admitted to the hospital, or I'd have to start administering his pain meds to make sure he didn't overdose.

"What do you mean, administering?" I asked.

"You'll separate them out into daily dosages. Make sure he takes them. Don't let him stockpile them like he's been doing."

Dad had been in and out of the hospital the whole time he'd been sick, but that wasn't really what Dr. Barton was suggesting. When he was talking about admitting Dad in this context, he was talking about hospice care; he was talking about checking Dad into the hospital for the last time.

"I'll need to ask him what he wants," I said.

"Sure," Dr. Barton said. "Of course."

I already knew what Dad wanted. I just needed to be sure.

* * *

The first week of me administering his drugs, he tore my room apart while I was at school, looking for his dose. He didn't find it. The next week he tore my room apart again. Still to no avail. I'd stashed his pills down inside my weight set, knowing he was too weak to get to them.

He started out complimenting me on being so good at hiding things. I told him it was a skill I'd learned back when he used to steal money out of my piggy bank to buy cigarettes at the end of the month, when we were low on cash.

The second week he told me the prescriptions weren't enough. He needed more. Especially during his AZT push. Surely I could see that.

"Dr. Barton sets the dosage, Dad," I said. "Take it up with him."

"What the fuck does he know about pain?" Dad wanted to know.

Seeing as how the overwhelming majority of Dr. Barton's patients were AIDS patients, I guessed he knew quite a bit about pain. But I didn't see the point in saying so.

The third week, I came home one day, and Dad and Kris were in the kitchen with a jar from my room on the table between them. The jar had been on the table next to my door. It was full of odds and ends—bits of string and beads, gears and pieces of toys. And, at the very bottom of that jar, I'd had one of my dad's daily doses.

"Son," he said as I came into the kitchen. "We need to talk."

"Mark," Kris said, trying to interrupt him.

"I think you have a problem," Dad said. "And it's my fault. You were too young for this kind of responsibility."

I stared at him for a minute, then looked at Kris.

"What's he talking about?" I asked.

"You've been stealing my meds," Dad said, jumping in before Kris could answer.

"I've been trying to get him to put it back," Kris said. "Before you got home. I'm sorry."

"It's fine," I said. "I'll take it from here."

"Jason," Dad said, "I know what it's like. But you shouldn't have to suffer for my shortcomings. Give me back the meds. I'll administer them myself. You can get help. You can get treatment."

Kris got up and went back to her apartment, giving me an apologetic look as she left the kitchen.

"I've called Dr. Barton's answering service," Dad said.

I looked at the ceiling and sighed. Then I started putting all the junk on the table back into the jar. I put Dad's meds in my coat pocket.

"Jason," Dad said. "This is serious."

"I don't take aspirin," I said, without looking at him.

"What?" he said.

"I don't take aspirin," I growled at him. "I don't take Tylenol. I don't drink. I don't even drink coffee. I never have. Never. Not once. Can you guess why?"

"I . . ."

"Yeah," I said. "So here's the deal. You can make this decision yourself from now on. I'll keep doing this for you, if you can get your shit together and let me do it. You pull something like this again, I'll tell Dr. Barton to admit you to the hospital. Do you understand?"

"Jason, I—"

"Do you fucking understand?" I hissed. "Do you fucking understand what I'll do if you pull this again?"

I wasn't looking at him. I was looking at the table. I stood there for a long time with my knees locked, leaning on the table and thinking about breaking it in half with my bare hands.

"I understand," Dad said.

"Good," I said.

I went to my room and put my junk jar back on the table next to the door. Then I stood in the middle of my room for a long time. I heard Dad go into his room and close the door. A muscle in my face was jumping. Finally I walked over to the corner next to my closet and picked up an ax handle I kept there. We'd brought it up from Eugene. It was a long, thin piece of hickory, the handle from an old felling ax. I looked around the room for a minute and my eyes settled on my bedroom door. I walked over and swung the ax handle maybe a dozen times, exhaling on each swing. The aged hardwood smashed the hollow-core door to pieces, cutting long horizontal gashes in the thin plywood. Then I walked over to my bed and beat on the mattress with the ax handle until I got tired. When I was gasping and sweating, I sat down on the bed and leaned on the handle to catch my breath.

This was what Han Solo would do. The door, rather than the sick old man. The doses, rather than the hospital. I could be a better man than my father. If I couldn't do anything else, I could do that.

After I'd collected myself for a few minutes, I got a roll of duct tape off the top of my dresser and used it to piece my bedroom door back together again.

* * *

When Dr. Barton got my dad's message he called our house, and I picked up. We talked about what had happened, and the likely outcomes if we kept doing what we were doing.

"This shouldn't be your problem," he said.

"It shouldn't be anyone's problem. But life doesn't work like that."

"No," he said. "But it really shouldn't be yours. This whole thing was a bad idea."

"What's the alternative? Put him in the hospital?"

"No. That was a bad call on my part. He can administer his own meds. I won't admit him. I'll see if we can get the same nursing service that administers the AZT to handle the narcotics. Or maybe we can give him the heavy stuff with his AZT, but leave him some Valium to help him sleep. One way or another, it shouldn't be something you have to deal with."

"What should I do in the meantime?"

"Just check him every so often when you know he's pushing the meds. If he doesn't breathe at least once every two minutes, go ahead and call an ambulance."

After I hung up the phone, I wondered if I'd actually call an ambulance when the time came. But it never did.

65

Alexis and I broke up after about a month. I broke up with her because I was tired of feeling like I was walking through a minefield. She talked me out of it, waited ten days, then broke up with me. I gathered that it was kind of a face-saving thing. Luckily, I had a shoulder to cry on. Marti and I had started spending a lot of time together. At first she was there for emotional support, but then we got to be better friends—and then we moved on to the late-night telephone confessions of mutual attraction. We knew we were on course for a cliché, but we were willing to be predictable. We spent a few months playing the "No, we can't—it'll hurt Alexis!" game, but at the end of the school year Marti called me to tell me that Alexis had announced she was dropping out of Garfield.

"She wants to move out on her own," Marti said. "Get an apartment."

"I guess that's mathematically possible," I said.

Like most of my friends, including Marti, Alexis had a part-time restaurant job. I got left out because I was still only fifteen years old. But I suspected Alexis would be in for a rude awakening if she tried to go from working ten hours a week to fund her perfume habit to working full-time and trying to pay rent and buy groceries and all that other crap.

"It might work or it might not," Marti said. "But she's not going back to Garfield. She's a hundred percent sure about that."

"So what does that mean?" I asked.

"I don't know. It still feels wrong."

We sat there for a while, just breathing into the phone.

"Why would she care though?" Marti said, finishing the argument for me. "If she's not going to be around school. I mean, if we're not all going to see each other every day. It shouldn't matter. She's back with Marshall anyway."

That was news to me, but not really surprising. Marshall was one of the band geeks Alexis had dated the year before. After they went out, he became the captain of the swim team, and now he was a hot ticket in the high school dating scene. He was six-three, he had washboard abs, and he was half Jamaican so he was always this offensively healthy light brown color, even in the dead of winter. If Michelangelo had sculpted in milk chocolate, he probably would have produced something like Marshall. I kind of hated him and wanted him to die, but cattiness between straight dudes wasn't socially acceptable in the 1980s, so I tried to keep it to myself.

"I don't think it will last," Marti said. "But I guess it means her grieving period is over."

The next day after school, Marti and I went back to my place. Having had a lot of time to think about what I'd done wrong with Alexis, I was ready when things heated up. Or I thought I was. I at least had a plan for pretending I was ready. Either way, we ended up having sex by the end of the week.

* * *

The lead-in to my first sexual encounter was, unsurprisingly, kind of weird and awkward. Marti came over to my house three nights in a row, and every night we went a little farther, but on the last night I just couldn't close the deal. I blamed it on my dad being in a drug coma in the next room. Since we certainly couldn't do it at her house, Marti took me camping that weekend.

The drive out to the country was inauspicious. The trip

took longer than we thought it would, so it was past dark as we were nearing our destination. The road went through a series of valleys, curving left and right, rising and falling. Which was why we didn't see the two cats that were sitting in the middle of the highway eating roadkill until it was way too late.

We both screamed. We both jammed our feet into the floor of the car so hard we nearly stood up in our seats. We both closed our eyes. The noise was like someone hitting a bag of celery with an aluminum baseball bat. When it was over I eased down into my seat and turned to comfort Marti, but she still had her eyes closed, her elbows locked, and her feet off the pedals. Which was concerning to me, since we were still going forty down a two-lane stretch of winding blacktop.

"Marti!" I shouted. "Pull over!"

"Okay," she whispered, peeking out of one eye and easing the car over to the side of the road. She relaxed back into her seat as the car slowed.

"Are you okay?" I asked after we'd come to a complete stop.

"Yes," she said. Her face was streaked with tears, but she seemed calm.

"Okay," I said, reaching into my backpack and taking out a hunting knife I'd brought with me. "I'll be right back."

"Whoa!" she said. "What are you doing?"

"Well . . . I have to go back and check on them."

"So what do you need the knife for?"

"I—Marti. If those cats are still alive, they're fucked. We can't leave them like that."

"No!" she said.

"Well, but—"

"NO! If you get out of this car with that knife, you are not getting back in."

I sat there for a minute thinking it over. It was hard to do the math: calculating the odds that either of the two cats was still alive after getting plowed under by a Volkswagen, against the hassle of getting left in the middle of nowhere by a girl I was supposed to be losing my virginity to this weekend.

"Okay," I said finally. "Let's go."

She put the car in gear and we continued on our way.

When we got to the campsite we put up our tent, gathered some wood, and got a fire going. I would have thought the cat thing would put a damper on the evening, but by the time we'd roasted some hot dogs and told a few ghost stories, the accident on the highway seemed like a thousand years ago. Marti had brought her portable stereo, and we left it sitting on the hood of her car, tuned to a local radio station, while we crawled into the tent and started making out. It was a decision I'd come to regret a half hour later, when Madonna's "Crazy for You" came on at the exact worst possible moment—not that I had any idea what that moment was. In spite of years of mandatory public school sex education, significant exposure to a wide variety of printed pornography, and a real-life personal how-to at age four, I had no idea what I was doing. At one particularly awkward pause in the process Marti looked up at me, raised her eyebrows, and said—very encouragingly, like she was talking to a pathological idiot—"Why don't you try some pelvic thrusts?"

That kind of clinical language might have been a turnoff for some, but I was mostly grateful for the clear guidance. I thrust my pelvis a few times. And had—for me, never having done this sort of thing on my own—a complete revelation about what that thing was *for*. Within about thirty seconds I abandoned all dignity and just started chasing this new feeling as fast as my body would let me. And when my moment of triumph finally came, I pushed down onto Marti, gasped, and said, "Holy *shit*! Jesus! *Wow*. I—*wow*. Marti. Goddamn. I see what all the fuss is about now. Holy crap, I can't believe people even put clothes on after that."

Marti was laughing uncontrollably by then, but in a nice way.

* * *

By the end of the summer, I was looking back on my decision to break up with Alexis as the last rational moment I would ever have about my interaction with girls. Things had seemed so clear that day. If something seemed like a bad idea, I just wouldn't do it. Alas, never again. Marti and I dated for two months, doubling my record with Alexis, but they were a very fraught two months. Alexis ran away from her parents' house and moved back in with Marti, which made the start of the relationship kind of tricky. Plus, contrary to her assertions that she was "fine with it," Alexis took to walking around Marti's house in a bikini and giving me long hugs whenever we ran into each other. I was pretty clear that Alexis didn't want me back. She was more interested in proving to herself, and to Marti, that she was the hotter property of the two.

I knew all this, yet I seemed incapable of not falling for it. I thought this must be what it was like to suffer some kind of traumatic brain injury. There was Marti, who'd been nothing but loving and loyal, and I was throwing her over for her snake of a best friend, who'd talked me out of breaking up with her just so she could be the one to dump me. For some reason, I thought I had moral cover as long as I didn't actually lie or cheat, so I broke up with Marti early one morning in her car, after she drove me home from a party. She saw it coming. She was crying before I even started.

"It's not you," I said totally unself-consciously. "It's me."

"Yeah," Marti said. "I know. And you know what? I deserve better. Get the hell out of my car."

I got out and went up to my porch. She sat parked in my driveway for five or ten minutes. Then I heard her scream, "Shit! Shit shit shit fucking shit, *fuck*!" before the engine roared to life and she slammed the car into reverse, executed a quick two-point turn, and raced off up the hill. I was proud of her. And she was right. She did deserve better.

66

Brandon worked at a Winchell's donut shop on Broadway, directly across the street from the corner where we waited for the school bus every morning. He worked there nights mostly, and the homeless kids on Broadway knew him—and knew his shop was a weapons-free zone. I spent a lot of evenings up there, keeping him company through his shift and watching street kids come in for coffee.

"No weapons in here," Brandon would say, if a kid looked like he was packing.

"Sure," the kid would answer. "I know the rule."

Then the teenager would pull a hunting knife or a cut-down baseball bat or something out of his pants and hand it over the counter to Brandon, who would store it in back until the kid wanted to leave. Once I saw a full-size machete. Another time it was a fiberglass club that could be unscrewed to form a pair of nunchucks. I saw hatchets, baseball bats, motorcycle chains, and saps. Some of the more exotic stuff was interesting, but none of it was surprising. That was just the world we lived in. Not a lot of guns yet, but pretty much everyone on the street carried a melee weapon of some kind to give them an edge if they got jumped. My tool kit included a couple of shivs, a good knife I could open one-handed, and my cheap-ass folding club. Brandon let me keep them when I came to visit.

One night, right before the start of our senior year, Brandon's cousin Ian came into the shop with a girl named Maria. I recognized her from Brandon's Guardian Angels crew. She was nineteen, but she looked younger. She was dressed in a gray wool overcoat, a skirt, and a sweater that were all too big for her. Her hair was dyed bright orange, and she had a sort of feral look to her face: up-slanting eyes, high forehead, and a heart-shaped face. Bad teeth. Not trailer-park bad, but it was obvious she'd never had braces growing up.

Ian and Brandon were family, but the relationship was pretty attenuated; second cousin three times removed or something. They certainly looked nothing alike. Where Brandon was short, round-featured, and fair, Ian was tall, skinny, and had dark brown hair. He wore an army field jacket, a T-shirt, and jeans; had kind of a *Taxi Driver* thing going on. I'd met him a few times before. He was interested in doing patrols with the Angels, but it didn't work out for some reason.

"Hey, Brandon," Ian said as he and Maria came into the store. "How's it going?"

"Ian," Brandon said. "How're you. You remember Jason?"

"Sure," Ian said. "Hey."

"And Maria," Brandon said, reintroducing me to Maria as she came in behind Ian. Maria and I waved at each other.

"We're just out on our date," Ian said. "And we thought we'd stop in and say hi."

Something about that wording seemed weird. Like Ian was overreaching. The sour look on Maria's face when Ian used the word "date" confirmed it.

"Have a seat," Brandon said. "You want some coffee?"

"Sure," Ian said.

Brandon plied Ian and Maria with coffee and donuts, and they ended up hanging around for more than an hour, until the end of Brandon's shift. Then all four of us went down to Brandon's place. Brandon's parents had split up the year before. His dad still had the house next door to mine, but his mom had moved into an apartment building at the end of the block and Ethan had moved out on his own. The building Brandon lived in with his mom had an activity room in the basement where we set up camp that night, with leftover donuts and a couple of two-liter bottles of soda.

It was one of those weird endless nights, like the time Eddie and I went downtown with Bobby and Barb and stayed out until dawn; just three guys and a girl sitting in a dark basement, talking and telling jokes between long silences. All three of us were flirting with Maria, but she wasn't giving much away. At some point Ian decided the way to get ahead in that game would be to challenge me to a wrestling match, and because we were all just that young and stupid, I took him up on it.

He had a lot of anger, but not much power. After I pinned him three times he took a swing at me, but I'd been practicing with Brandon, and on my own, for a couple of years. I slipped the punch and stepped back out of range.

"You try that again, you're gonna get hurt," I said.

"Sure," he sneered.

"Ian," Brandon said from where he was watching the bout. "He means it."

"Whatever," Ian said.

When we went back at it, he tried to punch me in the face again.

I stepped in and let the punch glance off my shoulder, then wrestled him to the ground and twisted his arm behind his back.

"We done?" I asked, applying pressure.

"Not yet," he said.

I pushed a little harder. Something made a grinding noise in his shoulder and he hissed. But he didn't cry or scream.

"We done?" I asked again.

"Yeah," he said. "We're done."

I let him go and stepped back. He stood up, holding his left arm up against his body with his right hand.

"Think that might have been it for my shoulder," he said.

"Sorry," I said, obviously not meaning it.

"Maybe we'd better call it a night," Brandon said. "The buses aren't running this late. Ian, Maria—you guys need a cab?"

I'd been holding off all night, waiting for Brandon to make some kind of move on Maria. But when we were all sitting in the lobby upstairs waiting for the cab to show up and Brandon still hadn't made any kind of gesture, I asked Maria for her phone number. I'd never done anything like that before—it was all based on stuff Brandon had told me about proper dating technique. Ian wasn't even on my radar. He'd clearly blown the whole thing when he decided to get physical with me.

Maria gave me her number and said she was free that Friday if I wanted to catch a movie or something.

* * *

Maria and I dated for about two months. She was a good girlfriend, but the fact that she was an actual legal adult with a job and an apartment and cats started to feel weird to me pretty quickly. I told Brandon I was worried that she was getting too attached, in view of how ambivalent I was about the relationship. Brandon repeated the advice he'd been giving me since before Alexis: when a girl tells you she's in love with you, break up with her. This time I followed his advice. When Maria accidently used the l-word around the two-month mark, I told her that was more commitment than I was looking for and ended it.

67

I joined the debate team in my senior year, for reasons that were beyond me. Brandon and Jane had both quit the team—probably to avoid Meadow—and I really had no interest in public speaking. Or public anything else, for that matter. But I wanted to get more involved with the school that I loved so much, and there was just no way I was going to try out for an athletic team.

I was surprised to learn that the term "speech and debate" encompassed a huge range of events, from expository speaking and editorial commentary to something called dramatic interpretation, which consisted of actors reading monologues or pairs of actors reading dialogues. Debates of the sort I'd imagined when I was thinking about joining the debate team were called Lincoln-Douglas debates, and they were so comparatively unusual that most tournaments didn't even offer them.

With so many events to choose from, I naturally went for the one that required the least preparation: impromptu speaking. There were usually three rounds per tournament, scored first through third, with everyone else being ranked fourth, no matter how many people were in the tournament. For impromptu speaking, each round had a topic list; each speaker would go up to the podium, look at the topic list, and take seven minutes to talk about one of the topics on the list. The usual approach was to take three minutes to think about it, and four minutes to talk.

I was terrible at it.

It may have been because of how I dressed, in jeans and

T-shirts, with my leather jacket, sneakers, and my hair tied back in a ponytail. Speech and debate was a very conservative sport. I once overheard a couple of judges saying they gave an automatic four to any boy who didn't wear a tie. But I was pretty sure that wasn't the real problem; I just didn't care very much. And I lacked aptitude. It amounted to the same thing.

I didn't mind. The tournaments happened all over the state, so I got to go on weekend trips with the eight or nine other nerds on my team, and the dramatic interpretation event attracted a lot of actresses, who seemed disproportionately to be hot nerdy girls who craved attention.

Meadow, the object of Brandon's infidelity against Jane, was one of those. She was tall and thin, with the kind of features that I imagined would work for her if there was ever a movie camera pointed at her: large eyes, small nose, big lips, small chin, long neck. She dressed kind of like a hippie, in natural fibers and earth tones, with a lot of big jewelry, but there was nothing random or casual about her. She coordinated her outfits very carefully. Her diction was downright obnoxious, and she had virtually no sense of humor on any subject. She was the first person I ever heard use the word "eclectic" in a sentence.

My initial thought about her was that she was clearly way more trouble than she was worth, but something about the way she looked at me suggested she might have a thing for bad boys, so I decided to keep the possibility open.

* * *

While there was a tournament almost every week and most of the tournaments were huge, not every tournament offered a full range of events to compete in. I went with my team to a tournament early in the season, only to find out when I got there that impromptu speaking wasn't available. Of course, the nature of impromptu speaking meant that I wasn't prepared for any other event either, but I signed up for editorial commentary on a whim.

"Hey," I said to Meadow, as our team gathered in the gym of the Podunk high school that was hosting the tournament. "You got a quarter I can borrow?"

"Why?" she asked, like I was going to spend it on drugs or something.

"I signed up for editorial commentary. I gotta run outside and get a newspaper."

"It's against the rules to just quote the paper," she said. "You have to write your own material."

"I will," I said. "But first I have to know what's happening in the world, right?"

She sighed and rummaged around in her shoulder bag until she came up with an embroidered change purse, and forked over the quarter.

"How long until they call the first event?" I asked.

She glanced up at the clock. "Half an hour."

"Great," I said. "Thanks."

I went out to the front of the school and found a newspaper vending machine with the *Seattle Times* in it. We were a hundred miles from the city, but I guessed not every small town in Washington could field its own daily. I put my hand on the change return button and yanked on the door handle as hard as I could. It was an old gag that didn't work with most of the machines in the city anymore, but this one popped right open. I grabbed a paper and ran back into the gym.

"Here," I said, handing Meadow back her quarter.

She looked at the paper, then at me.

"They were giving them away," I said.

I flipped through the A section until I found a story about a change in the gun laws in Florida. Evidently the law had recently been rewritten down there so anyone with a driver's license could get a concealed carry permit for a handgun, with no additional review. That one seemed pretty ripe.

"You got a notepad or something?" I asked Meadow.

She stared at me for a long time, then reached into her bag and handed over a spiral-bound pad.

"Thanks," I said.

I opened to a blank page and just started writing. I started out with a gag about a senile old lady blowing some panhandler's head off with a .44 because he tried to rob her. "He asked me for a quarter!" she screamed as the police took her away. Then I jumped into a description of the new law, and finished up with a little rap about how someone getting licensed to drive a car had to at least know what the traffic laws are, and that giving someone a gun without making them learn anything about when and how it was legal to use one was patently irresponsible. Then I tore the page out and handed the notepad back to Meadow.

"Thanks," I said again.

She tucked the corner of her mouth in disapprovingly.

They called the first event a few minutes later, and I went to the first classroom on my scorecard. I sat through a couple of other people's readings, then got up and did mine. When the round was over I walked past the judge's desk and glanced down at my card. It was my usual score—a four.

That was fine, I told myself. No biggie.

But when I went back out to the gym, two of the guys who'd been competing in my round walked up to me by the vending machines. They were both wearing blue button-down shirts, striped ties, and slacks. Tall skinny guys with bad haircuts—one blond, the other dark. They walked up to me like they were aping some kind of bad 1940s prison drama, and the dark-haired kid talked to me out of the side of his mouth while he pretended to look over the selection in the vending machine.

"Hey," he said. "I saw your round just now."

"Yeah," I said. "I recognize you."

"How do you think you did?"

"I looked at my card on the way out. I got creamed."

"Yeah," he said. "You get kinda nervous when you read, it looked like to me."

"Every time," I said.

"So here's what I was wondering," he said. "I was wondering if you might like to sit the rest of the tournament out."

"Huh?" I said.

"No offense, I think you probably know—your reading was . . . not so good."

"Yeah. So?"

"Well, the thing is, your reading wasn't great. But your piece—your piece was fucking awesome. Me and my buddy here were laughing our asses off. If you'd looked up from your sheet even once, you would have seen us. But this clearly isn't your event. So what I was thinking is, I'd buy your piece off you for, say, five bucks. But only one of us can run it, so if I buy it off you, you got no piece anymore."

"You wanna buy this?" I said, holding up my story. "For five bucks?"

"Shhh!" he said. "We're supposed to do our own work, man."

"Well, shit," I said. "You got it."

"Cool," he said. "Here's the money. Leave the story behind the Coke machine."

He slipped me a five-dollar bill and walked off with his buddy. A minute later, I dropped the paper behind the vending machine and went back to the table where my team was gathered.

"Hey," I said to my coach. "I think I'm done for the day. I don't feel great."

"Okay," she said. She was one of the history teachers at Garfield, and driving the team out to remote locations in a Seattle Schools van was just a way for her to earn a little extra cash.

"You okay?" Meadow asked.

"I will be," I said.

I never found out how the kid who bought my story did with it—if he won or lost. And it wasn't even the first time someone had paid me for my writing. Some weird kid in my eleventh grade American History class used to buy my homework assignments after the teacher gave them back to us, for a quarter apiece. That kid had said he liked my writing, but he'd also said he was a Satanist and that he was saving up his money to get his teeth filed into points, so I just figured he was using my work to wallpaper the little red room where he polished his ram's horn or whatever.

This thing at the debate tournament was a whole other kind of deal. And, for pretty much the first time in my life, I started to get the idea that I might be good at something that would actually make my life better.

68

One day that fall, Dad told me he'd picked up a bad case of lice at the free clinic. We used to get lice three or four times a year back in Eugene, but we hadn't had an infestation in a long time. Dad had gotten some special shampoo and soap, but we'd have to wash all our stuff in special poison laundry detergent and bug-bomb the house. I waited until the next time he went into the hospital, bombed the place, and washed all our clothing and bedding in the machines in the basement of Brandon's apartment building.

A few weeks later, Dad said we hadn't gotten rid of all the bugs, so I did the whole routine over again. I washed the dog. The works.

When it happened a third time, I was dubious, but Dad said the doctors at the clinic were having a real problem with it. He said they'd been sending notices out. The warning labels on the bug bombs said not to use them more than twice a year—that the buildup of insecticide inside a house could make humans and animals sick—but I didn't see I had much choice.

The next time Dad came home from the hospital he told me the house had been attacked by ninjas, his first night back.

"I saw one out my window," he said. "On the building across the street. It was incredible. I've never seen a human move like that. He was just like a shadow—he shot up the side of the building, using the drainpipe. Then he jumped from their roof to ours, and I saw him come down the side of our building, trying windows as he went. And he never made a noise. No noise at all."

I looked at the building he was pointing at—the one across the street. It was a good sixty feet away. The next time he told me he had lice, I asked him to show me. Show me some nits or some eggs. When I got back from school that day he had a tiny plastic bag with pieces of dirt he'd picked out of the rugs.

"See?" he said. "Look at the size of that thing!"

It was a piece of bark. I could also see a piece of dried leaf and some pine needles in the bag.

"Okay," I said. "Next time you're at the hospital, I'll bomb the house."

I called Brandon that night and told him the whole story.

"The thing I can't figure out," I said, "is how worried I should be. Like, we've got a gas cooking range. Gas oven. He smokes like a goddamn chimney. Who's to say he's not going to burn the house down? Or, God forbid, blow us all to kingdom come. Lizzie's downstairs. Having him come into my room and kill me in my sleep because he thinks I'm a ninja actually seems like the lesser of several possible evils here."

"Yeah," Brandon said. "I don't know what to tell you. Figure out a better way to lock your door."

"What about your dad?" I asked. "What's he up to?"

"Selling the house," Brandon said. "He'll kick back half to Mom, for back child support. Then he's going to use the rest to go to Thailand."

"Sex tourism, huh?"

"Probably. I don't know. We don't talk much anymore."

"Count your blessings," I said.

* * *

I lived my life in pieces. Marti and I had repaired our friendship, and Alexis and I talked on the phone every couple of months. I still went to Ryan's sometimes. Brandon and I hung out every so often. I had speech and debate. I had my dad. I had homework and school. There was hardly any crossover. Ryan still didn't even know my dad was sick. Marti knew. Alexis didn't. Brandon did, though we never talked about it. I called Maria once, because I liked the idea of being friends with all my ex-girlfriends.

"Why are you calling me?" she asked, after some initial small talk.

"I just wanted to see if we could . . . I don't know. Be in touch."

She sighed into the phone.

"You have something you want to do with me, call. You have something you want to say to me, call. You want to make yourself feel better for what you did ... deal with that yourself. Okay?"

"Okay," I said. But she'd already hung up.

<h1 style="text-align:center">69</h1>

The speech and debate team did our first overnight trip in November, heading up to Western Washington University, in Bellingham, about one hundred miles north of Seattle. We brought sleeping bags and camped out in a conference room in the old YMCA building, in the city center. Everybody but me seemed to have gotten some kind of memo about how the trip was going to work, because when I said I was heading to the bathroom to change into my pajamas, Karin, the captain of the team, said, "Don't be such a prude."

Karin was one of those girls who seemed like she'd been forty years old since birth, so I wasn't sure I'd heard her right at first.

Then Meadow pulled her arms into her T-shirt, did some kind of contortions, and stuck her arms back out through the sleeves—holding her bra in one hand. She stretched the shoulder strap and shot it at my head like a giant rubber band. Some of the other kids on the team tittered and began the process of changing clothes without actually getting naked. I had the uncomfortable feeling that I was about to see how nerds partied down.

"Okay," I said. "That's all fine. I'm still going to change in the bathroom."

"Booooo!" everyone called as I left the room with my sleeping clothes in a ball under my arm.

The rest of the night was a revelation. Meadow and Karin asked me for back rubs. I got a back rub from Meadow. We played truth or dare. There was even a suggestion that we should play spin the bottle. Nobody broke out any booze or weed and none of us actually ended up getting any play, but I started to get a picture of why Brandon thought these tournaments were such good places to hook up. We were all exhausted the next day at the tournament, but I could tell by looking around at my competitors that we weren't the only team who'd spent last night mainlining pheromones and pushing boundaries.

* * *

Bellingham had a reputation as a pretty liberal town, but the judges at the tournament that day were more of the same snooty white, polyester-clad church ladies I'd come to expect at these things. Not that I cared. I was used to losing and I'd had a good night, so the trip was already worth it for me. Then, in my second round, the first person to speak was a standard-issue exurban Young Republican: a compact white girl in a red gingham dress, blue cardigan, red bow in her hair. Thick glasses in round frames that made her eyes look slightly crossed, and black patent leather Mary Janes. She looked at the paper that told us what the subjects were, then kept her head down for a few minutes while she planned her angle of attack. I started doodling on the back of my notepad, trying to copy a picture of a dragon I'd seen in a comic book the week before.

"You see them in the city," the girl said. "You see them on

TV. Some days it seems like we see them everywhere. Men. Walking down the streets. Holding hands. Kissing."

My head snapped up.

"Everyone knows by now that there's an epidemic overtaking these men. God's punishment, some say. Or maybe it's just a disease. Either way, the question for the rest of us is simple: What should we do? Should we spend taxpayer money to search for a cure for this plague? I say no. I say that the wages of sin are paid by the sinners. This isn't our problem. Let them reap what they've sown."

She kept talking for another three and a half minutes, but I didn't hear much of the rest of it. I was caught up in a sensation I'd never experienced before. I'd read about it, I'd even seen it in movies, but I didn't know it happened in real life.

I saw red. My ears filled with the sound of an ocean. I nearly blacked out. I crushed my pen in my hand and dropped the fragments on the floor next to me.

It wasn't that I'd never heard this sort of thing before; I'd seen it on TV bunches of times. I'd seen it on *The 700 Club* with Pat Robertson. I'd heard Jesse Helms say it on the floor of Congress. It had been written in op-ed columns and on magazine covers and on posters. Talk radio hosts had said it. Eddie Murphy made AIDS jokes, and everyone at my school loved Eddie Murphy.

But all those people were, fundamentally, performers. They were safe—behind typewriters, behind TV cameras and radio microphones. They said these awful things precisely because they were protected from the consequences of it. I didn't forgive them, but I didn't take them very seriously either. And now here was this girl, saying it in a room full of people. And nobody was getting up and storming out. The judge wasn't gasping in horror and shaking her head while she scribbled reproachful notes on the girl's scorecard. This was just happening.

I could hear my dad's voice in my head. "People could come to our house, burn it down with us in it, and nobody would try to stop them or punish them for it. No law protects gay men."

When it was my turn, I walked up to the podium in a haze and picked up the piece of paper that was waiting for me there. Three subjects, but my vision tunneled in on one: the federal government should direct more funding toward AIDS research. I read it over and over again. What she'd done was within the rules. Speakers were allowed to argue against a premise. But it was the choice she'd made. She could have gone so many ways with it, and that was the one she picked.

When I looked up at the clock, five minutes had passed.

I looked at the girl in the gingham dress. She was smiling.

I cleared my throat.

"I know someone with an uncle . . ." I said. Then I stopped. I was gulping my air. My back hurt. I looked at the girl again. Looked her in the eye. "It's been said that the measure of our humanity—of our value as a people—is a function of how we treat the least among us . . ."

I stopped again. Billy wasn't the least among us. Charles wasn't the least among us. Neither was Scotty. My dad . . . well, maybe. But not the others.

"People should think about what they say in these things," I said, looking at a spot on the floor. "You never know who's listening."

Now the judge was shaking her head and scribbling on my scorecard. I went back toward my seat, grabbed my backpack, and left the room.

* * *

The whole team went out for dinner that night to celebrate a good tournament. Everyone on the team had scored unusually well—mostly ones and twos. With the exception of me. And Meadow.

I'd collected my card at the end of the day: two fours and a forfeit. The judge's notes in the second round said, "Totally unprofessional." Meadow usually ran ones and twos in these things, but at Western, for some reason she'd gone three-two-four. Clearly it could have been worse—she could have had my score—but it wasn't what she was used to. While the rest of the team read each other's cards and talked about their best line or the best moment of the day, Meadow and I sat quietly on the far end of the table staring at our food.

The keys to the van were sitting in the middle of the table, where the coach had dropped them. I looked at them, and looked at Meadow. And I wanted more than anything in the world to break something, so I stood up and said, "I need something from my pack." Then I grabbed the keys, went outside, and let myself into the van. I left the door unlocked and lay down in the back, where we dumped our stuff. Made a little bed for myself out of sleeping bags and settled in to wait.

Meadow came out a few minutes later. She didn't say anything as she crawled into the back of the van and settled down next to me. I moved my arm so she could rest her head on my shoulder. She reached up and took my hand, where it rested on her arm. We both sighed and settled into each other.

"Hard day," she said after a minute.

"Yeah," I agreed.

"What was yours? I know you don't care about your scores."

"Just some fucking...this girl. The question was about funding for...research. For AIDS research. She just—the shit she said. I can't explain it. I never thought I'd hear a real person say things like that. It just took everything out of me."

Meadow didn't say anything for a long time.

"What about you?" I prompted.

"I don't know," she said. "Problems with my mom. She's the most important person in my life. I love her. But . . . we're just having problems. I think it threw me off."

I thought that over.

"So . . ." I said. "You're having a hard day because you took a pasting in the tournament? Or because you're having problems with your mom?"

"I'm having a hard day because I'm having problems with my mom and I wanted to forget about it, and taking a pasting in the tournament reminded me of it."

Just a hint of impatience in her voice.

"Fair enough," I said. "Sorry."

But I was back in my own head, going over everything I'd just said to her about my own problems.

"The thing with the girl," I said, after a minute. "In the tournament. You know why it bothered me?"

"I don't know anything," she said. "But yeah. I can guess."

"What's your guess?" I asked. Challenging.

"Your dad," she said.

"Yeah. My dad."

She gave me a squeeze. "I'm sorry."

"I have mixed feelings about it," I whispered, almost to myself.

"Yeah," she said. "I'm sorry about that, too."

* * *

The rest of the team came out an hour or so later. I handed the keys up to the coach, and everyone else took their seats. Meadow and I stayed in back with the gear, pretending to sleep during the two-hour drive back to town. We dropped a few other kids off, but when we got to Meadow's place, I grabbed my bag and got out with her.

"I'll walk home from here," I told the coach.

"You sure?" she asked. "It's late."

"I'll be fine," I said. "It's a nice night. I'll walk home."

One of our teammates closed the side door of the van and the coach drove off to the next stop, leaving me and Meadow standing on the corner near her house, under the shadow of a giant maple tree that blocked out part of the streetlight above us.

"You are, you know," Meadow said.

"What?" I asked.

"Walking home from here."

"Sure," I said.

"My mom's home, and I'm not just bringing some guy back with me at eleven o'clock without any kind of warning. That's not what my home life needs right now."

"I got it," I said.

"Then why did you get out of the van?"

I stepped closer to her. She was eight inches shorter than me, so I had to set my feet almost a yard apart to get my face anywhere near her level.

"I just want to see what all the fuss was about," I said, thinking of Brandon and Jane and all the rest of it.

I leaned down slowly and kissed her. She wrapped her arms around my neck and I put my hands on the sides of her rib cage and lifted her up toward me. We kissed for a long time, without either of us taking it any farther.

"Well?" she said, when I finally set her back down. "Worth it?"

I shrugged. "I don't have the same things at stake."

But I was thinking about Brandon—and how he'd take this. Remembering what I'd wanted when I went out to the van earlier that night. I'd wanted to break something. I'd known what I was asking for when I lured Meadow out there, and now I thought I was probably going to get it.

70

Meadow and I negotiated our relationship over the course of a week, playing what I was coming to regard as the usual games about whether we were serious about each other and settling on yes. Once the deal was locked in, I told Brandon about it.

He just started laughing. He said if I wanted to date someone that unpleasant, I was welcome to it. But a week after I told him about Meadow and me, he announced that he was going out with Maria. Or, rather, he didn't announce it. I called him one morning to ask if he wanted to go to a double feature at the Neptune that night, and he interrupted me mid-sentence to say, "Ow! Maria! Stop that!"

Then there was a lot of giggling.

"Hey, Jason," Brandon said. "I'll have to call you back, all right?"

"Sure," I said.

I hung up the phone and spent some time worrying.

I didn't mind that he was dating Maria. Or I didn't think I did. But the way he'd told me seemed intentionally discourteous. I'd told him about Meadow in person. I'd offered to talk about it if he had anything he wanted to say to me. This thing with Maria—it felt spiteful. With anyone else, I would have expected it, but I was surprised Brandon cared enough about any of this to get mad. This was a guy who had a key chain with a picture of a cartoon character that was made of nothing but legs, boobs, a butt, and a vagina, and a caption underneath that said THE PERFECT WOMAN.

Except, the night I'd asked Maria for her phone number,

Brandon and I had both been flirting with her. I'd been the one to make the first move, but if Brandon had been serious about her, then watching me date her—and break up with her like a complete asshole—would have been pretty hard. I didn't think Brandon had a lot of scruples when it came to dating, but if I asked him I knew he'd tell me that he was at least a believer in the bro code: you don't date girls your friend is interested in, and you don't date your friend's ex-girlfriends. So maybe he'd been mad at me for a while, and this was just the first obvious sign. Maybe he was mad at me for breaking the code. Or maybe he just really wanted to be with Maria, and me dating Meadow gave him the excuse he needed to go ahead with it. That last seemed most likely, now that I was looking back at the problem I'd created for myself, rather than forward at the one I hoped to avoid.

Hindsight. Fuck.

I wished I was better at understanding normal people. I wished I could call Brandon and ask his opinion about all this.

* * *

My initial assessment of Meadow turned out to be accurate: she was far more trouble than she was worth. It was nice being with someone who had at least a theoretical understanding of my dad's situation, and Meadow was, indeed, very pretty. But she was simultaneously distant and demanding, and shockingly egocentric. After six weeks she told me she needed to take time off from the relationship to deal with an argument she was having with her mom about where she should go to college. I refrained from pointing out that I had some parental issues of my own that I somehow managed to balance while also being attentive to my relationship. When she called me back two weeks later to say she'd worked it out with her mom, I told her that I didn't want to get back together.

"Why not?" she asked.

"Honestly?" I said. "I didn't really appreciate how unhappy this relationship was making me until we took this break you demanded. I've been so much happier. It was like this enormous load was lifted."

A few weeks later she sent me a letter explaining that she was very proud of herself for having been brave enough to be with someone as damaged as I was, and that I would always be part of her "herstory."

71

I was alone with my dad, but I wasn't alone with his illness. In the three years since he'd been diagnosed, AIDS support organizations had been growing up steadily around the city. As they got bigger, they started helping him out—and, by extension, helping me. By 1988 massage therapists were coming by once or twice a week to give Dad back rubs. The Northwest AIDS Foundation did everything from loaning us the machine that Dad needed to take his AZT to sending a nurse to administer it. They also had caseworkers and social workers who connected us with other services.

One of those services was called the Chicken Soup Brigade. They started working with Dad when he got too sick to take care of himself. In my senior year, they started bringing him cases of a vitamin-enriched nondairy beverage called Ensure, that was designed for people who couldn't hold down solid food. They also brought prepared meals, like lasagna and enchiladas, and loaned us a microwave to cook them in. And at some point, someone decided to send us a housecleaner.

We needed one. As Dad got sicker, time meant less to me. When I was between girlfriends, I could go a few weeks without changing my clothes and not notice until the smell caught my attention. I would forget to go to school, or leave in the middle of the day and go for a walk. I wanted to be around other people, but I couldn't talk to them. I went to parks and coffee shops. I'd sit down, watch the people for a few minutes—then have to leave.

I kept punching walls. I tried to keep it a secret. Brandon was the only one who knew how bad it really was. But sometimes punching a wall or a telephone pole was the only thing that calmed me down; the pain in my hands took the edge off the panic. It didn't make it go away. Nothing did. It was in the background all the time, and it drowned out everything else. Taking care of myself was hard. Taking care of the house was impossible.

So Frank started coming to our apartment. He was a nice old man in his late sixties. He had short white hair, and he usually dressed in slacks and polo shirts. He came about once a week, did the dishes, swept, vacuumed, and sometimes cleaned out the refrigerator.

It bothered me having someone cleaning my house. It was embarrassing, because it was necessary. If I was home when he started cleaning, I came out of my room and started trying to clean ahead of him, so he wouldn't see what the place normally looked like. It was stupid, I knew. A waste of time. And it made me look like a crazy person. I couldn't stop doing it. My dad was in the hospital three weeks out of four, so this was mostly my mess. What Frank was actually seeing was how I couldn't even clean up after myself.

"You don't have to do that," he said one day, as I was sweeping the kitchen.

"I kind of do," I said. "I should clean up my own stuff."

"All right," he said.

After a couple of weeks, Frank and I got to talking. We talked about all kinds of things, but he mostly seemed interested in what I was going to do after high school. The conversation happened in bits and pieces over time. I didn't like talking about it. I had no idea what I was going to do after high school. I didn't even know how I was going to live. Partly, it was that I didn't believe I was going to. Partly it was just that I didn't understand the mechanisms involved. My dad had always paid the bills. He never had me help him with it or showed me how it was done. I didn't know how to find a straight job or get a place to live. I wasn't even allowed to have a bank account in my own name until I was eighteen. I wouldn't even turn seventeen till a few months after I graduated.

That left a year where I'd be a nonperson, with no place to go and nothing to do. In theory I was supposed to live with my dad's oldest brother, my uncle John, if my dad died before I was eighteen. That was the deal Dad and John had worked out after he was diagnosed. But I knew I wasn't going to do that. There was no point. If I went there, it was only a matter of time before I screwed it up so badly that I'd have to leave. And Uncle John would tell everyone it was my dad's fault, and my fault, and that we deserved everything that had happened to us. That we were beyond help, just like he'd been saying all along. May as well skip the middle part and not give him the satisfaction, was my thinking on the matter.

"Jason," Frank said one day while he was sweeping, "would you mind if I . . . offer an opinion?"

"Go ahead," I said.

He stopped and leaned on the kitchen counter. "You're sure? It's a bit strong. I wouldn't want to make you angry."

I sighed. "Go ahead."

"Well, all right. If you don't change course—if you don't have something waiting for you, even if it's just something to occupy you until you turn eighteen, you're not going to make it. You need to make a plan for next year."

I tried to think about what he was saying, instead of just flying off the handle.

"I don't have a lot of options," I said. "I can't afford college. And I'm pretty sure I've missed all the application deadlines."

"Well," he said, "that's true. But suppose it weren't? Which college would you want to go to?"

"Evergreen?" I said, naming a four-year college in Olympia, eighty or so miles away.

"Why Evergreen?" he asked.

"I don't know," I said. "I hear it's kind of a hippie school."

"I see," he said.

Of course, I didn't really want to go to Evergreen in the sense that they had a curriculum I liked, or anything like that. It was just one of two state schools I knew the name of. The other one was the University of Washington, and I knew for a fact that I was short of their admissions requirements. My grades weren't good enough, and I didn't have enough years of foreign language or math.

The next week, when Frank came to clean, he had an application for admission to The Evergreen State College, and a Free Application for Federal Student Aid.

"Listen," he said, when he showed it to me. "I know this is an inconvenience. But I'd consider it a personal favor if you'd fill these out."

"Frank," I said, "there's no way I can get in. The application deadline already passed. Even if I got in, I couldn't afford it.

Look, it says right here that the priority filing date for financial aid was last month."

"I know," he said. "And you're probably right. Let's call it a contingency plan. Please fill it out. Just to humor me."

I sighed.

"You know what I did before I retired?" he asked.

He'd told me before, but I'd kind of forgotten.

"Teacher?" I guessed.

"Principal," he said. "I had a lot of students over the years. Some of them work in colleges. You fill it out and send it in. Let me see what I can do."

"Fine," I said. That kind of networking, at least, was something I understood. And it wasn't like I had anything better to do. I filled out the forms and sent them in.

72

Grandpa had another heart attack that winter, and this time he ended up in Providence Hospital, in Seattle. This turned out to be sort of convenient. Dad was still technically living at home, but he spent about half his time at Swedish Hospital, a half mile away from Providence. So once or twice a week I could make the rounds to visit both of them in one day. Grandpa looked different this time than he had when he had a heart attack in Los Angeles. He was unshaven and haggard-looking. His toupee was on crooked. And he looked scared every time I came to see him. He held my hand and talked about his first wife, my dad's mother.

"I'll see her again soon," he whispered to me.

Margaret was standing a few feet away. I avoided looking at her.

Going to see my dad was a stranger experience. He looked better than Grandpa, but he was farther along. He'd never stopped hallucinating bugs and ninjas. Dr. Barton told me it was something called viral dementia. I thought the more likely culprit was chronic drug abuse, but it didn't really make any difference to me what was causing it.

Now, in the hospital, Dad was hallucinating other things.

"Frank tells me you're going to get a scholarship," he'd say when I came to visit him. "You've got a straight-A average. Things are going to be all right for you."

None of which was true, but I didn't see the point in getting into it with him.

"Sure, Dad," I'd say. "Everything's great."

Then he'd hold my hand and cry. Sometimes he'd bring up his dead mother. I thought it was nice, in a way, that he and Grandpa were on the same page for a change.

* * *

I still spent the odd weekend in Ballard, staying with Ryan and his mom, sleeping on the floor. Like Brandon, Ryan had developed a whole new scene—a whole new group of friends and new interests. He'd started doing a little light dealing late in his junior year, and by senior year we were spending a lot of time sitting in unfamiliar basements while he got high with people I'd never met before, and a few that I had. Ryan had started hanging out with this kid Wendell we knew from Mr. Fields's class. Wendell was a skinny little dude with curly blond hair, big features, and baggy eyes. He played bass and smoked his body weight in pot every week—and he knew a lot of dealers and users in the white trash north end drug scene. So one day while we were all sitting around watching TV I asked him if he ever heard anything about Eddie, and Wendell said yeah, he'd just heard something about Eddie recently, as a matter of fact.

"Really?" I said. "What'd you hear?"

"Heard he's dead, man," Wendell said. "Heard he overdosed on coke a few weeks ago, up in some squat in Shoreline."

Ryan looked at Wendell, then looked at me, then punched Wendell in the shoulder.

"Ow! The hell?" Wendell demanded, rubbing his arm.

"What'd you tell him like that for?" Ryan said. "You know they were friends back in Mr. Fields's class."

"Oh," Wendell said. "Yeah. I . . . sorry. I kind of forgot."

"Jesus," Ryan said. "I hope you get some bad news like that someday. Asshole. Jason, you okay?"

"Huh?" I said. "Yeah. Sure. Fine."

I hung around for an hour or so, then said my goodbyes and headed back toward Capitol Hill. I decided to walk instead of taking the bus. I walked the railroad tracks, from Salmon Bay to Fremont. I stopped on the way and punched the side of an old warehouse until my right hand was bleeding and I couldn't make a fist.

And maybe it was the weather or something, because it was just a few weeks later that Brandon called me at home and told me Marti had been trying to get in touch with me all day.

"I was visiting my grandpa," I said. "What's going on?"

"It's Alexis," Brandon said. "She . . . Listen, Jason, the thing is, she shot herself yesterday."

I felt it go through me, but it didn't stick. She'd shot herself. She might not be—

"Is she okay?" I asked. "I mean—"

"She's gone, Jason. She died."

I took a few deep breaths.

"Okay," I said. "Thanks."

"Call Marti," he said. "She needs to hear from you."

"Okay," I said.

I hung up the phone. I was alone in my room. And I was doing okay, except that it just seemed like too much. It was too much.

"Too much," I started saying, over and over again. "Too much, oh, Jesus, too much."

The words became sobs, and I tried to get up from my bed and walk, but my legs were broken by the words, and then I was just kneeling next to my bed, like a little kid saying his prayers, except all I was doing was sobbing and gasping and saying, "Too much. Oh, no, no—too much . . ."

* * *

Marti told me the story a few days later, over the phone. Alexis had been living with her new boyfriend, an older guy named Chris. They were both students at Shoreline Community College, where Alexis was getting her GED. I'd spoken to her a few months ago, and she'd sounded really happy. Marti said it was just a thing—just one of those things Alexis did sometimes. Chris had a single-shot .22 caliber rifle in his closet, and while he was at work Alexis took it out, braced the barrel against her collarbone, and pulled the trigger.

"Her collarbone?" I said.

"Yeah," Marti said. "It bounced off the bone, traveled at a downward angle, and hit her pulmonary artery. And she died."

I could picture it then. Alexis and her cries for help. Knife cuts to her stomach. A bottle of aspirin. A small-caliber bullet high on her chest—away from her vital organs. But .22s are dangerous precisely because they bounce. It must have been such a surprise, I thought, as she collapsed onto the floor and bled to death. It would only have taken a few seconds.

"So she didn't mean to," I said.

"I don't know," Marti said. "I thought that, too. But she was wearing her pearls. They were special to her. Like maybe she expected someone to find her."

"Her pearls?" I asked.

"Yeah," Marti said. "Her mom asked me to wash the blood off them. So Alexis could be buried in them."

I didn't have anything to say to that one.

The funeral was just for family, and a few close friends like Marti. The memorial service was a week later, and that one was general admission. I went with Marti and Brandon and a few hundred other people: people from the church Alexis hadn't been to in years and from her parents' circle of friends. Extended family. Her brother. And a bunch of us students from Garfield.

I cried for Alexis, like I hadn't cried for my dad, Billy, Scotty, or Eddie. Why I could cry for a teenage girl who'd basically killed herself by accident, when I couldn't cry for all these other people who'd so desperately wanted to live, was beyond me. Maybe I was really crying for myself. I didn't know. I didn't understand anything anymore.

* * *

Dad wasn't technically in hospice care yet so he still came home sometimes. I liked it better when he was in the hospital, but I wasn't willing to admit that to myself or anyone else, so I took care of him as best I could when he was around. I kept him from leaving the house in the middle of the night when he said people were coming to get him. I kept lying to him about bug-bombing the house when he was in the hospital. I just kept going. I didn't see any choice in the matter.

I tried to do better—in school, and with the house. Frank's concerns were starting to make an impression on me, and I knew I had to keep my shit together at least enough to graduate. It wasn't easy. I had dozens of absences in some of my classes, and there were new policies in place that required my teachers to fail me based on my attendance record alone. The policies were being tested this year. They'd be mandatory next year. I negotiated with my teachers individually to get them to give me passing grades.

"You shouldn't go to Evergreen," Dad said one day. "You should go to community college."

"I need to go to a four-year college," I said. "Community colleges don't have the kind of financial aid I'll need. Or dorms."

"You shouldn't go to Evergreen," he said. "I took care of you. You should take care of me."

"What?" I said.

"If you leave, they'll put me in hospice, at Swedish," he said.

"But—what about my grades, and my scholarship and all that? How good everything's going to be for me?"

"You owe me," he said.

"Okay, Dad. I'll think about it."

I knew he'd forget. Like he forgot about the bugs and everything else.

"You should drop out of school," he said. "Get your GED. It won't be long now. Just stay here and take care of me."

"Okay, Dad."

"I need you home," he said.

"Okay," I said.

But I kept going to school. I kept trying.

Then one day I came home and found my dad on his hands and knees on the kitchen floor, in a giant pool of his own blood.

73

I had to wait at least six months to get tested. I tried not to think about it. When I couldn't help thinking about it, I reminded myself of everything I knew to be true; the blood he'd had on his clothes was bright red from exposure to the air, and tacky to the touch—well below body temperature—and the virus doesn't survive well in those conditions. Sometimes I thought about why I'd done it, but I knew the answer to that question. I'd done it because it was what Han Solo would do. Not in the sense that he jumped heedlessly into dangerous situations, but because he was a complicated guy. If he was going to commit suicide, he'd figure out a way to make it look like an accident.

I kept going through the motions of Frank's plan, in case I lived. I took the SATs, though I did it on two hours of sleep. I went through a lengthy appeals process with the financial aid office after they processed my application, because their rules said it was scientifically impossible for two people to live on what my dad and I took in during the prior year. Or something to that effect. I had to show them Dad's bank records and all our food stamps and medical coupons and SSI stuff before they'd believe me.

Dad spent more time in the hospital. Grandpa was discharged and went back to Camano Island. I graduated; I walked with one of my school acquaintances, from Graphics class. Sometimes I worried about what was going to happen to me. Other times I felt like I'd already been killed, and I just didn't know it yet.

Frank got me a summer job as a laborer for a construction

contractor he knew. The contractor would take me out to places that had been forests five years earlier—places with names like Bear Creek and Beaver Lake—and drop me at a construction site in the middle of a thousand acres of bare earth, dotted here and there with the skeletons of four-thousand-square-foot houses that were made entirely out of two-by-fours and chipboard. On hot days, the wind scoured topsoil into a brown dust that covered everything. On rainy days, the earth collapsed into the old creek beds and roared downhill toward the nearest lake in a frothing brown and white stampede of mud and rocks. Rain or shine, the contractor would drop me off and tell me he'd be back for me in eight hours.

"Start a burn pile and get rid of all that trash and scrap lumber," he'd say.

He didn't seem to care much what I actually did, which was just as well, since I had no experience with having to work full days. I'd done plenty of task-specific work in my life—chopping firewood or clearing a patch of land—but I'd never had to get up every day and go do something I hated until it was almost bedtime. I found the idea pretty hard to adapt to. I stayed home one day out of every five. The contractor didn't seem to mind that either. I didn't realize until later that he'd probably only hired me on as a favor to Frank, and that a day I stayed home was probably just a day he didn't have to pay me six dollars an hour for busywork.

I hardly ever saw Brandon or Ryan, but Frank and I still saw each other around the house when he came to clean. He still talked to me about my future, and he started to give me more advice.

"Listen," he'd say. "Your dad will be gone soon. And you're going to be tempted to believe that everything that happens now has some kind of special meaning, because it's going to be the last time. The last argument, or the last hug. Whatever happened with you and your dad happened over the course of the last sixteen years. This part is just like a period at the end of a sentence. It's grammatically necessary, but it doesn't really mean very much by itself. Don't fall into the trap of believing it does. Your job during this part is just to get out of this with as little damage to your mind and soul as possible. It's what your father would want."

"No it's not," I said. "He told me I shouldn't go to college."

"That's his fear talking," Frank said.

74

I got into Evergreen, and I got a financial aid package that would cover my bills, but I still couldn't go. Even for someone with no income and no assets, the minimum student contribution was $1,500. Financial aid disbursals and tuition due dates were aligned in such a way that I needed to be able to front the cash for my first quarter on my own. That included rent, tuition, and the price of books. Between Aid for Families with Dependent Children and SSI, our household income for the year was about $6,000. My summer job added another $600 or so to the mix, but there was just no way I could come up with $1,500 on my own.

Frank stepped up again, like he'd been doing for months. He never told me about everything he was doing behind the scenes, but I gathered from things the admissions people said that he'd called people at Evergreen and gotten them to take my applications after their due dates. He'd wrangled a financial aid package for me and gotten me a job, and he'd cosigned a checking account for me at Sea-First Bank. He'd taken me to the Department of Licensing so I could get my first-ever photo identification. And now, when I told him about the financial shortfall over the phone, he said, "Jason, I'd be extremely grateful if you would take some money from me, just to get you across the finish line here."

"No," I said.

"I understand it's hard."

"No," I said. "It's not hard. It's easy. That's why I'm not going to do it. My whole life, I've watched my dad do things the easy way. Make the easy choices. He takes. He takes anything anyone offers him. I don't want to start off doing the same thing."

"That's why you'd be doing me a favor," Frank said. "And why you wouldn't be doing the easy thing. When I was about your age, I was supposed to go to college on a scholarship. The scholarship was contingent on me being valedictorian of my high school class. Which I was, except that I didn't have a suit. I was supposed to give a speech at graduation, and I didn't have a suit, so I couldn't give the speech, so I couldn't be valedictorian, so I couldn't get the scholarship. And there was a man I knew who found out about my situation. And he bought me a suit. And he told me that when he was a young man, someone had done something similar for him. And that all I had to do to repay him was to do something similar for someone else someday. So, you see, you'd be helping me settle my debt. And all you'd have to do to repay me would be to do something similar for someone else someday."

"Frank," I said, "you've done enough for me."

"No," he said. "It's only enough if it gets you out of here."

"What are you getting out of this?" I asked him. "I don't understand why you're doing this."

"I told you," he said. "I'm repaying a debt."

"Yeah. I don't know about that story, Frank."

"If you take on the debt, and repay me someday by doing something similar for someone else, does it matter if the story's true or not?"

"I don't know. I'm not used to thinking about things on this scale."

"Everything has to happen for a first time. How do you make other hard decisions?"

So I thought, what would Han Solo do? When I put it like that, the answer was obvious.

75

Kris helped me move my stuff to Olympia in September, but I never got all of it. The apartment was always there, waiting. The Section Eight payments happened automatically, and they were apparently enough to keep the landlord happy as long as Dad was alive. So I kept going back, to get a few more things.

I got the impression, from talking to Ryan and Brandon and people I knew from school, that most people my age were excited about this part. They were looking forward to freedom and adventure. I wondered what they were picturing when they thought about living on their own. I had no picture of where I was going, or what was going to happen to me. Even actually doing it—being in Olympia, in the dorm room I shared with some other first-year college student who'd been assigned to me by the housing office—didn't help me understand how any of this was going to work.

I had a tacit assumption that I was going to die. That wasn't what I told people. I told people I was going to get a teaching degree and come back to teach at my old high school. I told people I'd graduate from Evergreen when I was twenty-one, and get a head start on the rest of my life—which was going to be awesome. I told people I was excited about my future. And all of it was perfectly plausible. Like Alexis's plan to move out on her own: it was mathematically possible for atoms and molecules to arrange themselves in such a way that I'd be a young adult with a college degree and a good job. But from my perspective, I may as well have been describing the house I was going to build in the mystical land of Narnia. I didn't know what a happy ending looked like. I'd never seen a happy ending any more than I'd ever seen a fucking unicorn.

On the other hand, I'd seen bunches of young men die in the prime of their lives, alone, with nobody to take care of them or mourn their passing. That was what had happened to Alexis's mathematically possible happy ending; that was a future I could picture really clearly.

I went through the motions of living my new life. I got Kris to adopt Dad's dog, Thunder. She'd been taking care of him for most of the last year, so it wasn't much of a reach for her. I said my goodbyes to people in Seattle. I got a work/study job in the campus metal shop at Evergreen, and registered for classes and went for walks in the woods. I attended get-to-know-you events, orientations, and mixers on campus. I was pretending this was my life now—at the same time I kept finding excuses to go back to my old one.

76

In November of my first year at Evergreen, my dad sent me a letter:

DATE	PROGRESS RECORD · CONTINUED

Dearest Jason,

Son I have never lied to you before you cought me shooting that speed. I lyed to you, It was the biggest miskake in my life. I have never felt so guilty in my life. Jason there are only three words that I need to hear from you. They are I forgive you, Jason. I am a addict. I know alls it requires is self control I have never meant an addict yet who could say 'no' when confronted with certain circumstances

Love your father

The irony, from my perspective, was that I'd tried to forgive him a bunch of times. I'd tried to forgive him for lying to me, and for hitting me, and for terrorizing and abusing me. I'd tried to forgive him for letting me down. I'd tried to forgive him over and over again by having an honest conversation with him about any of the shit he'd pulled, and trying to get him to accept some responsibility for any of it. Or at least admit that any of it had happened. He only ever got angry; told me I was making it sound worse than it was, that my childhood had been great, and that I never appreciated what a good parent he was because I didn't have a basis for comparison. His parents lied to him about everything, he said. They didn't respect him enough to tell him the truth—about sex, or drugs, or "the system."

"I never lied to you about anything!" he'd shout. "Ever! You can accuse me of a lot of things, but I always told you the truth!"

Now here he was, delirious and dying, and asking me to forgive him for something he'd never done—for lies he'd never told. As far as I knew, Dad hadn't shot speed in ten years. The only time since he'd had AIDS that I'd "cought" him shooting anything was the time I walked in on him shooting sedatives into his PICC-line in the kitchen. I hadn't given him the chance to lie to me about that. I hadn't asked him a single question about it. I hadn't confronted him, or accused him, or questioned what he was doing. I knew there was no point.

Speed had been his drug of choice when I was little, back in Eugene. I assumed his reference to it was just some kind of drug addict's Freudian slip. A guilty echo. The incident in the kitchen was a proxy for all the other lies I'd caught him in. All the lies he wanted me to forgive him for now.

I called Frank and read the letter to him over the phone.

"What should I do?" I asked.

"What do you want to do?"

"I don't know. I don't want to tell him I forgive him. If he wanted that, he had plenty of opportunities. Now he's trying to blackmail me into absolving him for all the shit he's done over the years. I don't even see why he'd want that. He knows it'd be bullshit. What good does fake absolution do him at this point? If there's a time in a person's life when I'd think truth matters more than appearances, this would be it."

"Those are good points," Frank said.

"So what should I do?"

"What do you want to do?"

"Why do you keep saying that?" I asked.

"Because the only thing that matters now is what's good for you," he said. "Your dad's story is over. In six months or a year, this will be done for him. He won't be dealing with the consequences of what you choose to do now. You will. So you make this decision based on what you need."

"I don't know if I can do that."

"You're not understanding me. If what you need, in order to feel good about yourself later on, is to show him some mercy—then show him some mercy. If you need to tell him the truth, do that. But try to look at it in terms of what you're going to be able to live with ten, twenty years down the line."

It was on the tip of my tongue right then to tell Frank about getting Dad's blood all over me. I couldn't bring myself to do it. He'd worked so hard to get me out. I couldn't bring myself to tell him I might have screwed it all up—that I might have killed myself by being stupid and careless. Or by just not caring about myself enough to avoid a lethal mistake.

"All right," I said. "Thanks, Frank."

"Good luck," he said.

* * *

I went back to Seattle again a few days later. I didn't seem to be able to help myself. I visited Dad in Swedish Hospital, where he was staying while he waited for a spot in an AIDS hospice called Rosehedge House. I had no idea what I was going to say to him. I hoped he'd just forget, but as soon as I walked into the hospital room he looked at me with his dull eyes and bared his teeth in something that was supposed to be a smile. That same dull, give-me-a-hand-here smile he'd used when I found him in the kitchen covered in blood.

"Did you get my letter?" he asked.

His hopeful tone made me sick.

"Yeah," I said. "I got it."

"Do you have anything to say to me?" he asked.

I was breathing deeply, like I had when he threatened to have me committed. I stared into his eyes. They'd changed so much in the past five years. It was almost as if they'd gotten lighter; gone from dark brown to a kind of muted yellow. His face had collapsed in on itself. His skin hugged the bones of his face, like a damp washcloth draped over a skull. Only his eyes showed any life, and they were full of a slow-burning anger. Not the rage I'd seen on his face a thousand times, when he hit me or screamed at me. This was something deeper. More like hatred.

There was nothing in there to tell me what I should do.

"We can talk about it later," I said.

"No. I need to hear it now."

I could have the fight, I could leave, or I could give him what he wanted. Whatever else happened here today, I could see it wouldn't be a catharsis. He'd only ever let me forgive him for things he was ready to admit to, and he'd only admit to things that had never happened.

"I forgive you," I said.

"What?" he said.

"I forgive you," I said again.

He reached for my hand and held it in his.

I'd never hated anyone as much as I hated him then. I wanted to throw up. I wanted to crush him. I wanted to climb onto the bed like a rabid ape and jump up and down on his chest until his ribs burst out like a little nest, like a boat I could kneel down in while I wrapped my fingers around his neck and squeezed until the meat pushed out between my fingers like putty, until I was crushing his spine in my hands and screaming in his face. My guts cramped, pushing and pulling, tearing like something had torn loose inside me. I didn't know what.

I just knew I'd made a horrible mistake, and that I'd never be able to fix it.

*   *   *

I slept on Kris's floor that night and called Brandon to hang out the next day. He and Maria were sharing an apartment up on 15th, five blocks east of Broadway. I never saw Maria when I went over there to visit him. I'd run into her on the bus once, and she'd said he made her leave the room whenever I was coming over. He also didn't like her to call me or talk to me. Brandon and I still talked, but this had been a thing between us for months.

In my brief time at Evergreen, I'd learned a sort of problem-solving approach that I thought would help Brandon and me come to some kind of settlement on Maria. They did a thing there where they talked about their feelings as issues that needed to be addressed. Like "I'm finding your demeanor really threatening." And then whoever that was said to was supposed to dial it back. Maybe even apologize. Where Brandon and I came from—at Garfield, on Broadway, and in the houses we'd grown up in—admitting that kind of weakness was a death sentence. But at Evergreen, it was almost a kind of religion.

"So listen," I said to Brandon when I saw him. "We need to work this thing out. About Maria."

"I'm not sure what you mean," he said. We were sitting in his living room, which was only slightly less messy than his bedroom had been back when he was living next door to me. He and Maria already had a lot of pets, and the smell of them was strong in the apartment. But he had a couch, a few chairs, and some lamps. A few end tables. I could see the idea of a home underneath everything else.

"I mean I want to talk about this thing," I said. "Where you're mad at me for having been with her. And where you tell her to leave the room whenever I come over. And a million other little things you've done and said since you guys got together. It's like you hold it against me, how things went, but all I ever did was the stuff you told me to. Asked her for her phone number. Broke things off when she said she loved me. I was just following your rules."

He smiled at me, but it was a smile I knew. It was a smile I'd seen him practice in the Guardian Angels. It was meant to project professional distance. It was appraising. Patronizing. The silence stretched out between us until he leaned forward and braced his elbows on his knees, like he was going to tell me a secret.

"You know," he said, "I'm glad you brought this up."

"You are?" I said.

"Yeah. I am. Because there's something I've been wanting to tell you since school ended, and I think this is a good time."

"Okay," I said.

"You . . . use people, Jason. You use people, and you take from people. And you whine, constantly. You hear what I'm saying? The thing I'm trying to get across to you is, you're just not a very good person. Maybe it's not your fault. You've had a hard life. But I have to tell you, I'm just sick of it. For years, you want to get together at night and talk about your problems. You want my advice about every girl you have a crush on. You're afraid of being poor, but you're crap at holding down a job. You never make any of your own decisions, about anything. The whole time I've known you, all I do is give—and all you do is take. And now you come in here talking about Maria—it's like you're trying to make me feel guilty for being in love. On top of everything else. So here's what I'd like you to do. I'd like you to leave my apartment. And I'd like to never hear from you again."

"That's pretty surprising," I said. It wasn't what I meant to say. What I meant to do was, I meant to scream and cry and freak out and beg him to forgive me. But I sensed that it would only make things worse.

"To you, yeah, I imagine it would be. But here's the thing. I picture my life in five years. And one of the major ingredients in having it be a nice place—in having it feel good, and comfortable, and safe—is having you not in it."

I stared at him for a long time, trying to formulate some reply. Trying to think of some way of talking him out of it. I wasn't going to argue with anything he'd said. I didn't know if it was true, but it felt true—especially the last part. In a way, I was jealous. I wished I could imagine my life five years later, without me in it. I thought it would probably be a lot nicer than whatever I was going to end up with.

I didn't say anything else. I got up and walked to the door. I kept wanting to say "See you" or "Talk to you later" or something, but none of that was true. Even goodbye wouldn't really work. There was nothing good about this. It was just "bye," and, for some reason, I couldn't bring myself to say that, so I just left.

I had a strange realization later, when I was torturing myself trying to decide if the things Brandon had said to me were true. I realized that, in spite of my best efforts, not only was I no Han Solo—I was actually Luke Skywalker.

It was all there in the last movie, *Return of the Jedi*—the red-headed stepchild of the original trilogy. In the end of *Jedi*, Luke faces off against Darth Vader and the Emperor. He's accepted that Vader is really his father, and he tries to get his old man to redeem himself, but Vader blows him off.

"It is too late for me, son. The Emperor will show you the true nature of the Force. He is your master now."

So Luke tries to attack the Emperor—the sick old bastard who corrupted his father in the first place—but Vader defends the creepy predator. Then Luke and Vader go at it, with Luke getting increasingly frantic as the Emperor taunts him about how all his friends are going to die and the Rebel Alliance is going to lose.

"Good," says the Emperor. "Use your aggressive feelings, boy. Let the hate flow through you."

And, sure enough, Luke kicks his old man's ass. He even chops off Vader's hand, like Vader chopped off Luke's hand in *The Empire Strikes Back*. But that's the turning point. Because when Luke looks at Vader, lying helpless with his missing hand and his robot body, Luke looks at his own robot hand and realizes that he's already taken the first step in the process of becoming exactly like his father. Just like I was turning into my dad.

Once I spotted the pattern, the parallels seemed obvious. The contagion of whatever had fucked my dad up all those years ago had spread to me, and now I was becoming this rage-fueled need-machine with no self-control or enlightenment. I didn't make choices. I wasn't deciding my own fate. Things just happened to me. I was always reacting. I didn't have a Wookie sidekick, and I wasn't going to get the girl. At the end of this movie, everyone else was going to be celebrating the happy ending and partying down with the Ewoks, and I was going to go off by myself to cremate my father.

And if I somehow got saved, it was going to be because of this weird old man who came out of nowhere and helped me, for no good reason.

Christ. I couldn't even pick my own movie character metaphor.

77

When I finally got tested, I did it in Olympia, on campus. The Department of Health sent an itinerant phlebotomist to Evergreen once a week to give free, anonymous HIV tests to the students. We didn't have a real campus health center, so he took appointments in one of the science labs. I knew the test results would take two weeks. What I didn't know was that the tester was required to provide counseling.

"What's that mean?" I asked. "Counseling? What exactly are you going to make me feel better about?"

"It's not to make you feel better," said the Health Department guy. He was young, with longish blond hair and a beard. He was slightly overweight and frumpy in cargo shorts and a safari shirt. He had round glasses in plain steel frames, and he was wearing sandals. I'd forgotten his name as soon as he introduced himself, but I was leaning toward "Matt."

"What's it for then?" I asked.

"To prepare you for the possibility that the test may come back positive."

I sighed. "I'm prepared."

"Do you have a plan?" he asked. "Do you have a support system?"

We were sitting in one of the rooms where Evergreen students studied chemistry and physics, seated on either side of a narrow counter made out of a hard black mixture of concrete and asbestos. The counter had cabinets underneath and a sink at the end, and a half dozen chrome-plated fixtures that dispensed natural gas and compressed air. The natural gas was for Bunsen burners. I assumed the compressed air was for making balloon animals or something.

"Not that it's any of your business," I said. "But suppose I don't have a support system. Do I still get the test, or do I have to wait until I make some friends?"

"You get the test no matter what. I just have to ask these questions to help you think about them."

I leaned back in my chair and looked at him. He was maybe ten years older than I was, but he looked very earnest to me. Unspoiled by real life.

"No," I said. "I don't have a support system."

"Nobody you can call?"

"No," I said. "Not for this."

"So what's your plan? If the test comes back positive?"

"I don't think you're going to like it," I said.

"Try me," he said with a smile.

"I'll pretty much keep doing what I'm doing until I become symptomatic. Then I'll kill myself. Probably by hanging, but we'll see how it goes."

His smile changed gears, from friendly to patronizing.

"There are new treatments for this disease every day," he

said. "You don't have to be so dramatic. There are ways to live with this."

"Hey," I said. "Ask me why I don't have a support system."

"Excuse me?" he said.

"Ask me why I don't have a support system."

He sighed. Now he looked irritated.

"Why don't you have a support system?" he asked.

"Because I grew up with my dad. We moved all the time, and I never had any friends. I still don't have any friends. The only person who'd be my support system in a situation like this would be my dad. He'd be bad at it, but he'd do it. The problem is he's in a hospital, with end-stage AIDS, and he'll be dead in six months at the outside. I'm here to get tested because he passed out and cracked his head open seven months ago, and I got his blood all over me while I was taking him to the hospital."

I was having fun now.

"So," I said, "the reason I don't have a support system is because my dad, and most of the adults that I've known, ever, in my entire life, are all either sick or dying. Or taking care of someone who's sick and dying. And the reason my plan may involve suicide is because, unlike you—I'm guessing—I've actually seen what it's like to 'live with this disease.' I've seen it really intimately. I know what it looks like. I know what it smells like. I know what it sounds like at two o'clock in the morning. I know it takes a long time, and it's horrible and painful, and I'm not going out like that. I think we can probably agree that would be an informed decision on my part, right? That I'm not being dramatic? That I know what I'm talking about?"

He was quiet for a while. I wished I had a recording of this, so I could listen to it later. I'd been rehearsing this speech in my head for years, and it was landing on him exactly the way I'd always dreamed it would.

"I don't know what to say to any of that," he said.

"That's fine," I said. "You people never do."

"You people?"

"Yeah," I said. "You normal people. You people who tell me it's possible to live with this disease. You guidance counselors and cops and welfare caseworkers. Funny story. Last time I picked up the mail back at my old apartment, there were letters from the Section Eight housing and welfare telling us we'd been selected for audits. They'd have to go through Dad's bank accounts. Inspect our house. Interview my dad. Joke's on them, I guess. So sure, I can have a free AIDS test. But first I need counseling. From you. Because you've got some fresh insight about my situation. So okay, come on, Health Department. Counsel me. Tell me what I should do if the test comes back positive, with no family and no money and a slow painful death to look forward to."

"What do you want me to say?" he asked. "I want to tell you it's not that bad, but what do I know? You want me to tell you your answer freaks me out? That you're freaking me out? You are."

"I want you to tell me I'm right."

My own answer surprised me, but I knew it was true as soon as I said it. Just once, I wanted one of these people to look at me and tell me it was exactly as bad as I thought it was. I was sick of everyone watching TV while my family got trampled by elephants. I wanted some fucking acknowledgment, and if I couldn't get Ronald Reagan to come down here and beg my forgiveness for having sat on his thumb while Scotty died of yellow fever and Billy wasted away and my dad went slowly crazy, I'd settle for this earnest hippie telling me I was right. That a quick death might actually be my best option.

"I'm not sure I can say that," he said.

"So, it's not so much that you're required to give me

counseling, as that you're required to ask me some personal questions. The answers don't matter."

"No," he said. "I guess they don't."

"Just another hoop I have to jump through, to get my free thing. Because people like me should have to jump through hoops."

"I guess so," he said.

I could tell I'd burned him out. I'd get no more satisfaction from this one. Not tonight. If the test came back positive, I'd have another window. And a better motive. This was the problem with these government hacks; they handed out Band-Aids for severed limbs, then got indignant when they caught a little arterial spray. He wasn't here for me. He was here for the home viewing audience. I should have gone to Seattle, I realized. I should have gone to the clinic, paid $20 for a test administered by someone who might know what the fuck they were talking about, and saved myself this sanctimony. But I'd sung for my dinner. I might as well get fed.

"So what now?" I asked.

"Now we draw some blood," he said.

"Great."

He found the vein on the first try. I saw him again two weeks later. The test came back negative. He seemed more relieved than I was.

78

My dad died in January of 1990, less than a month before what would have been his fortieth birthday, and a few months after I turned seventeen.

He got into Rosehedge House before he snuffed it. The hospice was in a nice turn-of-the-century Craftsman house, just a few blocks from Bruce's condo. It had wood trim, and plaster-and-lath walls, like so many of the leftover houses we'd lived in over the years. Medical equipment in the hallways made the building feel cramped and overused, but sound moved the way it was supposed to in there, and the smell was right: one-hundred-year-old fir, wax furniture polish, and some subtle trace left behind by generations of past occupants; scented oils from the old country and extinct lines of ethnic cooking. I hadn't really appreciated how integral those houses were to our life—to the life my dad and I had shared—until I'd moved into the dorms at Evergreen, where the floor, ceiling, and walls were all thinly disguised ferroconcrete, and the only smells were carpet glue and fresh paint. I knew that, even if he was unconscious, being in the right kind of house would have made it easier for Dad to die. Would have made it less frightening.

I got the call the morning after it happened. I talked to a nurse, who said Dad had died in the middle of the night, that he had been unconscious for several days, and probably didn't feel much pain. I asked if they needed me to do anything, to take care of the body or Dad's things. He said they didn't. He said other people were handling it. I thought he probably meant Bruce and Kris, but I was happy to let anyone else deal with it.

I went to class later that day. I didn't really know what else to do. My instinct was that if I covered my mirrors and tore my clothes and sat on the floor, I wouldn't be able to get up again. I didn't feel sad—just numb, and impossibly tired. I was afraid to mourn in sort of the same way I would have been afraid to lie down in the snow and go to sleep. So I got dressed. I went to class.

We had a lecture and a seminar that day, about the use of shadows and negative space in Japanese aesthetics and culture; the difference between things revealed and things implied.

Dad had always covered his windows with curtains, or filled them with plants. He abhorred bright lights. Floor lamps were better than overhead lighting; kerosene and candles were better than electric bulbs. Day or night, his room was a star chamber dotted with constellations of dim light reflected in polished brass and tiny mirrors. Tapestries, photographs, and color prints of art deco paintings lurked in the shadows like cave drawings. Everyplace we'd ever lived, my dad's room had always looked like some dimly lit Arabian treasure chamber to me.

When I'd packed things up to move to Olympia, I'd had to open the curtains and turn on the overhead light. Everything withered in that bright glare, turning shabby and sad. All Dad's treasures—things he'd rescued from abandoned buildings and flea markets and carried thousands of miles up and down the I-5 corridor—in the clear light of day it was all just a bunch of worthless junk.

I had trouble sitting through the lecture on aesthetics. I kept needing to stretch, crack my knuckles, crack my neck. I couldn't get comfortable in my chair. I rolled my shoulders. I felt like I was in a box. After the lecture, the class split up into small seminar groups, and I went into my assigned room ready to tear something apart. I sat there holding on to it as long as I could, but all I could think was that none of these assholes understood— they didn't even understand what the lecture was about. They

406

could read about it, but they didn't get it. They didn't comprehend anything.

"I think Tanizaki is critiquing Western culture's obsession with technology," one of my classmates said. "And our lack of appreciation for subtlety and context."

"Which might be a valid critique for him to make," I drawled, stepping on the end of her sentence, "if he'd ever spent any time in the West. But since he didn't, either his critique is full of shit or you are."

The room caught its breath, and I suppressed a scream of frustration. Anywhere I'd ever lived up to that point, an insult like that would have been a clear invitation to everyone at the table to throw some hands. These useless pricks didn't even speak English.

"That was out of line," the seminar leader muttered, avoiding eye contact.

"Sorry," I sneered. "I guess I'm a little irritable today. My dad died last night."

The uncomfortable silence that followed gave me a warm, vicious glow, but it didn't burn hot enough to take my mind off anything.

* * *

There was a funeral in Seattle a few days later. I didn't even know who organized it. I'd told Kris and Bruce they could do whatever they wanted as far as I was concerned. Kris called me and told me the particulars. She gave me plenty of notice, but I was late anyway. I wore black jeans and a black T-shirt; I was carrying a white dress shirt that I'd meant to change into, but I never got around to putting it on.

The service happened in the chapel of a funeral home on Capitol Hill. The chapel was tall and deep, but very narrow, and made entirely out of concrete. Thick pillars supported the high ceiling, and banks of nondenominational stained-glass windows shone down from high on the north wall. There was standing water on the floor, like the place had been sprayed out with a pressure hose right before we came in.

My uncle John and his family sat with me near the front, in an uncomfortable wooden pew. My grandparents were boycotting the service because there were Buddhists speaking.

I didn't really pay attention to what was said or who talked. Afterward, I remembered the wall sconces. They had white plastic lilies in them. Dad had hated plastic flowers. The whole thing took about twenty minutes. I had the feeling we were getting some kind of welfare-funded pauper's funeral special, but realized later it was probably paid for by the Northwest AIDS Foundation or the Chicken Soup Brigade. Or maybe Bruce.

I went to the after-party at Kris's apartment. There was a lot of food. There was a sheet cake with a palm tree and a rainbow on it that had "Aloha, Mark!" written on it in frosting. I expected the party to be relaxing compared to the funeral, but mostly it was a lot of people I didn't know—people from Dad's support groups and service agencies. They all said nice things about him—generally to each other rather than to me, but I could hear them. After about an hour I decided I was just bringing everyone down, so I left. I walked to the Greyhound station, a half mile away, and waited for the next bus heading south, back to school. The benches in the terminal were full, so I sat on the floor and stared at the clock on the wall above the ticket office.

I realized I'd left my dress shirt at Kris's house.

It was funny. The whole thing was funny.

I wanted to call someone and make jokes about the funeral. I wanted someone to come pick me up and take me to a coffee shop. Or maybe to the beach. Someplace with a view. But Ryan was on the outside of this particular circle, and apart from him there really wasn't anyone else left. I hadn't spoken to Calliope in over a year. I wasn't even sure I still had her number. Marti and I hadn't talked since school ended, and she wouldn't thank me to call her now, for this. I had a lot of acquaintances, but hardly any friends. The people I'd been close to were all gone—and only about half of them were dead. So what did that mean?

* * *

Grandpa died three weeks later, of another heart attack. He died in his easy chair, in his living room, up on Camano Island. Probably he was watching baseball when it happened. I'd moved by then to a place where I didn't have a phone, so I didn't get Uncle John's messages until after the funeral. It didn't upset me much. Grandpa had been sick for a while, and anyway, it was how everything was going now; everyone was dying or moving on. My whole universe was closing up shop.

79

I told most of my classmates at Evergreen that my dad had died of tuberculosis. It was the lie he and I had settled on when he first got sick. And not just because of homophobia. A 1985 *Los Angeles Times* poll had said that a majority of Americans favored forcing AIDS patients into quarantine camps. Then a U.S. congressman named Dannemeyer had actually suggested doing it. In the pre-Internet age, Xerox copies of newspaper articles about that kind of thing were passed around the AIDS community like banned books. It all seemed crazy, but World War II hadn't been that long ago and nobody wanted to find themselves sitting in a bunkhouse in central California, surrounded by guard towers and barbed wire, thinking, "Wow. They actually did it." I knew I was safe from that kind of thing, now that Dad was gone, but fear of how straights would react to the truth about anything was a lifelong reflex by that point.

Staying in the closet about my own family background kept me at a boil for months, and then years, but I had other problems. It was true that my old life had ended when my dad died, but I carried fragments of it around inside me afterward, like pieces of shrapnel I'd picked up in some unpopular covert war, and they ate at me in ways that surprised me. I kept thinking I was going to wake up some morning and breathe a sigh of relief because nobody was going to come into my room in the middle of the night and start screaming at me. Or hitting me. Or trying to smash my head in with some kind of blunt instrument. I didn't have to worry about accidental fluids exposure anymore. I'd survived my dad. But surviving a trauma and being able to live with it were two different things.

I started to shake apart. It was little things at first. I'd always had trouble sleeping, but at Evergreen it just spiraled. By the end of my first year, I was going days at a time without rest. And when I finally did sleep, it was rarely for more than four or five hours at a time. Other things followed. I'd been kind of jumpy for years. But now I couldn't sit in a room with my back to the door—couldn't relax at all in a room where the door was open. When I did sleep, I slept fully clothed. I kept a knife under my pillow. If someone startled me—if they came up behind me or talked to me while I was reading—my hands snapped up in front of me, like a boxer, ready to fight. Sometimes I'd start shouting obscenities at them. I overreacted to normal stimulus. All the time, in every situation, I was so angry I was vibrating

410

with it. I couldn't regulate the volume of my own voice. I couldn't concentrate.

And I couldn't explain any of it.

People talked a lot about post-traumatic stress disorder in the eighties, when everyone suddenly started giving a shit about Vietnam veterans. I'd seen the symptoms in everything from Rambo movies to *Magnum, P.I.* reruns: flashbacks, hypervigilance, insomnia, mood swings, increased fight-or-flight response. But it was only ever talked about as something that happened to soldiers. There was nothing in my background that would justify me being as messed up as I seemed to be. The physical violence, with my dad—it hadn't really been that bad. Or I didn't think it was, anyway. And I'd seen other people who had it so much worse. The idea that I might be suffering from a delayed stress reaction didn't seem credible, even to me.

In the absence of a good reason for being like I was, I made up a lot of ridiculous lies about the hard life I'd had on the streets and the horrible acts of violence I'd committed and witnessed there. Some of the people who were afraid of me also started feeling sorry for me. Unsurprisingly, this also made me angry.

By the end of my second year, I was behind on my rent, unemployed, and I was only passing about half my classes. Evergreen didn't have grades—they issued written narrative evaluations to students at the end of every academic term. But other schools converted those evaluations into grade equivalents, and I knew I was running about a high-D average. I figured I was doing myself more harm than good staying in school, so I dropped out and went back to Seattle.

That was when things started to really suck.

80

I spent my first six months in Seattle camped out in Kris's hall closet, before I moved into an apartment I couldn't afford with a guy I barely knew in a neighborhood up north of Ballard. I didn't have a bed because the dorms at Evergreen came with them, and I couldn't move or store one anyway. So I slept on the floor, wrapped in the Pendleton blankets Dad had bought with his inheritance when I was four years old, and I used my wadded-up army surplus field jacket as a pillow.

I looked for work that could tolerate my mood swings. I spent a year using toxic chemicals to rinse laboratory glassware in a small, poorly ventilated room with no windows. I hated the job, but I could have as many bad days as I wanted to in that room. Nobody tried to talk to me. Nobody told me they were scared of me, or accused me of anything, or asked me what was wrong with me. When that job ended, I worked four part-time jobs at once, washing dishes, running a cash register, making pizza, and covering a few nights as a pantry cook.

The cash register job required more contact with people than I would have liked, but the environment was uniquely suited to my temperament. I worked the downtown bar rush two nights a week, serving pizza and ice cream to drunk suburbanites, college students, and the criminals who preyed on them. My boss carried a gun in a shoulder holster, and we kept a baseball bat next to the register. When I caught a customer pissing in a back stairway of the restaurant, I grabbed the bat and made him clean it up with a roll of paper towels. Afterward I was horrified by my own willingness to do serious violence over something that really wasn't that big a deal. I told my boss about it at the end of the night, assuming I'd be fired on the spot, but he just told me I'd done the right thing and that being ready to mess people up was part of the job.

A week later, my boss told me he wanted me to help his cousin remodel another pizza restaurant, a few blocks away. I spent three weeks on that job, working side by side with the cousin. We talked about all kinds of things. He asked me a lot of questions about my background. Then, after three weeks, he took me to lunch and told me he wanted to promote me.

"To do what?" I asked.

"I'm looking to move into patents," he said. "To buy them from inventors. But I need someone who can convince them to sell. I hear you're a guy who knows how to talk to people."

I laughed.

"Where'd you hear that?" I asked.

"The way I hear it, you convinced a guy to clean up his own piss," the cousin said.

I stopped laughing.

"This is no small-time operation," the cousin assured me. "We're vertically integrated. You work for me, you've got a house, a car, clothes. Medical and dental. The works."

"What about a lawyer?" I asked, to make sure I understood what he was saying. "Bail. That kind of thing."

"That shouldn't be necessary," he said. "But if it came up, I'd have you covered."

"I'll need to think about it," I said.

I gave notice a few days later and got another job making pizza in a different neighborhood.

I spent a lot of my spare time exercising, shadow boxing and doing calisthenics. If I wasn't working out, I was reading. I read novels, and nonfiction books about revolution: Emma Goldman, Bobby Seale, and Malcolm X. I read books about tree spiking and industrial sabotage. I read history books about the

Students for a Democratic Society and the Weather Underground. I didn't know what I thought I was preparing for, but the feeling that some kind of doom was just around the corner followed me everywhere. When it didn't arrive on its own, I started to think about what I could do to hurry it along. When I turned twenty-one I got a permit to carry a concealed pistol. I never did buy a gun, but I spent more on knives, saps, and throwing stars than I did on clothes.

I kept circling the idea of doing something irrevocable. And while I thought about that I did stupid, pointlessly dangerous things. I walked fifteen hours—almost fifty miles, in a fall rainstorm—wearing a T-shirt and jeans. I went out in the middle of the night and crept through the camps of the homeless men who lived in the woods above the railroad tracks. Or I walked on the tracks from Seattle to Edmonds, the next town up to the north, with the ocean on one side and cliffs and deep ravines on the other. It was an easy walk by daylight, so I'd start at 10:00 p.m. walking in the dark as quietly as I could, so I'd be able to hear the chirp of the tracks if a train approached. When the engines went by, I'd crouch on the edge of the stone seawall while the cars roared past just a few feet away.

I didn't know what the hell I was doing. But I didn't have any friends to talk to about it, or family to have to explain it to, so it seemed not to matter. It seemed like I could go as crazy as I wanted to and there was no societal mechanism to reel me back in. I kept expecting someone at one of my jobs, or even a random stranger on the street, to tap me on the shoulder and say something like "It's none of my business, buddy, but you need therapy."

It never happened though.

At some point I ran into Brandon's cousin Ian—the guy whose arm I'd maybe dislocated on the night I asked Maria for her phone number, all those years earlier. I bumped into him on Broadway, on Capitol Hill. He looked the same in most respects, but his eyes were strung out as hell.

"What've you been up to?" I asked.

"Not much," he said, scanning the street over my shoulder, not making eye contact. "Joined the Army. Rangers."

"Yeah?" I asked. "I've been thinking about doing that. How was it?"

"I got discharged," he said.

"What?" I asked. "Like—thrown out?"

"Yeah."

"What for?" I asked.

"Well, you know," he said. "Those guys are a bunch of fucking hypocrites. They're supposed to be training us to fight—to kill—but then they get all freaked out when you want to get good at that part of it."

"Uh," I said, "so . . . what actually happened?"

"Officially it was some weird subclause in some regulation. But really it was because my sergeant found out I'd sharpened my entrenching tool."

"Your entrenching . . . you mean those little shovels? Like they use to dig foxholes?"

"Yeah," he said, his eyes focusing on me for the first time. "You sharpen one of those up, it's basically a battle ax. It'll split you from here . . . to here."

As he finished the last sentence he put the first two fingers of his hand on my left collarbone and slid them down my torso to my right hip. Something about the gesture was disconcertingly intimate.

"Okay," I said. "Well, good to see you. How's Brandon doing?"

"He's still with Maria. They've got a place up the hill."

"Right," I said. "Well, that's good. I'm glad they're doing well. I'll see you around, man. You take care of yourself, okay?"

"Roger that," he said. He was already looking somewhere else, and I was glad to get out from under those eyes.

It wasn't until I got home later that night that I started to wonder if most people would think Ian and I were pretty much the same guy.

* * *

The idea that I might come across the same way Ian did bothered me for a lot of reasons, but one of them was that even I knew I wasn't totally beyond help. There were days—sometimes even two of them in a row—where I still wanted to be Han Solo, and believed that was possible. I just didn't know how. And I worried what would happen if I joined something, like the military or some church, to try to find my way. Because I recognized in myself the potential to be a zealous convert to any organization or philosophy that promised me direction—and it scared me. Better to stay away from those who might claim to have all the answers; messed up as I was, I knew I'd probably believe them.

Still, I felt like I was waiting for the universe to give me a hint. Left to my own devices, I cobbled my divine mandate together from cheesy movie dialogue, fortune cookies, and things I saw spray-painted on walls or written in bus shelters with felt-tipped markers. When I was walking down the Ave, in the University District, and some gutter punk handed me a homemade leaflet that said, "Why pay the government to tell you what to do? Take back your life!" I knew that was a message I should think about. When I heard George Carlin say, in a stand-up routine, "That's the whole secret of life: not dying!" I thought, Yeah, that's the stuff. A few years later, *The Shawshank Redemption* came out, and no lesser personage than Morgan Freeman told me to "Get busy living, or get busy dying." I knew I had my walking papers.

Of course I also knew that I was making the whole thing up; that my intermittent bouts of optimism were just a reflection of my own gradually improving mental health. But, functionally, I didn't really see the difference between taking my cues from Morgan Freeman or from Jesus the space alien. Emma Goldman's advice, that "The ultimate end of all revolutionary social change is to establish the sanctity of human life, the dignity of man, the right of every human being to liberty and well-being," seemed as complete, to me, as anything I'd read in the King James Bible or heard at Grandma and Grandpa's churches.

Mr. Freeman had told me to get busy living, but, just like before I went to Evergreen, I struggled to understand what a happy ending—a real life—would mean for me. When I'd asked my dad how regular people went on about their business while a family in Cambodia was being trampled by elephants, he'd implied that ignoring suffering was a core tenet of the straight paradigm. Calliope had told me that our secret superpower—hers and mine—was to hear all the screaming and horror that straight people tuned out. The cheerleaders for the American dream told me that if I worked hard and sacrificed, I could be normal someday. But I couldn't bring myself to want that. The rage I'd felt toward the straight world, for standing idly by while AIDS destroyed my home and my community, wouldn't allow it. I could feel the crashing of giant feet on the earth and hear the sounds of human suffering. I had an obligation to listen, even if it kept me from ever being normal.

But what was I supposed to do, then, in order to get busy living? Join the patent-mafia and start strong-arming inventors?

I found my answer in the gospel of Frank. And it was only when I was out on my own, lost and looking for direction, that I realized I'd already been baptized into his religion.

Frank and I had lost touch while I was at Evergreen. Or it might have been more accurate to say he'd let me go. Not because he wanted to, but because it had been our arrangement;

there were no strings attached to the help he gave me. So he sent me a few letters telling me I was welcome at his house for Thanksgiving, or for Christmas, if I happened to be in town, but that I shouldn't feel obligated. And when I didn't respond, he let that be that. I appreciated his forbearance. Those years had been hard enough without having him watch me stumble and fall, over and over again. But I understood now that Frank's gift to me wasn't the money he'd given me, or the help with my school applications. It was the promise he'd let me make, that I'd pay it all forward some day.

In a certain light, Frank was as straight as they came. He was an old white guy, a retired professional, married, with a grown son. But his career path, as an educator, had been in public service. And when he retired, instead of going on cruises or traveling in Europe, he'd volunteered to clean houses for a group of people that the rest of the country wanted to banish to quarantine camps. He hadn't done any of it because Jesus told him to. He'd done it because it was right. Or maybe because someone had done it for him once. He would have been a good example in any case. But then he helped me, when nobody else could or would. And when I took his help, I promised to follow his example.

When I was three, my grandma had told me that all I needed to do in order to be saved was to invite Jesus into my heart. Later, I understood that the ritual she was talking about was really just a metaphor for internalizing a value set or an idea. I hadn't been willing to take the plunge with Jesus the space alien. But Frank W. Ross—there was a guy I could commit to.

* * *

Once my path was clear, I just started to put one foot in front of the other. I enrolled in a community college. I set my sights on a four-year college. I got back in touch with Kris and Lizzie, and the three of us got a house in Ballard. We did Christmas and Thanksgiving together. Whenever Kris bought ice cream, I ate it all—and they let me get away with it. They teased me about it.

I built bookshelves in my room. I decorated.

I didn't just turn into a happy person overnight, and I never went straight. I was still angry. I still had days and nights when I imagined some unnameable doom hanging over me. But when the fear came close to paralyzing me, or I thought about taking a step closer to the cliff edges that seemed to surround me on every side, there was always my promise to Frank to pull me back.

I couldn't save a life from prison. I couldn't save a life if I was dead.

I started putting one foot in front of the other. It really was that easy.

It was the hardest thing I'd ever had to do in my life.

Acknowledgments

A guy like me, writing a book like this, needs to thank people who helped me with the book, and people who helped me live long enough to write it. Rosina Lippi has the distinction of being in both groups. She's read multiple drafts of my work, provided invaluable feedback, encouraged me, and made introductions. This book wouldn't exist without her, and it for damn sure wouldn't have been published. So for this book, for things that have come before, and for anything that comes after, Rosina—thank you.

I give my heartfelt thanks to my agent, Jill Grinberg, for kicking ass, taking names, and being so very, very patient with me. I'd also like to thank my editor, Joy Peskin, who looked at my one-page bio and saw this book underneath it. If it weren't for Heather Hobson, my hands wouldn't have stopped shaking long enough for me to type any of this out. Her honesty and trust helped me write about things I usually don't even like to think about. Stephen McCandless, the enabler, helped me get out of my head and get going.

My wife, Tricia: to say she deserves my thanks doesn't begin to cover it. The spouses of writers are a uniquely underappreciated breed of survivor.

John Damon got me started loving stories; Corinne Schmutz convinced me to try my hand at writing some.

Frank W. Ross saved me once, and a thousand times since then.

A portion of the proceeds from this book has gone to establish the Frank W. Ross Memorial Scholarship Fund. You can support the fund with a tax-deductible donation. Please send your check made out to Pride Foundation, with "The Frank W. Ross Memorial Scholarship Fund" on the memo line, and mail to:

Pride Foundation
The Frank W. Ross Memorial Scholarship Fund
2014 E Madison Street #300
Seattle, WA 98112

Or go to www.pridefoundation.org and click DONATE NOW to make a tax-deductible credit card donation. Be sure to enter "The Frank W. Ross Memorial Scholarship Fund" in the comment box.